Political Theories of Modern Government, Its Role and Reform

Other books by Peter Self

Administrative Theories and Politics
Econocrats and the Policy Process
Planning the Urban Region

Political Theories of Modern Government, Its Role and Reform

Peter Self

Australian National University, Canberra,
and
London School of Economics and Political Science

London
GEORGE ALLEN & UNWIN

Boston   Sydney

George Allen & Unwin (Publishers) Ltd,
40 Museum Street, London WC1A 1LU, UK

George Allen & Unwin (Publishers) Ltd,
Park Lane, Hemel Hempstead, Herts HP2 4TE, UK

Allen & Unwin, Inc.,
Fifty Cross Street, Winchester, Mass. 01890, USA

George Allen & Unwin Australia Pty Ltd,
8 Napier Street, North Sydney, NSW 2060, Australia

First published in 1985.

British Library Cataloguing in Publication Data

Self, Peter
    Political theories of modern government: its role and reform.
    1. political science   2. Democracy
    I. Title
351′.001   JC423

ISBN 0–04–320174–1
ISBN 0–04–320175–X Pbk

Library of Congress Cataloging in Publication Data

Self, Peter
    Political theories of modern government.
    Bibliography: p. 212
    Includes index.
    1. State, The. 2. Political science. I. Title.
JC325.S45   1985   320.2   85–6076
ISBN 0–04–320174–1 (U.S.: alk. paper)
ISBN 0–04–320175–X (U.S.: pbk.: alk. paper)

Set in 10 on 11 point Times by Grove Graphics, Tring, Herts
Printed and bound in Great Britain by
Mackays of Chatham Ltd., Kent

Dedication

To Bernard Schaffer whose learning and wit lit up every subject he tackled.

CONTENTS

INTRODUCTION

The governments of modern Western societies present a rapidly changing spectacle. Throughout this century, governments have grown rapidly in their size and functions, and have become much more complex in respect of their policies and goals. These developments seem to have been propelled by inexorable processes of economic and social change, as well as by the demands of political groups and parties. Government has become the dumping ground for innumerable social problems which (seemingly) can be tackled by no other means. One might therefore expect that the operations of governments would occupy a high place in public interest, and that their policies should be able to rely upon the general support of public opinion.

In fact, the performance of modern government has come under increasingly severe scrutiny. Economists compare it unfavourably with the operation of competitive markets. Political scientists describe how strong interest groups use public money or powers for their own advantage. Marxists have seen government as a more or less pliant servant of capitalism. Students of administration have observed severe 'overload' in the machinery of government and have pointed to many forms of bureaucratic inefficiency or policy perversion. These criticisms are often qualified and are not unanimous, and may of course be mistaken, but they do seem to correspond with a good deal of more general comment upon the failings of governments.

It therefore seemed a worthwhile task to attempt an overview of some leading schools of thought and opinion about the performance of modern democratic governments. The 'theories' of this book's title are not precise and detailed, but represent broad schools of thought about the nature of government. Thus government is viewed in turn through the lenses of economists concerned with the behaviour of rational individuals in political situations; of pluralist thinkers who see government as divided into numerous groups and organizations, both private and public; of the new theorists of corporatism who deal with the growing integration of public and private interests; and of modern theorists of bureaucracy.

Each school of thought strives in the first instance to *explain* the character and behaviour of government, not to criticize it. Explanation moves to criticism when the performance of government is compared with some standard that is regarded as desirable and attainable. Each theoretical approach brings with it a typical reform agenda and a set of often diverse prescriptions. So this book is concerned both with *why* governments act as they do and with *how* they might do better, as viewed from different perspectives.

The final two chapters present my own conclusions about the future of government in modern democracies. A critical issue here is what are the jobs which governments really need to do in modern societies, as opposed to functions that can be left to economic markets or to private initiative. A further key issue is how governments can amass the political support necessary for them to do their work effectively and fairly. I make no secret of my own views that some substantial political reforms are necessary if democracies are to obtain and to tolerate the kind of governments that they will require in the future.

This book has been written at a time of political pessimism and confusion. The current attempts within Western democracies to reduce the scope of government, and the accompanying tendencies towards extremism of both the Left and Right, suggest a degree of crisis over the conduct of government. Whether and how this crisis is overcome is a political, not an academic, question. All the same, this review of theories suggests to me that while governments of the future should be a little leaner, they need to be still broader than now in their scope and responsibilities; and that they will not perform better until a more active and equal form of democracy is established.

In essaying this series of broad reviews, I may often do less than justice to individual authors and to particular arguments. My defence is that the subject itself is incorrigibly large and the literature is sprawling, and that as it is, other possible perspectives upon government have had to be left out. I shall be happy enough if someone else can deal with the same subject matter more fully. In the meantime, I put forward this book as hopefully offering some guidance and insights into a complex, changing and important subject.

My thanks are due to many individual scholars who kindly commented upon parts of the book. In particular I thank the

Introduction

following for their helpful contributions: Bernard Crick, Eva Etzioni-Halevy, Robert Goodin, Leonard Hume, Margaret Levi, Richard Rose, Philippe Schmitter, Hugh Stretton, Martyn Webb, Glenn Withers and Maurice Wright. Naturally, none of these individuals has any responsibility for my eclectic opinions.

I have also learned much over many years from my students in seminars at the London School of Economics and Political Science, and from my colleague, Patrick Dunleavy; and I have benefited also from seminars at the Australian National University and the Universities of Sydney, Queensland and Western Australia. I have had the helpful support of colleagues and staff in the Urban Research Unit, Research School of Social Sciences, Australian National University: in particular of Janet Penny, who made many helpful comments on style, and Wanda Dziubinski who organized the typing.

I am more than grateful to my wife Sandra for typing an early version and for putting up with the subject for quite a while. Finally, this book is dedicated to the late Bernard Schaffer, who not only offered helpful comments, but whose friendship was over many years a continuous source of stimulus and delight.

Canberra, *November 1984*   Peter Self

1

MODERN POLITICAL THOUGHT

WHAT IS POLITICAL THEORY?

This book is concerned with theories about the behaviour, performance and reform of modern governments. The governments in question are those generally described as 'Western democracies' which have capitalist or 'mixed' economies. Foremost in my mind are the English-speaking democracies of the United Kingdom, Canada, the United States, Australia and New Zealand, with a particular stress upon the first of these, which I know best. In a general way (and sometimes specifically) the analysis applies also to other democracies in Western Europe and Scandinavia. However, the coverage does not extend either to Communist states or to Third World countries which would require a different kind of analysis.

Throughout the book I shall attempt to relate the theories to the broader social context in which they have arisen. Thus the next chapter takes a general look at the environmental changes – technological, economic and social – which have impacted upon the scale and functions of modern Western governments. Superficial as such a survey must necessarily be, it will hopefully offer some insight into the basis (and also the limitations) of the theories discussed in the following four chapters.

Each of these four chapters deals with what may be described as a school of thought about the nature of modern governments (although one chapter, the corporatist one, deals with several such schools for reasons which will emerge). Moreover, these chapters proceed in sequence to different and broader (which need not mean superior) levels of analysis. Chapter 3 reviews explanations of government behaviour derived from individual motivations, particularly those of the rational, self-regarding individuals posited for purposes of analysis by the 'public choice' group of economists; Chapter 4 reviews the pluralist analysis of the influence of organized groups and individual public agencies; Chapter 5 moves to the level of the 'corporate state', used here as a focus for several theories concerned with the development of government as an encompassing and integrated system subject to strong structural pressures; while Chapter 6 takes up theories dealing with the efficiency and power of modern bureaucracies.

It may be objected that a series of brief reviews cannot do justice to the fullness and variety of the various 'schools of thought'. The criticism must be admitted. In an age of massive academic publishing (motivated perhaps more by the 'publish or perish' imperative than the expectation of a large readership), when for example there are over fifty major works and a multitude of articles bearing the general impress of the 'public choice' school, it would be absurd to attempt coverage in depth in one chapter.

But the objector should consider two points. The first is that a student or general reader faced with a massive flow of writings emanating from authors espousing quite different schools of thought, and following different methodologies, will very likely not be able or even attempt to relate the theories together. Students are more likely to stay within the frame of discourse recommended by their teachers, or else to use different frameworks for different subjects (say, public choice theory for a public policy course, and neo-Marxism for theory of the state), without being more than vaguely aware of their gross inconsistencies. Those who wish to dig deeply into a school of thought are free to specialize, but for many a broader view of theories about modern government is surely helpful, and is all too hard to obtain within the modern academic world.

Secondly, my aim in any case is not a pedagogic exercise of analysing the writers. Rather is it to examine and draw upon various theories for the contributions which they can make to a better understanding of the nature of modern government and the prospects for its future evolution and reform. Consequently, the last two chapters put forward my own conclusions about the future role of governments, and about the kind of political reforms which are needed if governments are to work better.

Before proceeding further it may be useful to inquire what we *mean* by political theory. A distinction is sometimes drawn between traditional political philosophy and modern political theorizing. The former is said to be concerned with large general questions about the nature of the state, political obligation, the rights and duties of individuals, the nature of a good society, and so on. By contrast modern political theories of a 'scientific' or sociological form are claimed to be empirical, specific and 'positive' rather than ethical in their nature.

This distinction does not stand up too well under examination, but it derives some of its plausibility from the nature of modern politics (Runciman, 1963). Thus it is only in the last century or so that the development of modern parliamentary regimes, mass electorates, political parties and pressure groups has established politics as a specialized and complex type of activity. Similarly, while the foundations of the study of comparative government were laid over 2000 years ago by Aristotle, past types of government bear only a very limited resemblance to the enormously complex structures of the governments of Western democracies.

While politics as a profession has become much more specialized, politics as a motive to governmental action has increasingly (and particularly in the last few decades) invaded almost every aspect of human life, and indeed of animal life as well. Almost any issue is capable of being and often is politicized. By politics here I am not referring to the 'small p' which exists in any organization, in clubs or in families, except (which is an important proviso) where such activity is closely or clearly related to the functioning of government. But there are important respects in which the activities of the political system have become diffused, expanded and absorbed into society; or, as some critics would say, society has been absorbed into the political system.

Thus governments now provide an enormous variety of services, many of which were once provided and still are often also provided by private organizations. The number of regulatory agencies is legion, and the number of laws and administrative regulations which theoretically require, although they often do not receive, the compliance of citizens is past anyone's reckoning. There are vast numbers of 'hived off' or semi-independent public agencies, and also government sponsored or regulated private agencies, all sometimes lumped together in the inaccurate term QUANGO (inaccurate because the term actually refers to quasi non-governmental agencies). Then again, bureaucracy contains many specialists who might be doing much the same work for private organizations, and vice versa; and groups of public servants increasingly organize themselves and behave like private pressure groups, unless expressly prohibited. Private interests as well as public bodies have their spokesmen within government, and quasi-judicial inquiries (such as, for example, public inquiries in Britain) have often to resolve disputes between a mixed bag of different public and private bodies. All these are familiar features of the administrative state or, as some would conceive it, the pluralist state.

Thus the empirical features of modern political systems are novel and complex, and attract the attention also of a novel army of analysts and researchers. The information now available about political systems is by historical comparison enormous and growing rapidly, even if some inner secrets remain carefully guarded. Political theories must thus cope with massive empirical data of a novel kind.

Some years ago now the theme of the 'end of ideology' also gave a new slant to political theorizing. This thesis seemed to make the broader ethical issues of traditional political philosophy much less interesting or relevant. Indeed, Sheldon Wolin (1960) feared that political philosophy might be on the way out, and offered his book as a memorial to the kind of discourse which was once engaged in by reflective thinkers. The 'end of ideology' theme was sustained by the supposed convergence of politics towards the general goals of economic growth and modernization; by the appearance of a host of experts offering technical solutions to political problems; and by the pragmatic and incremental character of modern party politics.

All these arguments seem less persuasive in the 1980s now that political conflict has heightened and experts (notably economic experts) are less trusted or followed. All the same, most policy making in Western democracies continues to follow incremental lines, droves of experts continue to offer technical advice, and extremist goals or theories command rather little assent. Hence it could still be argued that modern political theories must deal with a realm of possible choices which are narrow or marginal by comparison with the issues of political philosophy. However, this proposition has frequently been true of practical policies, save in periods of revolution, while the rapidity and uncertainty of change in modern societies suggests that political stability and pragmatism may be resting on weak reeds.

In any event, this type of analysis misses the reasons for the continued relevance and indeed re-emergence of philosophical and ideological issues. A political theory has to make some choice of methodology and it is difficult indeed to separate this choice from the old issue of an individualist versus a collectivist (or 'systems') type of approach. The choice of approach in turn strongly influences both the kinds of explanation given for the political system, and the remedies offered for correcting its failures. The more systematic and rigorous the methodology, the stronger becomes its influence upon the subsequent analysis.

We are not dealing here with purely pedagogic positions. Behind

4

methodology there often lies ideology, in the sense of a 'world view' of the nature of man and his social relationships. Behind the individualist approach lies a long history of social contract theories, which explain the nature of the state from reflections upon the intrinsic nature of man, and which prescribe the functions and limits of government by reference to individual rights or individual preferences. The converse position is to derive government from social norms or values which can be used both to explain and to prescribe its scope and character; or alternatively (and very differently) to explain political development in terms of historical laws and of necessary power relationships between classes, nations or other groups.

I am not saying that one cannot escape the methodological and ideological traps of dogmatism. I would accept that there are better and worse ways to seek objective knowledge. The point to note here is the recent increase in the ideological content of theories of government. The rebirth of social contract theories, and of theories of individual rights and their perversion by government, is matched by the rebirth of Marxist thought about the necessary subservience of modern Western governments to the imperatives of capitalism. Of course social contract theories can be used in a defensible rather than dogmatic style of philosophic analysis, and not all political theories are intentionally ideological. My point is that the rebirth of ideology may very possibly be connected with a rise of political conflict, and growing criticism of or disillusionment with the performance of modern governments.

A short consideration of methodology at the start of this book therefore seems desirable. Those who find discussions of methodology boring or superfluous can turn to page 16 where the main argument begins.

One can distinguish between propositions which are open to refutation or modification by empirical evidence, and propositions which consist of circular chains of abstract logic or of metaphysical statements that can not be tested. This distinction is difficult, because theories sometimes mix their propositions or shift from one level of argument to the other.

The most familiar example of this dualism is Marxism. An assertion that governments serve the interests of capitalism can be made an empirical proposition if I will entertain evidence that it is false wholly or partly, and that it is truer of some periods and of some states than of others. On the evidence available, my own opinion is that the interests of capitalism are one important explanation (but only one) of modern governmental behaviour.

5

Again, I do not believe that the interests of capitalism as perceived and acted upon by government depend wholly upon inescapable structural pressures, since it seems likely that something at least depends upon particular interactions between capitalists and government agencies which can be empirically investigated.

However, if it is held that capitalism necessarily dominates and controls government everywhere until revolution intervenes for 'structural' causes which do not turn on the motives of individual actors and can be known only by their alleged effects (which in turn must be assumed due to capitalism), we enter a philosophic theory beyond the reach of evidence. Modern neo-Marxists are of course well aware of this problem and introduce a variety of qualifications, such as the conflict between different 'fractions of capital', and the concept of 'the relative autonomy of the state'. However, the state is often conceived to be 'relatively autonomous' only in the sense that some appearance of impartiality and a mild degree of autonomous action is supposed to be once again useful to capitalism.

If we explain these relationships by elitist theories which envisage the co-option of politicians by capitalists, we are closer to a testable theory. Admittedly, the influence of capitalism may not depend simply upon direct contacts between capitalists and public officials, but upon the way that these officials think it necessary to support capitalism for the sake of their own objectives. However, the nature and extent of these structural pressures are unlikely to be constant, and need investigation. Empirical testing in the social sciences is difficult and rarely conclusive, but if theories are to be true, they must utilize and account for such empirical evidence as can be found, and not occupy a hermetically sealed box of circular argument.

Another type of political theory is that of the public choice economists. The methodology used here is that of neoclassical economics. Axioms or postulates are first stated, together with certain initial conditions, and deductions are then made about consequential behaviour. One necessary assumption is that individuals act rationally, i.e. they have adequate information and order their preferences consistently. Another assumption is that individuals are 'utility maximizers', which means crudely that they will always seek 'more for less', e.g. more satisfaction for the same outlay or a smaller outlay for the same satisfaction. If these assumptions are now applied within an appropriate environment, such as fully competitive markets, some consistent predictions can be made about economic behaviour.

6

The 'scientific' character of economics, in so far as this really exists, stems from the statistical uniformities of behaviour which result from a vast number of exchange transactions conducted through the medium of a common numerator (money), and motivated by a simple yardstick of individual economic advantage. The instrumental and egoistic nature of market exchanges in modern Western societies is not just a question of theoretical assumption, but is on the whole socially expected and acceptable. An instrumental concept of economic exchange requires the support of particular laws and culture; for example, it was much less applicable in the Middle Ages and may indeed, as some liberals fear, be becoming slowly less applicable today. Economics can offer general laws and predictions only to the extent that enough individuals do in fact behave like 'economic man'. Beyond this point, economics has to descend from its perch into the same limited and qualified empirical generalizations which characterize the other social sciences.

The question raised by the public choice economists is how far politics can be treated as an exchange relationship governed by the same instrumental and egoistic motives as are often assumed in economics. James Buchanan argues that an individual is the same person, and can therefore be expected to behave in the same way in his political and his economic relationships (Buchanan, 1965). But is this true? The problems of much weaker measurement and prediction in politics need not invalidate the economic approach itself, although they raise many problems about its application. However, the public choice theorists themselves have demonstrated the paradoxical and mutually frustrating results which seem to follow logically from rational egoistic behaviour, not only in politics but in many contexts outside the rather special context of competitive free markets (Schelling, 1978).

This being so, can we assume that political man does behave like economic man? How does he avoid the traps of egoism? Even if we can usefully assume that 'political man' does often act egoistically, we must locate him in a situation of much greater complexity and uncertainty over the nature of his interests than is the case with market exchanges. This situation may move us away from the possibility of generalized predictions based upon simple assumptions into the real world of varied institutions and cultures.

A question is: does this economic methodology represent a philosophic position which is sealed off against contrary empirical evidence? In principle it is certainly not the intention of these theorists to deny evidence or to be dogmatic. One problem may be that the 'scientific' status of economic methodology itself has been much exaggerated. Because it uses the hypothetico-deductive methods which characterize the physical sciences, economics has been able to some extent to share also their prestige. However, as Blaug (1980) points out, theoretical economics is not at all adequately open to the test of falsification by empirical research which is crucial to the physical sciences. In applying the same methodology to politics, some members of this school set up an abstract model, quote any empirical evidence which supports their deductions and ignore any which does not. The results may still be interesting where *enough* behaviour (as with economics) conforms with the predictions, and concessions are made to empirical realism. However, when applied to politics, this methodology can produce an artificial and insulated style of reasoning, whose mathematical formulations conceal the barrenness of the actual argument, and whose starting point is a narrow view of human nature.

What then is the status of political theories? If the theories are genuinely empirical, as they claim to be, it is probable that the theories will also be limited, partial, and time and space specific. It may be a great intellectual nuisance (although possibly a practical benefit) that social phenomena have multiple causations to which precise weights cannot be assigned; but if that is the state of the world, it had better be recognized.

To some extent the theories to be discussed do recognize this limitation. Modern governments do not stand still and generalizations made for 1970 have to be modified for 1980. It is meaningful, for example, to say that there was a growth of pluralism after 1945, in the sense of a growth of organized and influential pressure groups, followed by a growth of corporatism, in the sense of an incorporation of private interests into government; and we can inquire into the relation between these developments. But we do not need to assume that 'pluralism' and 'corporatism' when fully spelled out are more than partial explanations of system behaviour, and to some considerable extent they may co-exist.

Different levels of explanation may therefore be complementary as well as contradictory. It is reasonable to say that consciousness and purpose can be predicated only of actual individuals. On the other hand, individuals acquire their tastes, norms and ambitions through processes of socialization, and we can say rather little about the behaviour of an isolated individual. Social behaviour is structured by historically acquired conditions of a given

8

technology, economic system and set of institutions. Consequently, while political behaviour can be analysed as the product of individual interests or group interests or corporate pressures, an adequate understanding of such behaviour requires us to move between these different levels of analysis.

Some types of political theory, however, do claim a universal applicability which may derive from the assumption of invariant features of individual behaviour (e.g. public choice theory) or of a unique and necessary historical law (e.g. Marxism). Such theories may be empirically interesting, but only if the testable conclusions (however rough the testing) are separated from the methodological dogmas. This is not an easy process.

It should be clear that modern political theories have not disentangled themselves from the traditional concerns of political philosophy. Behind questions of methodology there lurks still the classical question of the relationship between the individual and the collectivity. Methodology is still linked with value judgements. While the functioning of modern governments is a subject for empirical theories of a novel kind, it can still be judged ethically by reference to concepts and standards which were familiar to Plato and Aristotle.

POLITICAL POWER AND VALUES

The last section has raised the old question of the relationship between 'positive' theories, which claim to describe the world as it is, and 'normative' theories, which suggest principles or goals of human behaviour. This book (and the theories it discusses) are concerned in various ways with *both* the explanation and the evaluation of the behaviour of modern governments. What is the connection between these two forms of argument?

In principle it is not hard to offer a satisfactory answer. Normative judgements are void and utopian, if not actually meaningless, if they cannot be applied because of the nature of human behaviour. They therefore have to take account of how individuals do behave under different conditions or political systems, and the best way to apply a normative theory, say about democracy, is to test it against systems which are claimed to be democratic. The tests will be useful and suggestive rather than conclusive, because there can be no final knowledge about the elasticity of human nature or behaviour.

Conversely, the argument that individuals do habitually behave in a certain way is inadequate grounds for ruling out the claim that they ought to behave differently, unless it is indeed impossible for them to do so. Thus we reach the common-sense proposition that positive and normative judgements are logically independent but empirically related. The nature of that relation is one of the oldest themes in political discourse. For example, conservatives frequently say that the selfish or sinful nature of man is an immovable barrier to the goal of equality, while radicals often believe the opposite.

Logically it is possible to separate the two types of proposition. For example, pluralism as a normative theory may hold that all groups in the population who share any significant common interest ought to be proportionally represented; while as a positive theory, pluralism may find that some groups are a great deal more successful and influential than others. Unfortunately there is a frequent tendency among political theorists to conflate the two propositions. Partly this comes about through wishful thinking or rationalization. It is tempting to suppose that what one would like to be the case corresponds with reality, and to adduce any selective evidence which helps. The use of 'ideal models' leads often to the problem of whether an author is describing the fully realized properties of an actual system, or an ideal standard by which an actual system should be judged.

How then are we to describe the theories with which we shall be concerned later? We need to recognize that the 'positive' and 'normative' elements in a political theory often get mixed. If we are dealing with a coherent and persuasive mixture of the two, the result can be called an *ideology*. An ideology links some general explanation of human nature and behaviour with conclusions about the right or best course of action for an individual to follow. Logically, the normative conclusions need not follow from its explanations of behaviour.

For example, even if I were to accept historical determinism, I need not equate my moral duty with assisting the course of history. (If I am a complete determinist, the issue is of course logically meaningless.) Again, if I assume that individuals are basically egoistical, I need not conclude that it is morally right to accept a highly unequal society. The force of the conclusion depends in each case upon how strongly the basic theory is held. In practice, few people believe wholly in either historical determinism or individual egoism, and in each of these cases the ideology is more influential over suggesting certain limitations upon my freedom of action than upon closely specifying how I ought to act. Ideologies do not extinguish individual choices or moral dilemmas, but an effective ideology offers a helpful guide to action (or inaction) for the person who accepts it.

10

This is not a book about ideologies, but the assumptions of political theorists, if tenaciously held, do amount to ideological positions. Barry (1970) contrasts the egoistic assumptions of economists with the assumptions of sociologists about social norms. The former approach analyses the logical choices and strategies which a self-regarding individualist will employ under various institutional conditions, whereas the latter approach deals with the influence upon individuals of socially prescribed roles and norms. Both these approaches – the economic and the sociological – are capable of some empirical testing and both types of theory may be partly true and even in part compatible; but limits are set by the dominance of the initial assumption. If individuals are basically rational egoists, why do they respect social norms which contradict their rational interests? If the influence of social norms is so strong, why do individuals often disregard them to pursue personal gain? Of course we may conclude that the empirical evidence supports one approach more than the other, and Barry is inclined to award higher marks on this score to the economists, but we still have the problem of incompatible assumptions.

However, it would be wrong to equate an individualist explanation with egoism, or a collectivist one with the maintenance of social norms. Liberal individualism need not assume that the individual is only concerned with the maximization of his satisfactions or utilities, but can recognize the existence of altruistic or idealistic motives to action. In collectivist theories, the contrast of theories is still sharper. There is a world of space between the theory of Talcott Parsons (1951) that political behaviour is governed by normative beliefs about the public interest, and the Marxist theory that it is the reflection of the class struggle. Therefore, either economic interests are secondary to social norms or else these norms are a mere rationalization (deliberate or not) of economic interests. The only common element is the belief that it is systemic properties – the requirements of social integration in one case and the nature of historical laws in the other – which govern political behaviour.

Another way of looking at this subject is to draw a distinction between theories about the use and distribution of power and theories about the influence of personal or social values. Political science is sometimes described as the study of power, and the theories to be considered later are often presented in these terms. However, 'power' on its own is an inadequate explanatory notion because it leaves out the social meanings which people attach to its use. Authority represents an exercise of power which is supported

11

by social beliefs and norms; and when these supports weaken, the exercise of authority becomes challenged. A 'values' approach to politics is concerned with the procedures and goals which individuals or groups accept as being desirable or necessary, and which they suppose may justify the use of the coercive power of government.

Each type of theory which we shall consider later is concerned with questions of both power and values. In each case, there is also a difference between what may be called a realist and an idealist approach to politics. The 'realist' approach is concerned with material interests and power relations, whether these are treated in units of individuals, groups, classes or nation states. Such theories purport to be 'positive' not 'normative', that is to express human behaviour in an objective way, but their assumptions may of course be false or too dogmatic (as was suggested earlier). Explanatory theories do not necessarily lead to any normative conclusions or reform proposals, but in practice they usually do so, either by a common-sense appeal to shared values (for example, if bureaucrats are shown to be greedy and unreliable, should they not be fewer?); or else by an ideological form of association (for example, if historical forces make some development almost inevitable, is it not better to hasten it along?).

'Idealistic' or normative theories start from the opposite end of recommending certain political goals and values as being right or desirable. The values in question may be individualist, pluralist or corporatist. The theory in question becomes more plausible or realizable if the values specified can be shown to be widely held; but in any case the theorist will need to specify the institutional or other changes which will assist the realization of these values. Thus, explanatory theories have to be invoked to show how values might be realized and the relationship between prescription and explanation must once again be demonstrated.

Individualist theories of a 'realistic' kind often but not always describe human behaviour in terms of the egoistic motivations and material interest of individuals. Logically, this view of the world need not be associated with any particular ethical conclusions, but this view of the individual as a somewhat isolated seeker of his own satisfactions is often associated with a correlative belief in the right of the individual to be as free as possible from external constraints. From this standpoint, an individual's acceptance of coercion by government will depend upon the benefit to his private interest. By contrast, an idealist approach holds that the individual has some moral responsibility also to consider the interests of all

12

other individuals within his or her society. Empirically speaking, this approach leads to a quest for the laws and institutions which will fairly balance the rights and duties of individuals and promote the realization of their personalities.

Pluralist theories of a realistic kind view organized groups as existing to advance a collective interest, usually of a material kind, under conditions of mutual competition or conflict. The related normative theory looks towards a political system which, like an idealized market system, brings about a tolerable balance between these competing group pressures. On the other hand, idealistic pluralism envisages the emergence of organized groups by a process of free association and sees their desirable goal as one of mutual co-operation rather than competition. Empirical investigations may or may not confirm the existence of such groups and may suggest how they could be encouraged to develop.

'Realistic' corporatism is rooted in the analysis of the consequences of power struggles between nation states or economic classes or both. Its normative implications may be nationalistic or revolutionary socialist. Idealistic corporatism recommends values of social order and justice which will support the integrated pursuit of collective goals, and it investigates empirically the institutional developments which might help to bring about this result.

This treatment of 'realist' and 'idealist' positions is much simplified since the elements can be mixed in many ways. Moreover some theories attempt to be wholly positive and do not offer any normative conclusions, just as some idealistic positions (which lie outside the scope of this book) are wholly philosophical and abstract.

Just the same, this brief summary has some historical relevance for the chapters which follow. Modern theories of government on the whole purport to be 'realistic' rather than 'idealistic' in their character and assumptions. The hard-headed hypotheses of the public choice economists have tended to displace traditional forms of liberal individualism. The American school which analyses pluralism as a form of competitive struggle for material stakes has largely taken over from the more idealistic theories of the English and European pluralists. The analysis of national corporatism as a product of power struggles has largely replaced the once fashionable idealist theory of the state.

Neither 'power' theories nor 'value' theories taken on their own seem to offer an adequate account of political behaviour. This is because, as Duverger (1964) says, politics is intrinsically geared towards both more selfish and more altruistic forms of behaviour than occur in competitive economic markets. The coercive power of the state represents an enormous prize for those who can capture it. It can provide financial subsidies, free or cheap services, powers of self-regulation and exclusion of competitors. There is thus great scope for manipulation by self-seeking groups and individuals. No doubt in modern democracies these manoeuvres are controlled and regulated to some extent by constitutional and administrative procedures. The nastier aspects of personal patronage, private benefits and corruption are less evident than in some societies, but they still exist and perhaps are growing. In any case, behind the rhetoric of public interest, there lurks an array of private interests seeking their advantage.

Yet for all its dismal or sinister features, politics elicits also considerable resources of human idealism and altruism. The general reason for this is obvious. The powerful apparatus of the state can in principle be captured for ideal or altruistic purposes as well as for selfish ones. No doubt in the annals of history the latter motivations have counted for more, although often motivations may be mixed. In any event the language of politics would be meaningless if this were not the case. If all political ideals were rationalizations of interests, the pretence ought to have been seen through by now. Instead, the frequent alternations of idealism and cynicism, and the conversion of the former into the latter, show how often ideals are frustrated — whether by structural features of the political system or by the opposition of self-regarding interests.

Because of the weakness of individual action, group identification is a necessary and ever-present feature of political life. The individual may identify with a group *simply because* he supposes it will serve his private interest, but it would seem more usual (and the word suggests as much) that the individual psychologically incorporates both meanings of interest, and assumes (since the benefits are collective anyhow) that they should be jointly pursued. Equally an individual supporting a cause group makes an altruistic type of identification. Certainly these group identifications are often qualified and may be rescinded, particularly in the case of cause groups where individual judgement plays a stronger and more critical role. Of course these examples of identification do not imply that the individual will necessarily play an active part in the organization, because of the probably unrequited costs to him or her.

None the less the number of active political participants in modern democracies is large in absolute numbers, even if statistically a small proportion of the population. As one might

14

predict a very high proportion belong to the middle class and higher income groups. For such individuals the costs of participation are less (because of their greater resources and knowledge), and the psychological benefits are greater (becaue of their schooling in a public or voluntary service ethic). There is as noted an altruistic element in working for both an interest and a cause group, but in the latter case there is the further attraction (or if one is an egoist, marginal repulsion) of having an altruistic objective. This fact may help to explain the appeal of cause groups among the middle classes. If one is going to be altruistic anyway, it makes sense to do it for a good cause. The same reasoning might support the hypothesis that any altruism among the traditional working-class would be funnelled into a Labour or left-wing party, viewed as a cause group for the remedy of injustice.

Loyalty to an organization or cause is a self-reinforcing phenomenon unless frozen out by disillusion, because of the individual's growing psychological investment. Also, as has often been pointed out, loyalty to the original interest or cause can be easily displaced upon the organization itself as a result of personalized satisfactions or loyalties. It would seem that crises of loyalty are more frequent and traumatic in politics than in other occupations. This result is to be expected and is amply documented in political annals. The faithful horse in Orwell's *Animal Farm* (1955) stands for all the dumb loyalists in history who have gone on working unselfishly for a party which has betrayed its and their ideals. The politician who has a 'crisis of conscience' between his party and his principles, or who must sacrifice personal interest or reputation for his political cause, is a real, even if a relatively rare figure.

It is in these situations that the challenge or 'charm' of politics, to which intellectual politicians sometimes refer but which seems meaningless or cynical to the outsider, reveals its crisis points. These arise because politics as a vocation offers uniquely sophisticated opportunities for behaviour ranging from the principled to the cynical, from the idealistic to the egoistic. Politics is a speculative activity with a long time horizon of objectives and (usually) a short time horizon of effective power. There are myriad points where trade-offs must be made between a sacrifice of either influence or goals, and the issue judged within a speculative scale of future opportunities. There are strong temptations either to claim or deny (as personal interest suggests) the responsibility for decisions whose effects are both slow and uncertain, and also to dodge the decisions themselves.

Political theories of modern government

Max Weber well understood the crisis of responsibility faced by the German politicians of his later years, and believed that in preferring the semblance to the reality of authority they had relinquished power to the bureaucracy (Gerth and Mills, 1948, pp. 77–128). Perhaps Weber was right, and perhaps modern democratic politicians are failing in the same kind of way. Hirschman (1970) has pointed out how leading figures in the US Administration opposed to the Vietnam war failed to exercise the only effective 'voice' open to them – resignation. But however pessimistic one's opinion about actual politicians, the intrinsic characteristics of politics cannot change. It will always present Duverger's 'two faces of the state' – the faces of coercion and community, of massive selfishness and periodic idealism.

FROM BENEVOLENT TO MALEVOLENT STATE?

Ideas and theories have their own history. Closeted in universities, academics are often refining theories inherited from an earlier age or derived from fascination with some abstract methodology, but whose relevance to the changing world outside may be somewhat marginal. None the less, one would expect some correspondence between the course of political events and that of academic theories, particularly in a period when applied social and political science has mushroomed and yielded much matter for intellectual digestion.

The history of political ideas over the last forty years (say roughly from 1944 to 1984) suggests a steadily deteriorating evaluation of the functioning of modern democratic states. Necessarily, this is a very broad statement. There were certainly theories current in 1945 which took a very jaundiced view of the state's growing powers – Hayek's *The Road to Serfdom* (1944) is one outstanding example (and Hayek, 1973, later agreed that the results had not been as bad as he feared). Equally there are writers today who take a cheerful view of the problems of 'big government', arguing that Western states are weathering fiscal crises tolerably well and that democracy is spreading to countries like Spain and Portugal (Rose, 1984). Also, national traditions of political thought diverge among Western democracies. American thinkers have always had a more distrustful and negative view of government than have British ones, and the continental European concern with state sovereignty has little resonance in English-speaking countries. (In using the word 'state' myself I do not mean to take up this issue, but approximate its meaning to that of 'a nation's political institutions and governmental system'.)

It is also relevant that in 1945 the Western democracies triumphed in a world war. This experience certainly strengthened the bonds of collective sympathy and national sentiment, and led to a somewhat heady belief in the possibilities of 'democratic planning'. If democracies could organize effectively to win a major war, could they not equally well dispose of nagging problems such as unemployment, poverty and personal insecurity? It could be said that the political 'price' of the war was a dose of political radicalism and a large programme of publicly organized welfare schemes and physical reconstruction, a development particularly marked in Britain where postwar planning was incubated as early as the black days of 1940. Inevitably, as had happened before, some of these hopes were bound to be disappointed when private interests, frozen during wartime, reasserted their political weight. The collectivist or idealist sentiment was strong enough to make this process of reassertion very gradual. A major victory for radical collectivism in Britain was the acceptance by the Conservatives, who regained power in 1951 and remained there for thirteen years, of most of the welfare measures initiated by the postwar Labour Government.

With these reservations, the theme of a shift in political thought from the benevolent to the malevolent aspects of government remains a valid one. The trend can be seen in the evolution, appearance and re-emergence of leading schools of political thought. Theories of pluralism, developed initially in and about the American environment, started out with an optimistic view of the consequences of the rise of organized groups for democratic stability and balance, veered towards a stress upon the capture of government by powerful private interests, and contributed finally (in Europe particularly) towards a concept of 'corporate pluralism' in which integrated private and public interests dominate government to the exclusion of other groups. The transition from a fairly benevolent to a distinctly malevolent view of pluralism can be mapped in a comparison of two major American works, Truman (1951) and Lowi (1979).

The public choice school of economists, which grew steadily in numbers and output from the late 1950s, represented a frontal attack upon any idealist theory of politics. This attack was clearly mounted in Buchanan and Tullock (1962). The basic assumption was political individualism or egoism of an instrumentally rational type. Conventional beliefs about the public spiritedness of politicians and bureaucrats were given a possibly well-deserved hammering, and we were back in Bentham's world of conflicting egoisms but without Bentham's assumption that democracy would solve the problem.

However, the writings of the public choice school were also relatively mild and optimistic at first. Anthony Downs' path-breaking *An Economic Theory of Democracy* (1957) reached the fairly comfortable conclusion that there were sound reasons of rational egoism for voters to trust their representatives with considerable discretion, and for parties to satisfy the median preferences of voters. The Buchanan and Tullock book was concerned (as Buchanan has continued to be) with the design of an ideal constitution which could establish a satisfactory trade-off between the rational individual's requirements for public goods and the injury to his interests from state coercion. One can contrast these earlier works with the increasingly black picture of political and bureaucratic perversions painted by Tullock (1965), Niskanen (1971), Ostrom (1973), Breton (1974) and others.

Marxist theorizing has never of course dried up, but the renaissance of this school in the 1970s is a striking phenomenon. In most academic environments in the West the study of political economy is now dominated by one or other of the polar opposite schools of neoclassical economists and neo-Marxists. Often the former dominate economics, the latter sociology departments, with politics departments split or (as has always been the case) eclectic and economically illiterate. The two schools agree only on the important feature of 'economism', or the dominance of politics by economic motives or forces.

The new Marxist theorists are too numerous and subtly diverse to list here. One interesting development has been the powerful incursion of this school into the subject of urban politics and planning, led by a pioneering work by Harvey (1973) which contrasted liberal and Marxist concepts of the functioning of cities. This strong Marxist interest in urban questions has been inspired by the growth of urban activism which may suggest that cities are the flashpoints of capitalist crisis or revolution (Castells, 1978). Other reasons for this interest are the availability of public research funds under community action programmes, and the greater ease of research in a local than in a central government setting. Another major development in neo-Marxist thought has been the study of public finance, perhaps most notably in James O'Connor's *The Fiscal Crisis of the State* (1973).

For all their elaborations, Marxist theorists naturally continue their historic mission of explaining the growth of government in terms of its utility for capitalism, and its failures in terms of capitalist contradictions. The resurgence of Marxism in the West seems further strong evidence for the growth of more critical opinions about the role of government.

Bureaucratic theories have also become increasingly critical and harsh. Weber himself may have been neutral or hostile to the growth of bureaucracy, but his concept of bureaucracy as an efficient and rational tool for the conduct of government became the classic entry point into this subject. So long as bureaucracy could be assumed to be responsive and accountable to political leadership, the Weberian theory seemed satisfactory enough to most democrats. However, the growing autonomy and political irresponsibility of the higher bureaucracy has been a theme of many studies, exemplified by Jean Meynaud's *Technocracy* (1968), although the thesis has as often been denied.

At the same time numerous studies of alleged bureaucratic 'dysfunctions' have knocked holes in the Weberian concept of bureaucratic efficiency. The themes include the perversion of political goals by government agencies (Gawthrop, 1969); the co-option of agencies by private interests (McConnell, 1966); the over-spending of bureau chiefs (Niskanen, 1971). 'Managerialism' stresses the power of bureaucratic gatekeepers over the clients they are supposed to serve. 'Access theory' deals with the weak position of clients, and the 'irony of equity' whereby the correction of one kind of discrimination leads to another (Schaffer and Lamb, 1981). Some of these assertions will be questioned later, but there are enough of them to suggest that the face of bureaucracy looks increasingly malevolent, at any rate to those who study it.

We can also observe some significant changes in the general character of political and economic thought. In 1945 the idealist theory of the state still cast a long shadow. Britain may perhaps be a special case of idealist influence, but an interesting one inasmuch as the dogmatic and authoritarian features of continental Hegelianism had been transformed by the Oxford idealists into a gentler, more pragmatic belief in the instrumental virtues of government. T. H. Green's conception of the role of the state as one of 'removing obstacles to the good life' combined a liberal belief in the value of self-improvement with a strong role for government over providing the necessary material and educational basis for all citizens to have the opportunity for personal growth. The corollary was a strong emphasis upon the obligation of citizens, especially privileged ones, to contribute to the altruistic ends of government. This high-minded doctrine inspired the ethos of the Oxford-educated political and administrative elite (Richter,

1964), and reached a wider audience through such textbooks of political philosophy as Sir Ernest Barker's (1951).

Today the idealist theory of the state has almost vanished. Modern political thought is concerned primarily with obstacles to the expression of individual preferences or the assertion of individual rights, and the question of duties to the state has slid into the background. Moreover, philosophically speaking, idealism has become outmoded in favour of a much more circumscribed, 'realistic' and materialistic conception of human nature. It may be that the impacts of Darwinian, Marxist and Freudian theories have finally worked their way into the popular consciousness. It is a curious fact that *On the Origin of Species*, *Das Kapital* and *The Interpretation of Dreams* lie side by side on one table in the British Museum, since these three volumes successively suggest the subordination of human will and values to biological, economic and psychological laws. If human behaviour is indeed closely circumscribed by environmental laws, there can be less ethical objection to either the assertion of individual wants or the exploitation of man by man. It is not hard to conjecture the impact of such beliefs upon the special province of politics, with its intrinsic alternations between coercive and idealist motivations.

The changing impact of economic thought upon politics can be charted more specifically. By 1945 belief in the value of market systems had taken a heavy battering from economists themselves. The answer of modern economics was to move to a positive position of regarding market theories as hypothetical predictions, and not in any way as a commendation of the market system. This position could not of course alter the implications for public policy of new theories about the actual workings of markets.

These new theories suggested the existence of an enormous amount of market failure when contrasted with the neoclassical model. The theory of imperfect competition (Robinson, 1948) analysed the growth of private monopolies; Keynes' (1936) famous theory explained how massive involuntary unemployment could result from the workings of the market system. The inegalitarian tendencies of markets had always been known, but received massive new testimony from the depression of the 1930s. Welfare economists were developing theories about the impact of numerous market 'externalities', often but not always producing an adverse effect upon the welfare of third parties – the best known examples being the indirect costs of air, water and noise pollution.

All these market failures or 'imperfections' seemed to call for massive governmental interventions, and economists themselves were active over assigning to government a very large and benevolent role. Those like Hayek who demurred spoke from a traditional liberal stance, and stayed outside mainstream economic thought, now divided between the interventionist welfare school and those who had moved to a purely descriptive economics. Thus a powerful school of economic thought helped to prod post-1945 governments into massive attempts at economic management and intervention, and their influence can be seen in the enormous increase of economists in government as both professional and political advisers.

The assumption that governments could and would act in an impartial manner to correct the defects of markets was and is a highly unrealistic one. Not only does it suggest that there are unique social welfare solutions to these problems, but the assumption also neglects politics itself. The stage was thus set for the appearance of the public choice economists who, working with the same methodological tools, were quick to point out that politics would produce quite as many or more failures and imperfections of welfare maximization as do market systems. Whatever the limits of the economic theory of politics, it did at least inject more realism into the debate about the state's economic role. Today the normative concern of economics has been shifted from market failures to political failures, while simultaneously some of the traditional virtues of markets have apparently been rediscovered, at any rate by comparison with political results.

The effect of this history upon the reputation of government has been severe. Increasingly politics has revolved, and elections have been fought, around issues of economic management. Yet governments have patently been unable to resolve many of the problems of the economic agenda, or to perform their assigned role of economic managers to general satisfaction. Not a little of the evidence for popular disillusionment with the major political parties might be traced to this situation.

I do not mean to fall into the vice of intellectualism or to exaggerate the significance of academic theories. The more interesting question is not how a theory arises but whether it is true, and the truth or falsehood of some of these theories will be scrutinized later. Some of these developments in political thought may no doubt be explained, as suggested earlier, by the sociology of knowledge – by a development of academic specialisms which may be only weakly related to the world outside. Still the volume of evidence in this section does suggest a considerable deterioration in *perceptions* of government, whether or not this change is justified.

Political theories of modern government

It would be absurd to suppose that governments *have* actually changed from benevolence to malevolence over forty years. The likeliest examples of truly malevolent governments in the modern world would be the Nazi and Fascist regimes of the 1930s. No such fierce criticisms can be thrown at modern Western governments. Rather would it be better to modify the title of this section and say that we have moved to a more pessimistic view of the capacities and performance of government.

Why should this be? One possible answer is the thesis of 'overload' (Rose, 1980). As governments take responsibility for solving more problems (for reasons discussed in the next chapter), the weight upon political and administrative machinery grows. If much more public regulation is required (as it is), bureaucracy becomes less liked and popular compliance weakens. Pressure groups increase the demands upon governments. Additionally or alternatively, economic changes and conflicts squeeze governments within a vice of contending pressures which they cannot resolve. It is to further examination of these possibilities that the book now turns, returning at the end to the issue of whether there will need to be more or less government in the future.

2

ENVIRONMENTAL CHANGE AND GOVERNMENTAL RESPONSE

THE EXPANSION OF GOVERNMENT

It is a familiar and now well documented fact that governments expand as societies grow richer. Even the economic recessions of the 1970s and early 1980s can be seen as only a hiccup in this general trend, at any rate unless the depression proves permanent. The reasons for this fact are not difficult to find. Depression involves government in higher social security and welfare payments, and in job creation schemes for the unemployed. While welfare payments may become more stingy under the taxpayers' backlash, there is still the problem that a fall in the gross national product (GNP) makes it harder to reduce the share of that product absorbed by the rather inflexible requirements of government; indeed the proportion of total (measured) wealth going to government may actually increase, even if total public expenditure in terms of constant prices is held steady or is slightly reduced.

One hundred years ago Adolph Wagner formulated his 'law of increasing expansion of public, and particularly state, activities'. His explanation was as follows:

> That law is the result of empirical observation in progressive countries, at least in our Western European civilization; its explanation, justification and cause is the pressure for social progress and the resulting changes in the relative spheres of private and public economy, especially compulsory public economy. Financial stringency may hamper the expansion of state activities, causing their extent to be conditioned by revenue rather than the other way round, as is more usual. But in the long run the desire for development of a progressive people will always overcome these financial difficulties. [Quoted from Musgrave and Peacock, 1967, p. 8.]

Wagner's last remarks about government taxation being usually determined by expenditure needs, rather than the other way round, seems a shrewd anticipation of post-1945 government behaviour, and his final conclusion is cold comfort for right-wing governments seeking permanent tax reduction.

Wagner's explanation of government growth is couched in somewhat Hegelian terms of social and political progress. It is possible to give more specific explanations in terms of environmental variables impacting upon government. There are fairly close correlations between indices of economic development, per capita wealth, urbanization and education. All these factors, severally and jointly, create demands for more public spending. Thus technology, urbanization and the growth of mass communications all bring about a massive increase in the number, complexity and impact of social and economic interactions (in economic terms, a multiplication of 'spillovers' or 'externalities'); hence pressures for public regulation and management. Rapid economic change and social mobility produce a need for a network of social security, while education both absorbs large public resources itself and increases demand for public goods of a welfare and cultural kind. Higher incomes per head create a demand for services like education, health, social security and leisure facilities which could not be afforded in earlier times. They also, of course, underwrite the possibility of government expansion.

It is the last point which reveals the limitations of these naturalistic explanations of government growth. Up to a point the explanations are convincing and fairly obvious, particularly in relation to the needs for mandatory collective regulation produced by urban and economic change. However, they do not explain why many services in increased demand, such as education, health, cultural and leisure facilities, etc., are often mainly provided by governments instead of by private entrepreneurs or voluntary co-operatives. These goods, like indeed the bulk of public services, are not 'pure public goods' in the classical sense, because their consumption can be subdivided. The usual answers given are either that many of these services are primarily directed towards the needy (which is only partially true); or else that there is a public or community good in the provision of services like education and culture. These arguments return the explanation for government growth back to the notion of social and economic progress held by Wagner, and away from a more or less automatic environmental impact upon government.

A second problem is to understand the relation among the 'environmental variables' which impact upon government. This issue emerges (or rather it should emerge) in connection with any theory which treats government as a 'black box'. These theorists inquire how much of the growth in government can be explained by factors outside the political system. The factors in question include all change external to the working of government itself, whether technological, economic or social. But how are these types of change related to each other and to the political system? One might reasonably assume that in a democratic system changes in social and political values are so interconnected as to be almost inseparable, so that this aspect of social change is uniquely close to the 'black box'. However, social opinion can be said to change with social structure, social structure with economic systems and economic systems with technological developments. All types of change are also subject to feedbacks from government policies, as when government promotes supersonic airplanes or medical innovations, regulates the building industry, legislates for equal opportunity or influences opinion through a propaganda film. Therefore, unless one takes a rigidly deterministic view of these various relationships, it is extremely difficult to seal up the 'black box' of government as an independent variable, or to specify all the connections (even in principle) which will occur between the variables including government.

This restriction does not mean that no progress in analysing the growth of government is possible. But before proceeding, it will be useful to look briefly at the 'black box' type of theory. Such theories generally sidestep the problems listed above by simply seeking correlations between objective indices, e.g. public expenditure data is matched against indices of income per head, literacy or educational attainment, urban concentration, etc. Using regression analysis, one can now inquire how much of the growth in public expenditure might be explained by these external indicators, and what precisely is left to be explained by the political process.

The most thorough exercises of this type have compared data for American states. Dye (1972, Ch. 11) reports that differences in per capita income can explain about four-fifths of the differences between state expenditures. This finding seems to leave rather little to be explained by the policy process itself, and Dye found that political factors such as degree of party competition and levels of voter turnout had little apparent effect upon total expenditures, although they were of some significance for welfare (in an upward direction). Others have questioned these findings, but assuming they are soundly based they do not actually tell us a great deal about the significance or insignificance of the policy process, for the following reasons:

(1) A fairly high correlation between income levels and total public expenditure is of course to be expected. This correlation is likely to be much stronger between states in a federation than between national governments, because of similarities in both the economic and cultural environment and in the political process itself. (There is perhaps a tendency for political scientists in federations like the USA and Australia to take a rather exaggerated view of the differences among their respective states; possibly Dye's findings are a corrective to this tendency.)

(2) Actually the correlation described by Dye has weakened, and he gets his results only by including the growing item of federal grants-in-aid as an extra exogenous factor. His justification is that federal aid is 'outside money' to the states, and thus constitutes part of their given economic resources. However, the distribution of federal aid is itself a function of political bargaining, and also represents a political movement towards more equalization between state expenditures. To some extent anyhow, it shifts the political process upwards.

(3) The analysis covers only gross expenditures, and says nothing about the quality or distribution of public services; nor does it tell us anything about the extent, methods or equity of systems of public regulation or any other activities which cost relatively little. All these important aspects of government output and performance seem more likely to be directly influenced by the policy process than does overall expenditure.

What this American state data tells us about economic influences upon government output is useful but limited, and not very surprising. When one turns to international comparisons there is, as one would expect, a general tendency for public expenditure to go up with levels of development or 'modernization'. But the trend is a very general one, and much more striking are the large differences among the taxing and spending habits of rich countries. Over ten years (1966–76) tax revenue as a proportion of GNP rose in the USA from 26·83 to 29·29 per cent, in Sweden from 36·44 to 50·89 per cent, and in Japan from 17·63 to 20·91 per cent, yielding per capita figures of US$2,199, 4,595 and 1,049 respectively (Larkey *et al.*, 1981). Thus Sweden with only slightly higher personal incomes than the USA taxes them more than twice as heavily, while Japan raises in taxes well under a quarter of the Swedish figure. Moreover, over these ten years the rate of revenue growth was much higher in already heavily taxed Sweden than in either the USA or Japan.

How is one to explain these differences? Wilensky (1975) and others have shifted attention from economic indices to the structural characteristics of societies. Wilensky found that most Western European countries spent (in 1966) at least twice as much as their GNP upon social security as did the USA, although they were considerably poorer societies. There were also lesser but still significant differences among the European countries, while Canada and Australia were in between the European average and the USA (Wilensky, 1975, p. 122).

These differences were largely explained by the author in terms of characteristics of the 'middle mass' and the 'working class' in each society. The existence of wide educational and employment opportunities, of extensive experience of self-employment and of 'social distance' between the middle mass and the poor (due, for example, to racial differences), are said to create resistance against welfare spending; whereas the existence of a well-organized working-class movement, itself participating in welfare administration, will boost such spending. These differences in social structure do, he contends, explain the striking differences between the USA and Sweden over social security, without any need to bring in ideology as an explanatory variable. It seems doubtful whether his own explanation of the attitudes of social groups really does exclude ideology, and certainly social attitudes and beliefs about welfare are strikingly different between the USA and Sweden. (The data the author uses to exclude ideology seem to me too limited and aggregated to be persuasive.)

The Wilensky study directs us to the close relationships between social structure, public opinion and the policy process. The problem is that the existence of continuous 'feedback' from government into the social system virtually excludes treating either end of the process as an independent variable. Other studies, such as that by Heclo (1974), have shown that the date at which a programme starts is important for the growth of government spending, and that this date is related to party politics and bureaucratic influence. The creation of a free national health service in Britain in 1947, in advance of most other countries, was certainly strongly related to Labour Party policy, and the existence of the health service since then has had a considerable impact upon spending patterns, including probably a displacement effect upon other programmes. It has also heavily influenced public expectations and attitudes.

Some theories of the growth of public spending focus upon a generalized relationship between structural pressures for governments to spend more and the tolerance or acquiescence of public opinion. The Peacock and Wiseman (1961) theory that high public spending in wartime acclimatizes the public to its continuation into peacetime, comes into this category. So does the general proposition that the acceptance of Keynesian demand management lowers resistance to such spending, both inside and outside government, because of its presumed beneficial effect upon the economy. Equally, of course, the climate of opinion can go into reverse, as happened with the growth of monetarism and taxpayers' revolts in the late 1970s.

Many theories concentrate instead upon the policy process itself, and particularly upon its alleged tendencies to produce excessive and distorted levels of public spending. Public choice theorists have been prolific on this theme, and some of these theories are considered in the next chapter. One obvious problem here is that significant environmental pressures upon government may be getting left out or discounted. Thus one is returned again to the need for an interactionist perspective. Unfortunately the interactions seem far too complex for any general theory to be adequate. Tarschys (1975) has analysed the complexity of possible explanations. The useful survey of theories by Larkey *et al.* (1981) concludes that more specific empirical hypotheses are needed, using better cross-national data.

For these reasons, this chapter will not assume that government can be treated as a 'black box', nor attempt to measure the impact of different environmental variables. But it will assume, since the evidence to that effect is formidable, that environmental changes have had a potent effect upon the growth and work of government. At the same time, the self-exciting tendencies within the political system, and their feedback effects upon public demands, must not be forgotten. The rest of the chapter, therefore, will survey on this basis some major environmental impacts upon government, and note some linkages between environmental explanations and those of the political theories to be discussed subsequently. Table 2.1 may help the reader to follow the discussions of the next three sections.

Table 2.1 Influences upon government behaviour

Environmental explanation	Demands upon government	Responses by government	Effects upon government	Problems for government	Links with political theories
A Technological change	Correction of 'externalities'; treatment of scale and risk	Extensive regulation; new technical services, e.g. R & D.	Growth of bureaucratic size and discretion	Regulation and enforcement	Emergence of new political conflicts; *pluralism*
B Economic change (1) Capitalism	Need for government support; growth of monopoly and oligopoly	Nationalization, subsidies, contracts etc.; regulation of competition	Growth of bureaucracy; growth of public expenditure	Fiscal overload	Contradictory demands upon government; *Marxism*
(2) International competition	Need to direct economy	Economic planning, technological development, merger policy	Growth of planning and development agencies	Co-ordination; inefficiency	Problems of effective national integration; *corporatism*
C Social change (1) Structural	Need to replace family and local support networks; more personal affluence and mobility	Rapid growth of public social services	Growth of professionalism; growth of public expenditure	Fiscal overload	Conflicts and co-operation with clients; *pluralism*
(2) Values	Assertion of individual and group rights; increased tolerance/indifference	Anti-discrimination laws; public participation	Growth of new public agencies and networks	Regulation and enforcement	*Public choice*

Political theories of modern government

The impacts of technology upon government are many and various. They include:

(1) The need to provide supporting services, e.g. airports, air traffic control.
(2) The need to control adverse side-effects, e.g. noise, pollution
(3) The need to adapt existing services and bureaucracies to the effects of technological change, e.g. mobile crime squads.
(4) The need to undertake or sponsor many high-risk, high-cost forms of tecnology, e.g. nuclear energy.
(5) The need to respond to the social and economic uncertainties and risks associated with technological change, e.g. genetic engineering.
(6) The need to cope with political conflicts surrounding technological change, e.g. cable television.

Unless we espouse technological determinism, these impacts are not of course automatic. They hinge upon the existence of incentives to utilize new technologies. In Western democracies, such incentives are plentiful. There is the profit incentive to produce new goods which consumers will buy. There is the military incentive to keep up to date with armaments. There is the welfare incentive, for example to improve health through medical innovations. There is the scientific incentive towards new knowledge, linked often with the belief that such knowledge will 'pay off' in due course.

There are political pressures favouring the development and use of technology, among capitalists and businessmen, the military, scientists and doctors. These pressures exist also within government, where they may be restrained by political and administrative awareness of the consequent costs and problems. There is also political opposition, notably from firms and workers who will be adversely affected, members of occupations who must change their ways or lose their jobs, and many members of the public who dislike change, especially rapid change. Despite these contrary pressures, an accelerating rate of technological change has occurred in Western societies. This fact merits the consideration of political theories. Here it need only be said that the faster such change is, the more are the problems 'dumped' into the lap of government.

Environmental change and government response

A homely but telling example of this process is to consider the case of the motor car. The use of the car has spread rapidly in Western societies because its considerable utility as a consumer durable is matched by its remarkable adaptability to mass production. Entrepreneurs such as Henry Ford and William Richard Morris (Lord Nuffield) spotted this fact and became two of the success stories of modern capitalism. The consequent impacts upon government have included:

(1) A massive volume of road construction and maintenance. Theoretically, roads might be commercially provided and sometimes are (toll roads), but practical problems of charging largely preclude this solution.
(2) Many laws have to be devised and enforced for traffic regulation, motoring offences, car licences and insurance, taxation, etc.
(3) A major expansion and reorganization of police forces to cope with motoring offences and mobile criminals.
(4) Large bureaucracies of traffic controllers, parking attendants, etc.
(5) Hospital and health services have had to cope with a volume of road casualties much greater in the aggregate (since 1945) than total Western casualties in World War II. Much of this extra medical care, in some countries almost all of it, falls upon public authorities.
(6) Environmental hazards to the safety, health and convenience of pedestrians require protective public action of various kinds.
(7) The growth of private transport reduces the efficiency and increases the congestion costs of public transport, creating a case for subsidies and other supports.
(8) Town planning is being transformed by problems of adapting cities to cars and vice versa.
(9) A complex set of political demands and pressures has assembled around the use and control of motor vehicles and their economic and social impacts.

These various activities utilize all the distinctive powers of government for coercion (e.g. traffic control), eminent domain (e.g. road building), and subsidization (e.g. public transport). Moreover, it is hard to know how government could avoid being involved with all these functions, once cars are allowed to proliferate.

31

In the USSR and other Communist countries this proliferation has not been allowed. The ruling elite have preferred to avoid heavy investment in motor plants and highways, and to rely upon the collectively cheaper and technically more efficient choice of public transport. The policy was supported by town planning which limited the growth of Moscow and surrounded it with a ring of satellite towns. This example shows the fallacy of 'technological determinism'. The use of inventions can be controlled. Such elite decisions, whether good or bad, could not have been made in Western democracies, but the pace of change might have been controlled, and more balanced systems of transportation favoured, if enough politicians and experts had shown foresight. Equally, of course, the use of cars is now spreading in the USSR from the elite itself slowly downwards, since the advantages of such an attractive individual durable cannot be permanently suppressed – although its design might be drastically changed so as to reduce its adverse impacts.

ECONOMIC CHANGE

Some part of government interventions in the economy can be explained by more or less inescapable technological problems. For example, problems of airspace and wavelengths mean that there must be some public regulation of airlines and television stations; severe pollution of water or air can hardly go wholly uncorrected; and if the risks and costs of some technological developments are to be undertaken at all, probably government must underwrite them.

These necessary features of public intervention do not explain *how much* regulation or economic support will eventuate, or *who* will be the beneficiaries or the losers from governmental action. This subject takes us into a different ball game, namely the pressures emanating from within the particular economic system of production and distribution. The explanations that can be offered become more dubious and controversial, and their connection with various political theories becomes closer.

Up to a point the facts themselves are not in dispute. Governments have become increasingly 'responsible' for the operations and management of the economy. Their interventions have taken several main directions:

(1) Assuming responsibility for major items of infrastructure, such as railways, ports, airports, electricity, gas, telecommunica-

tions, water supplies. In Western European countries such as Britain and France, these services are nearly all nationalized. In most cases their administration has also been transferred from local governments or private companies to national or regional public corporations. In the USA, and to some extent elsewhere, many of these services remain as private monopolies operating under public regulation.

(2) Taking over unprofitable industries whose commercial viability has been eroded by technological and market changes. This 'ash-can socialism', as the Americans call it, variously includes coalmines, steel plants, ship-building, aircraft, motor vehicles and other industries. The instruments are again public corporations or publicly owned companies. This process has also gone a long way in Britain or France, but little distance in the USA where the best example of ash-can socialism is Washington's rescue of the rump of a once great railway system. The process is partly reversible, as actions by Conservative Governments in the UK reveal, yet the feasibility of a full reversal of policies remains dubious.

(3) Governments have given extensive aid to industries, in the form of free or cheap technical and advisory services, substantial support for research and development, investment grants or loans, tax rebates, export credit schemes, etc. Many of these supports are intended to boost productivity and exports. Government aid in the European countries also has had a strong regional dimension which has recently declined. In the USA again there is less direct economic support except to agriculture, and much less of a regional dimension, but the federal government helps firms with big military and other contracts and provides tariff protection, while state and local governments offer incentives to attract industries.

(4) Governments have taken special measures to rescue large firms in distress, such as Rolls-Royce and British Leyland in the UK or Lockheed in the USA. They have sponsored and subsidized a wide range of job creation schemes. They have promoted public or mixed enterprise companies for the purpose of stimulating the economy and creating jobs.

(5) Governments have subjected firms to a growing array of controls for protecting the health, safety and welfare of workers, consumers and the general public. How adequate these measures are, and how far they constitute a burden on industry (or are simply passed on in higher prices) are matters of keen debate. In the USA, by contrast with Europe, the

weight of these controls constitutes the main grievance of business interests (Goldstein, 1978).

(6) Governments have increasingly and ambivalently concerned themselves with the working or non-working of economic competition. To some extent, particularly in the USA, they have adopted an anti-monopoly stance; but in practice they have often not only tolerated but actively promoted the emergence of large private monopolies or oligopolies.

This list adds up to a massive amount of public ownership, intervention and support with some striking differences between countries and some apparently contradictory tendencies. Allowing for the common technological problems, how are we to explain the process as a whole? At this point a brief look at three political theories may be helpful.

A *pluralist* analysis would concentrate upon the gains of government actions to particular interests. It would argue, for example, that government will step in to rescue a large firm like British Leyland because of the large number of jobs and the big investment which are at stake. It would not do the same for smaller firms with less political clout or visibility. Pluralism would deal with the growth of government support and services by pointing to the accumulation of special interests which result from such measures – a theme also known as 'politics make policies'. Pluralism would deal with the conflicts over regulation by pointing to the respective strength of special and general interests. For example, a large majority may be in favour of strong pollution controls, but the details and practicability of enforcement entail bargaining with industrialists who are able to win large concessions.

There would seem to be considerable political logic in the pluralist analysis. However, it does not fully explain why capitalism requires or accepts such a large degree of public intervention and support, or why the majority of taxpayers are prepared to pay for it.

A *Marxist* analysis addresses this issue. It argues that the diminishing profitability of capital compels capitalism to seek the support of the state. The state responds by bailing out unprofitable firms, helping export markets and absorbing redundant labour into its growing bureaucracy (O'Connor, 1973). Much of this thesis appears plausible. Governments have aided industries in a great variety of ways, and have often modified controls so as to protect profitability. It can certainly be said that the growth of the

34

government's role has been squared with the maintenance of capitalism, and that what governments do is strongly *constrained* by capitalist interests.

However, it is a large leap to say that all this has happened *for the sake of* capitalism. This thesis seems to prove too much, and to be somewhat contradictory. The measures that help some capitalists often harm others. For example, state policies which promote mergers, or try to rescue particular firms or industries, involve injury to the other firms and industries. The state's large costs have to be paid, and heavy taxation of business profits is hardly in the interest of capitalism as a whole. It is the other side of the state's largesse. It could, of course, be argued that it is the smaller and weaker capitalists who are injured, and that potential businesses are strangled for the sake of existing ones, but this comes closer to a plausible pluralist analysis than to a Marxist one. The Marxist thesis is only rescued by strong assumptions about the necessary internal development or 'logic' of the capitalist system, and its continuing compulsive power over the state even as capitalism weakens. Such strong assumptions cannot be verified and seem implausible if adequate alternative explanations can be provided (see Ch. 5).

The Marxist analysis can be helped out, however, by an analysis directed towards the *logic of international competition*. In a world of intense international and military competition, governments do not stand on the sidelines. They try to do what they can to improve the balance of payments, and to support prosperity and employment in their own country. This aim involves not only special measures to boost imports or to protect the home market, in so far as international treaties (and perhaps their own ideology) permits, but also to stimulate greater competitive productivity and efficiency in their own industries. As capitalism becomes increasingly integrated and internationalized and firms become larger and more diversified, governments get involved in a struggle for world markets which is quite different from the competitive market model. The USA, with its superior resources and enormous home market, sets the pace, and the governments of the smaller Western democracies are forced (or suppose that they are forced) to emulate the policies and techniques of the American multinationals.

The treatment of monopoly is a fascinating test case of the development of national economic policies and interventions. The liberal ideology condemns the effects of monopoly upon consumers' choice and competitive efficiency, and governments give lip-service to this principle, but their actions frequently proclaim the contrary.

Political theories of modern government

In an early postwar work, Galbraith (1957) gave a comfortable pluralist explanation of government ambivalence towards monopoly and imperfect competition. He claimed that governments intervened to strengthen the bargaining power of weak sections of the economy, such as agriculture, while dampening down by anti-trust legislation or other means the stronger concentrations of economic power. The first proposition is certainly true. Governments have legislated widely to confer coercive monopoly powers upon farm organizations, for example. The second proposition is very doubtfully true even of the USA, about which Galbraith was primarily writing, since anti-trust legislation is frequently ineffective. Oligopoly may speed up technological development and capital accumulation, but it is a considerable distance from the competitive model.

In Britain, blows have occasionally been struck against monopolistic practices. A committed minister and liberal-minded civil servants pushed through the abolition of resale price maintenance against considerable opposition (Bruce-Gardyne and Lawson, 1976, Ch. 4).

A Monopolies Commission has, on occasion, resisted the domination of a market by a single firm, although it has had to accept the frequent existence of oligopoly. However, British governments have deliberately promoted large-scale mergers in the aircraft, shipbuilding, defence contracting and other industries, and have set up such bodies as the Industrial Reorganization Corporation and the Public Enterprise Board to assist mergers for the purpose of stronger international competition. Economic planners in France have been more systematic. According to Shonfield (1965), they have worked to the 20–80 rule, meaning that 20 per cent of firms in an industry ought to account for 80 per cent of the output. Once again oligopoly, if not full monopoly, seems to be acceptable to government, and one closely related to competitive international competition.

The growth and nature of the state's economic interventions might be explained by a mixture of theories. Pluralism surely helps to account for the massive variety of assistance and protection given to agriculture, since farmers (as their numbers fall) have organized themselves increasingly effectively and often occupy, or are supposed to do so, a pivotal electoral position. Pluralism also helps explain the special help given to big companies in distress, and the way that many government initiatives (such as nuclear energy or supersonic aircraft) escalate under the influence of vested interests in the maintenance of contracts, jobs and scientific skills.

Environmental change and government response

In an economic market such ventures as Concorde could not possibly be sustained when their costs became clear, but in a 'political market' the impact of disappointed interests may be politically more painful than the taxpayers' eventual and generalized grievance. But the 'structural' conditions of international capitalist competition also have much explanatory power. They can explain public policies towards monopoly and mergers, government initiatives to create strong national companies or 'flag-carriers' and large public spending upon advanced technologies. Of course, governments may often be very mistaken or inefficient in judging how to maintain economic prosperity and there is plenty of evidence that they are so.

This account has left out the influence of ideology upon government economic interventions. *Laissez-faire* policy was strongly underpinned by the belief in the beneficence of free markets, a belief which particularly benefited employers but also had a general effect upon restraining the growth of government. Conversely socialism in principle appealed to the material interests of organized labour, but also carried an influential ethic which distrusted the profit motive and wanted to replace economic competition with co-operation. Socialist beliefs explain the faster pace of government intervention in some societies, but have been followed by disillusionment over the apparent inability of public ownership to alter the structure or behaviour of society.

SOCIAL CHANGE

Changes in social structure and values over the last forty years have had profound effects upon politics and government. These changes represent an acceleration of trends which have long been apparent, and which are closely associated with changes in the economic system. It is rather a dogmatic view, however, which assigns no independent force to social behaviour and values. Moreover, their impact upon government policies is in some ways more straightforward than is the impact of the economic system.

The size of family units has gone on shrinking rapidly. Households of extended kinship are now rare except among ethnic minorities and the very poor. Within the nuclear family, wives have greater independence, children leave home earlier, and the aged more often live on their own or in homes, or if rich enough they move to a retirement colony in some sunny clime. There has been a very large growth of single-parent families. One striking example of these changes is that the average household size in London has almost exactly halved since 1945, from about four and a half persons to about two and a quarter.

Geographic mobility has also much increased. One aspect is greater mobility between cities and regions, caused by shifts in industrial location and massive labour redundancies, and by the growth of more mobile career patterns among executive and professional groups. Large urban areas have both grown and spread. Within them there is a greater specialization of lifestyles according to income, age and marital status. The unattached young, single-person families, and the aged are more inclined to locate in inner areas, the rich often patronize exurbia, the middle mass migrate among numerous suburbs according to income and status. One individual will often move between a variety of locations in the course of his life (Berry, 1973; Self, 1982).

The relevance of economic change to these developments is obvious enough. Rapid shifts in industrial location, the growth of service employment, and the merger of firms are obvious causes of increased mobility. Increased job opportunities for women and juveniles have been an influence upon the fragmentation of households. But the pressure moves the other way also. Reduction in the size of the family unit has been much faster than economic developments would seem to require, and has compelled many employers (particularly while there was near full employment) to change their policies over hiring and conditions of work. Again, greater executive and professional mobility is not just a result of larger and more centralized firms, since it applies to the public service and to such a detached vocation as the clergy.

Associated with these structural changes are changes in attitudes and values. These include much more stress upon the freedoms and rights of individuals, as opposed to those of the family or any collectivity. The movements for sexual freedom, women's liberation, the rights of youth and greater racial equality all build upon this theme. This stronger individualism goes with greater tolerance or indifference toward other peoples' behaviour, and with more anti-authoritarian attitudes within and towards all organizations. There is more value placed upon private pleasure and consumption, and more (although qualified) acceptance of the value of change itself.

These social changes have been matched by a decline in the political importance of family influences and traditional loyalties, and by a growth of more individualistic political attitudes and behaviour. Greater occupational differentiation and geographic mobility has weakened class identifications. For example, more affluent industrial workers who have moved to a new town may go on voting Labour for a time (Goldthorpe, 1968), but their allegiance is much less certain and is liable to shift. American and British data reveal a considerable decline in party membership, and an increase in the number of 'floating' voters who shift between the main parties, or turn often only temporarily to a minor or new party. Single-issue voting also has increased (Crewe *et al.*, 1977; Nie *et al.*, 1979).

These changes in political behaviour provide more credibility for the public choice theorists' assumption of individualistic or egoistic behaviour. This assumption would have made much less sense historically, when so much political behaviour was grounded in family, community or class attachments. It is doubtful how far this more individualistic political behaviour also meets the assumption of rationality posited by these same theorists (see Ch. 3).

The decline of wider group loyalties also links with the growth of pluralism. The rise of interest and cause groups is a response to the increased specialization and fragmentation of economic and social life. Participation may be a problem because of the 'free rider' problem, but representative or not, pressure groups proliferate and flourish. They also take up slack in the activities of political parties by focusing demands more specifically.

The effects of social change upon demands for public expenditure have been considerable. Working mothers have wanted day-nurseries and nursery schools. The care of old people has been increasingly handed over to local authorities and the health service. So has the care of all those people who suffer physical or mental incapacity. The concentration of deprived people with restricted mobility in the inner areas of cities, whence more prosperous and mobile wage earners have fled, has led to special public programmes of aid for these areas. Increased mobility and the cult of private consumption have contributed to the growth of crime and juvenile delinquency. Lack of parental control has damaged educational performance. The bills for remedying all these special problems have been handed to the state, but public service performance has not matched the scale of social demand, despite the large growth of expenditure. Services of support, amelioration and correction which were once provided imperfectly but at little cost by kinship or community groups are now provided professionally but at considerable cost by public authorities.

Housing policies are an interesting example of social impact. The demand for housing has escalated since 1945 largely because of the dramatic reduction in the size of households. This fact led to an escalation of the waiting lists for public housing in Swedish, British and other cities (Self, 1982, Ch. 2). The city governments seemingly accepted it as their duty to try to meet this social trend. The subsequent rundown of public programmes exposed the extent of the unmet housing needs of single-parent families and other fragmented groups.

Social change has affected the nature of the welfare needs with which government tries to cope. The old belief that public welfare is primarily the requirement of a group labelled 'poor', who have distinctive and intractable lifestyles, lives on in theories such as Banfield's (1968), which fed the prejudices of the American anti-welfare lobby. Poverty has remained a basic problem, but less so as a class phenomenon and more so as the by-product of the numerous casualties of economic and social change.

The state's frequent assumption (in principle anyhow) of massive social responsibilities represents a replacement of erratic and voluntary kinship care by systematic professional care. One result has been the rapid growth of professional social workers who in turn form lobbies pressing for higher standards, broader coverage and better remuneration for themselves. Thus the effect of public social services is not hard to picture in pluralist terms. The creation of a service stimulates social changes (such as the break-up of households) which increases the need for it; coverage in one area or for one group leads to pressures for universalization; and the providers are themselves a strong lobby. This 'spiral effect' may help to explain why social services have gone on expanding fast in a well-provided country like Sweden, and lagged in an ill-provided country like the USA.

For many years social services have expanded much faster than either total public expenditure or GNP. In Britain for example, between 1958 and 1973 total public expenditure in real terms doubled, but the national health service grew by 141·0 per cent, education by 274·5 per cent and personal social services by 506·1 per cent (Klein, 1975, p. 14). Taking the averages for eight member nations of the Organization for European Co-operation and Development (OECD) between 1954 and 1980, the proportion of GNP spent by governments trebled in the case of health, more than doubled for social security and almost doubled for education (Rose, 1984, p. 213). A high proportion of this extra spending went to increasing the numbers of teachers, doctors, social workers, etc., so as to provide broader coverage and better staffing ratios. The latter seems to have had rather little effect upon service performance, but it may of course be the case that increasing social problems require professionals to do more work for the same results. The cost of personal social services also rises relatively because they are labour intensive − whereas industry continually sheds labour. Sweden is a country with an exceptionally high level of public social services, and whose planning, housing, transport and other policies are imbued with careful attention to the needs of the aged, the handicapped and mothers with young children. Sweden can only manage its welfare achievements by being both nearly the richest and also the most heavily taxed country in the world.

The differences among Western democracies over social policies are at least as great as over economic policies. Social security schemes are most developed and expensive in the continental European countries, such as France, Germany, the Netherlands and Belgium. Educational expenditure is high in the English-speaking federations of the USA, Canada and Australia. Personal welfare services are highly developed in the Scandinavian countries. Health services provide the most striking differences, with most countries offering some form of national health insurance while a few still baulk at more than a very restricted coverage (e.g. the USA), and another few such as Britain try to provide a free health service directly. Social priorities exercise some displacement effect upon other services and also reflect different social attitudes and beliefs. Education is associated in public opinion with notions of individual opportunity and economic growth. Only a few countries such as Sweden have fully embraced the philosophy that the state should rescue the casualties of social change.

The pressures for an upward spiral of social service spending can be thwarted or put into reverse by a strong enough resistance from politicians expressing the interests of taxpayers or public opinion. The strength of this opposition may be related to Wilensky's notion of the 'middle mass', with the paradoxical consequence that as the middle mass gets larger and wealthier, welfare spending of a redistributive kind might actually decrease. On the other hand, contributory social security schemes, especially if they are earnings-related, do not attract so much criticism as personal welfare services, so that expenditure upon such schemes could simultaneously increase. In terms of voting theory, this (doubtful) hypothesis could be presented as a shift in the position of the median voter.

Economic depression slows up these social changes. The rate of household formation will be reduced if personal incomes do not grow, and larger family units will therefore persist for longer. Unemployment and lower activity rates mean that able-bodied people (both women and men) have more time to care for children and the aged. Unemployment may increase crime but less personal mobility and affluence may reduce it. Some part of the social demand for many public services will therefore also be reduced, and if supply of these services is also cut, social change will be further inhibited.

This analysis is not meant to be judgemental, but to suggest how changes in economic and social structure work their way into social values and public opinion, thence into the policy process and the outputs of government; and how 'feedback' from these government operations tends cumulatively either to accelerate or decelerate the original social changes. It seems that on the whole the governments of Western democracies follow and accentuate social trends, rather than trying to control or direct them.

Changes in social values have other important impacts upon government. Stronger assertion of the freedoms or rights of individuals and minorities has brought about extensive anti-discrimination legislation and the creation of public watchdog bodies to support it. The growth of anti-authoritarian attitudes has softened discipline within bureaucracies and led to the provision of new mechanisms for public participation and protest. Simultaneously, the values of individualism, anti-authoritarianism and greater social tolerance or indifference increase the difficulties of enforcing the growing volume of public regulations. The massive growth of tax evasion is an example of the difficulties of achieving compliance with the purposes of law.

This analysis may seem to conflict with public opinion surveys which reveal a continuing trust in government institutions (Rose, 1984, p. 180) and a hardening opinion against subversive movements (Rose, 1984, p. 241). However, there may be no inconsistency. Democratic institutions may still receive generalized support and loyalty, at the same time as individual attitudes towards particular laws or programmes become more critical or evasive. Opinion may harden against subversion not because the public is less critical of government but because it seeks protection against the tendencies to political violence and disruption. Interestingly, the survey which showed more popular confidence in governmental than in private institutions gave the highest ratings to the police and army (bulwarks against subversion) and the next highest to strongly normative institutions imbued with traditional respect – the legal system, education and the church. By contrast confidence was relatively low in parliament, the civil service and large private companies, although lower still over the press and trade unions.

We can tentatively conclude that the phenomenon of governmental 'overload' in Western democracies is a real one. A large number of problems have been dumped into the lap of government as a consequence of changes in the technological, economic and social environment. These problems have been translated into political demands and bureaucratic programmes in ways which have caused the costs of government to rise much faster than the growth of national economies. For six Western countries the average annual growth in public expenditure between 1951 and 1980 has been estimated at 6·9 per cent, whereas the increase in the take-home pay available for private consumption was only 3·1 per cent. (Estimates by Rose and Peters; see Rose, 1984, p. 220.) When economies contracted, change in take-home pay became squeezed to a smaller or negative figure.

Of course, this strong growth in public expenditure may be quite sensible and justified in terms of the balance of social needs. We must entertain the suspicion, however, that a mixture of political and bureaucratic pressures may have caused an extravagant growth of some programmes. At the same time, governments may be failing to achieve other desirable objectives through weakness of political support or bureaucratic failure (see Ch. 7).

Democratic governments may have retained their generalized support and legitimacy, but public opinion has certainly become less willing to underwrite the costs of public programmes. Equally, there seems to be a growing mismatch between the demands placed upon government by citizens and the 'supports' which those citizens will give toward effective achievement and enforcement of public policies. There may also be severe strains in the capacity of modern bureaucracies to deliver services effectively and equitably. These possibilities, which were the subject of the pessimistic theories quoted in Chapter 1, will be the subject of further investigation.

ENVIRONMENTAL CHANGE AND POLITICAL THEORIES
This survey of the impacts of environmental change has already led to some consideration of various political theories. A very simplifed table (Table 2.2) may help the exploration of these theories in the next four chapters.

Table 2.2 *Political Theories*

Theory	Type	Demands upon government	Responses within government	Effects upon system	Problems for system	Possible remedies
A Public choice	Action	Individual wants or preferences	Varied according to institutional setting; strong tendencies to political distortion and bureaucratic expansion	Oversupply and distortion of public goods	Control of political and administrative behaviour; aggregation of individual preferences	(1) Return services to market (2) constitutional restraints on government; (3) improve political control to reflect preferences; (4) dismantle bureaucracy or strengthen incentives; (5) cost-benefit analysis
B Pluralism	Action	Multiple group demands	Creation of new agencies; consultative machinery; administrative fragmentation	Development of organizational interests and pluralist alliances; incremental policy making	Uneven balances of political and organizational power; issues of overload and co-ordination	(1) Extension of system to represent missing interests; (2) political entrepreneurship to express latent interests; (3) modification by general laws

C1 Corporate pluralism	Action-structural	Selective and unequal group demands	Incorporation of private interests; stronger control of resource allocation	Dominance of organizational interests (public and private); government co-ordination [corporate planning]	Executive domination and political exclusion of unfavoured groups	(1) Return to pluralism; (2) improve access to decision makers; (3) Return to constitutionalism and general laws
C2 Marxism	Structural	Requirements of capitalism displaced on to government	Economic supports to bale out capitalism; social supports to legitimate capitalism	Growth of government fiscal overload; integration of government and capitalism [corporate planning]	Structural contradictions and conflicts due to overload and subservience of government	Revolution (peaceful or violent)
C3 Nationalism	Structural-action	National interests as affected by international capitalism and competition	Government support for economic and technological developments and efficiency; economic protection, mergers, etc.; tendency to military spending	Corporate planning to integrate public and private interests for national goals	Structural conflicts between capitalism and nationalism; government inefficiency	(1) Strengthen national political integration; (2) bureaucratic reform and efficiency
D Elitism	Concealed action	Coalition of key actors	Political and bureaucratic secrecy and discrimination	Hidden maintenance of elite interests	Legitimacy and control of dissent	Democratic reform?

Political theories of modern government

The table needs some brief explanation, although its usefulness is mainly as a reference point. 'Public choice' and 'pluralism' are treated as single theories, but 'corporatism' is divided into three categories: C1 represents a development of pluralism, C2 follows Marxist analysis and C3 treats corporatism as a form of nationalism. It may be objected that this stretches the meaning of corporatism rather a long way. That may be true, but the problem is that corporatism is intrinsically a rather weak and flabby concept. It is treated here, as is explained in the relevant chapter, as a generalized description of the movement towards a close integration of private and public interests, and towards the overall integration of governmental action for certain ends. As such, it can become the subject of three different explanatory schemes.

Logically, theory D should be bureaucracy, to correspond with the chapter on that subject. However, the problem is that the other theories, as well as the various environmental types of explanation, all point to a growth of bureaucratic numbers, influence and discretion. Bureaucratic theories therefore overlap considerably with the other theories, and do not fit easily into the above scheme. Bureaucracy would need to be treated separately in the scheme if one held that bureaucrats are the dominant power-holders and actors in Western democracies. This belief will need some consideration later, but it is not held in this form by any prevalent political theory (although 'managerialism' comes close to it), and my own belief is that this view of bureaucracy is exaggerated.

On the other hand, 'elitism' is listed in the chart although it gets no separate chapter. It is included for purposes of reference and comparison, but elitism is not in my view as adequate or interesting a political theory as the others. If elitism refers (as it usually does) to a coalition of key actors, such as the 'military-industrial complex', who are said to maintain their joint power and interests by various devices, then it is dealing with much the same phenomena as my chapter on 'corporatism'. The difference is that a 'power elite' is a political not a structural force, which usually makes frequent use of secrecy, propaganda and the manipulation of institutions. Normatively speaking, elitism is much less interesting than the other theories because unlike them it offers no remedies for the state of affairs which it describes.

The various headings of the table should be self-explanatory as the discussion proceeds. They are intended to suggest in a general way what a theory says about the nature of the demands upon government, how government responds, what further effects occur, the typical problems which result and some of the remedies which follow from the theory in question.

'Type of theory' needs a little more explanation. Theories are divided into 'action' or 'structural'. Action theories focus upon the policy process itself, while structural theories look to environmental factors such as technology, 'modernization' or the economic system, in order to explain government behaviour. The categories are simplified, because theories are often mixed.

Public choice theories pay little attention to environmental changes, except as the impact upon problems of rational individual choice. Pluralist theories are also 'action-oriented', being rooted in the interests and goals of groups or organizations. 'Corporatist' theories are mixed. As a development of pluralism, corporatism adds structural constraints to the goals of groups and organizations. Marxist theorizing is primarily, but not wholly, structural. The nationalist theories of corporatism assume strong structural constraints upon economies, to which governments respond, either submissively or purposefully. In elitism the elite is purposive and gains results by political means, but generally conceals its intentions.

3

THE INDIVIDUALIST STATE

THE ECONOMICS OF POLITICS

The reduction of economic and political life to the interplay of basically egoistic individuals was a central theme of the nineteenth-century Utilitarians. Bentham argued that nature had placed all men under the sway of two sovereign masters, the pursuit of pleasure and the avoidance of pain. By studying these individual motivations, one would understand how the social system worked. A satisfactory system was one where the structure of incentives (to obtain pleasure and avoid pain) brought about the maximum possible net sum of individual pleasure, counting each person as one. Bentham's 'felicific calculus' offered in theory a rudimentary way of measuring this goal.

The economic theory of *laissez-faire* claimed that free competitive markets, policed by suitable laws for the protection of property and contracts, satisfied these conditions so far as the accumulation and use of wealth were concerned. The same ideas were applied by Bentham to penology, with such familiar conclusions as that the aim of punishment should be deterrence not retribution, and that consequently its certainty was more important than its severity. The Benthamite theory was curiously weak about politics, merely assuming that a fully democratic system would displace the 'sinister interests' which blocked, in the economic sphere, the ideal of competitive markets. Utilitarians such as James Mill and Bentham were somewhat naive about the relationship between 'is' and 'ought'. If human nature was as egoistic and hedonistic as they supposed, how were public spirited reformers such as themselves possible at all? How *could* a satisfactory social system be designed from such unpromising material? (See Halevy, 1928.)

John Stuart Mill did not quarrel for the most part with the political economy of the earlier Utilitarians but he did reject their psychology. Man and, much to the point in Mill's case, woman were capable of more elevated goals than pleasure, and pushball emphatically was *not* as good as poetry even if the quantity of pleasure was the same. J. S. Mill reverted to the Aristotelian goal of the development of human faculties to their highest level, and the cultivation of individual freedom and responsibility. J. S. Mill is important here, because his quarrel with Bentham closely parallels the modern divergence between welfare economists whose goal is the maximization of individual 'utilities' (= satisfactions or pleasures), and modern liberals such as Hayek who stress the superior value of individual freedom, responsibility and judgement.

The welfare economists are direct descendants of Bentham, while modern liberals owe a large debt to J. S. Mill, although the latter being more cultivated are much more aware of their pedigree. Hayek, for example, is a keen admirer of Mill, while most welfare economists seem ignorant of their large debt to Bentham.

The neoclassical economists such as Walras brought the theory of free market competition to its peak of formal mathematical perfection. At equilibrium point, the marginal 'utilities' of all participants in the economic game would be equalized and harmonized. There would be maximum all-round satisfaction, provided all participants acted egoistically, competitively, and rationally, i.e. that each calculated his own interest precisely. Of course these conditions never could be fully satisfied, but the theory demonstrated the logical structure and (at least by implication) beneficial nature of a fully competitive market system. Ironically perhaps, these economists were writing when the competitive structure of markets was becoming undermined by the growth of great monopolies or oligopolies.

Modern descriptive economics has tried to fight clear of the psychological and ethical assumptions of earlier economists. The economic term 'utility' is a pale and equivocal version of the Benthamite notion of pleasure. A consumer's utility represents what he likes or chooses, which are not the same thing. The theory of 'revealed preference' makes no assumption about an individual's motives, and merely registers the statistical uniformities of aggregated economic behaviour. None the less economic behaviour can be predicted only *to the extent* that such uniformities exist, and these uniformities have to be explained by an appropriate motive. In the background still lurks the figure of rational maximizing economic man.

This historical background helps to illuminate the modern invasion of political science by economists in the neoclassical tradition. The main carriers of this invasion are the public choice theorists, who have built up a flourishing academic industry primarily in the USA. The tools of these thinkers are the logical deductive methods of economics, which proceed from basic assumptions or axioms and statements of initial conditions to deductions about social behaviour. Like formal economics, they make a heavy use of mathematical description, even though their equations seem often to advance the actual argument very little. None the less their methodology has a tighter logical structure than do most forms of political analysis, and is able to draw upon the supposed 'scientific' superiority of economics over other social sciences.

There is, however, one crucial and paradoxical respect in which the public choice theorists depart from mainstream economics and revert to the psychological and philosophical concerns of the Utilitarians. The simplifying assumption of egoism, now muted in economic thought, is carried boldly by these theorists into the seemingly much less tractable sphere of politics. In viewing the political system as a product of the interaction of self-regarding individuals, they are in a sense tackling the agenda which Bentham overlooked. They are also, as the last two chapters have suggested, striking a sympathetic chord in modern political thought. In modern 'Western' societies, political behaviour has certainly become more individualistic even if not narrowly egoistical. Moreover, disillusion with political behaviour has created a climate that is hospitable towards a realistic view of politics as an activity concerned, in Lasswell's (1950) famous phrase, with 'who gets what, when, how'. If the actors in this political process can plausibly be designated not as groups or classes but as individuals, then a formal deductive account of how they will behave so as to maximize their personal gains in different institutional settings acquires at least a *prima facie* credibility. Such an account seems to need no more than a few basic assumptions about individual motives, plus a careful stipulation of the initial institutional rules, to yield some plausible deductions which can then be put to the empirical test.

The public choice theorists apply the logic of market behaviour to the political realm. Politics is seen as a market for the demand and supply of public goods. Buchanan argues that the individual is the same person in his economic and political relationships, and that he will make his decisions according to the same criteria. His motivations are hypothesized (rather than asserted) to be those of a rational egoist; in other words he will judge public policies or party programmes according to their probable benefit to himself. Admittedly, the conditions of political choice are different from those of market choice; but if both activities are viewed as forms of mutual exchange, based upon similar motivations and objectives, it will follow that there are considerable similarities between the two processes. The problem for public choice then becomes one of matching the theory of economic markets with an equivalent theory of political markets.

Up to a point a market theory of politics is persuasive, at any rate when applied to Western capitalist societies. Many writers, such as Schumpeter (1943), have stressed the close cultural and institutional linkages between capitalism and parliamentary democracy. Marxist theorists have made precisely the same point, from the opposite viewpoint of arguing the dependence of liberal democracy upon capitalist interests (MacPherson, 1962). Instead of the power relationships of class interests and conflicts – a form of analysis quite familiar to the great classical economists – the public choice theorists concentrate upon the features of open-ended individual competition in both economic and political realms. They tend to overlook or assume away the possibility of a basic class, ethnic, or other type of group domination, in favour of a universe of interacting atomistic individuals. They cannot of course ignore the existence of inequalities of wealth or power, but these are often treated as differences to be justified, not as impediments to their mode of explanation.

Following this approach, voters can be likened to consumers; pressure groups can be seen as political consumer associations or sometimes as co-operatives; political parties become entrepreneurs who offer competing packages of services and taxes in exchange for votes; political propaganda equates with commercial advertising; and government agencies are public firms dependent upon receiving or drumming up adequate political support to cover their costs. Of course, the political market is cruder than the economic one. Much political exchange takes place not in terms of votes, which like money can be counted, but in terms of influence, which cannot. Measurement is very much more restricted in politics than in markets. But one can still conceptualize politics as a bargaining process between individuals possessed of different degrees of power or influence, which they trade off as 'political opportunity costs' in their pursuit of different goals.

This conception of a political market is not the special property of public choice theorists. It is a recognizable version of pluralist liberal democracy. Indeed public choice theory has difficulty over articulating a political system of this kind, because individual egoism will continually inhibit or destroy effective political action by pressure groups, parties, political leaders, etc., thereby producing a much darker and less predictable Hobbesian type of political universe. Leaving this issue aside for the moment, we will revert to the central argument.

At first sight, anyhow, Buchanan's comparison seems to overlook the role of social norms in different institutional settings. An important fact about economic markets is that within the limits of legality egoistic behaviour is fully acceptable, indeed it is socially justified and commended by the requirements of a competitive system. No doubt some people who object to *apartheid* will not buy South African oranges, but in the system as a whole such deviations are very minor. Even a socialist buying a hi-fi set will seek out the (to him) best bargain, regardless of the nationality or employment practices of the supplying firm. He might regard such matters as appropriate for *political* action, but not as affecting his market choice; and public opinion generally would sanction this position. This illustration suggests one major difference between markets and politics. Politics is the legitimized sphere for resolving normative social conflicts, whereas an idealized market system is self-regulating and ethically neutral, given the enforcement of basic laws of property and contract.

It does not follow that political man is moral in a way that economic man is not. Just because directly egoistic behaviour is for the most part much harder in politics than in economic markets, a point seized upon by the public choice theorists themselves, group norms and allegiances have to count for more if effective collective action is to result. Political choice for an individual often centres around conflicts between different group interests and loyalties, whose ultimate pay-offs to that same individual are highly speculative and uncertain. One problem, therefore, for the public choice theorist is how the egoistic assumption of market behaviour will work out under the very different conditions of political life.

For reasons familiar from the history of Utilitarianism, 'egoism' also proves to be a slippery concept on which to build political theory. This concept is sometimes defined narrowly so as to cover only private material gain, in which case socially defined goals such as reputation or duty will be relevant only to the extent that the material costs of ignoring them exceed the benefits (Laver, 1981). This is hardly a realistic definition of political behaviour, since it seems clear that human beings and especially politicians often intrinsically value the esteem or deference of others. Man is not an isolated individual concerned solely with private consumption. Alternatively, egoism can be extended to cover such values as the maximization of income, deference, and safety (Lasswell, 1950). This formulation is more plausible, but it makes prediction much harder since the goals are contradictory; as Lasswell points out, safety seems to be negatively correlated with deference. Finally, one can include in egoism the 'psychic satisfaction' of helping others, but this gambit makes nonsense of the concept. If almost all behaviour can be described as egoistic in some sense, there is little scope for prediction.

The difficulty with egoism is that it has to be contrasted not simply (or primarily) with altruism, but with conformity. The conformist may act from fear of sanctions or from a wish for the good opinion of others or from a sense of duty, but it is hard to assess such motives or base predictions upon them. The egoist by contrast calculates his private advantage, which equates him with rational economic man. It also makes prediction much easier – if the assumption is true. There has always been plenty of both egoism and conformity, but the volume of egoism may be greater in some periods (like the present) and in some cultures (like the USA).

Public choice theorists are also well aware of the necessity of social norms for maximizing the sum of individual satisfactions. It is only in very special conditions, such as properly policed competitive markets, that individual interests can to some extent (but by no means wholly) be harmonized spontaneously. Elsewhere the interplay of individual wants produces frequent mutual frustrations (Schelling, 1978). However, public choice theorists are much better at explaining how egoistic behaviour undermines social norms, than how these norms get established in the first place.

A good illustration of the mutually frustrating effects of individual egoism is the well-known 'tragedy of the commons' (Hardin, 1968). In this example, a group of villagers graze their livestock upon a common pasture. Once social restraints get broken, each individual has a progressive incentive to expand his share of the grazing, and no new equilibrium point can be reached until the pasture is completely ruined. There are numerous comparable situations in modern life. For example, a group of wealthy exurbanites may well support town planning controls which reduce the value of their land, for the sake of protecting their locality and way of life against unwanted intrusions, but if one or two owners manage to sell their land at a profit, it becomes increasingly in the interest of other owners to do likewise. Mishan (1967, pp. 233 – 40) applies the same logic to transportation controversies. Once enough individuals have purchased a car, public transport starts to run down, so that more individuals feel compelled to buy a car or to use it more, and so on; yet he contends that most individuals would prefer a mixture of better public transport plus some restraints on car usage.

This last example suggests how very widespread 'tragedies of the commons' have become under modern conditions of functional interdependencies, and of tendencies towards the erosion of common natural and social resources (an example of the latter is the deterioration of a slum, when it becomes decreasingly worthwhile for any owner to maintain his dwelling). The tragedy of the commons example serves:

> as a paradigm for situations in which people so impinge on each other in pursuing their own interests that collectively they might [surely, *would*: P. S.] be better off if they could be restrained, but no one gains individually by self-restraint. [Schelling, 1978, p. 111].

Thus public choice theorists run into considerable problems over the definition and relevance of 'rational egoism' for political behaviour. The most fruitful way of dealing with this problem is to restrict the initial hypothesis, and accept that the economic motive of maximizing one's own material benefit is not the only individual motive in political and organizational contexts; but it may still be a significant and powerful motive, especially in some types of transaction, whose strength can be tested through careful empirical research. Olson's work is the best example of this approach (see next section). On the other hand, many writers in this school start from a more comprehensive hypothesis of egoistic behaviour, and support their deductions by no more than a plausible selection of possible evidence. It has to be stressed, of course, that these theorems of public choice thinkers do rest upon hypotheses – they are not meant as dogmatic assertions; but they become dogmatic if they take the form of logical deductive reasoning which is not submitted to the test of falsification.

An alternative public choice approach, which sidesteps these problems about individual motives, is to investigate the strategies which rational actors will pursue to realize some unambiguous goal or consistent set of preferences. The theory of games accords very well with the 'rationality' assumption of the public choice school, because a game is constructed as an exercise in logical choice and the goal of winning is unambiguous and not usually harmful either. For these reasons, the theory of games can make some interesting predictions about the strategies which rational players will adopt, and how these strategies will work out.

The same analysis can be applied to 'games-like' situations in real life, such as the behaviour of committees. We need not bother with the motives of a committee member in order to analyse his optimum strategy for achieving a given order of preferences. The study of voting rules yields information about the potential influence of individual committee members, for example, the representatives of small nations in the UN Security Council turn out to have negligible capacity to influence decisions (Riker and Ordeshook, 1973, Ch. 6). The 'size principle' suggests that a coalition will usually be the minimal size required for winning, since otherwise the benefits will be unnecessarily diffused. If an overlarge 'grand coalition' does happen to occur, it will dissolve quickly; for example President Lyndon Johnson won the 1964 election by a vast majority which quickly dissolved (Riker and Ordeshook, 1973, Ch. 7).

The last example simplifies the logic of choice by making assumptions about political aims which may not be true. For example, a large majority may find policy implementation easier and may not dissolve. Application of the games theory to international conflicts runs into tougher problems. Up to a point one can analyse possible rational strategies for contesting an international issue, but governments are not individuals, stakes are real and behaviour under crisis is not closely predictable. Life in fact is not a game. The predictive power of this type of theory can cover only the pursuit of clear goals in closely rule-bound situations, or general inferences about the likely effects of different rule systems.

On the other hand, this type of analysis is normatively interesting for its contribution to democratic concepts of equity and fairness. How to aggregate individual preferences is a classic problem of public choice theory. Arrow's impossibility theorem supposedly demonstrated that there is no way of performing this task which fully satisfies a set of democratic criteria (Arrow, 1963). Nevertheless, there are better and worse ways of combining preferences and study of the many alternatives can be of real help to democratic theory. In political and real life terms, Arrow's problem is actually a rather minor obstacle to popular democracy when compared with the problems of structuring the political agenda so that individuals have the opportunity to make effective choices. But this problem also can be tackled up to a point through logical analysis of alternative systems.

Political theories of modern government

This section has shown how an economic approach to politics opens up issues about individual motives and behaviour, social rules and norms and the logic of collective choice. It has also suggested some of the difficulties and limitations of making egoistic assumptions about political behaviour. In the next section I consider some of the implications of a public choice approach for political and organizational behaviour, followed by a section dealing with the supply and demand for public goods, a subject of key interest for this brand of political economy. Finally I review some of the normative principles for the reform of government put forward by public choice theorists.

It should be stressed that my approach is selective. It is not my intention to give a detailed review of a diverse and prolific set of writers, whose common ground is limited to their economic methodology. As with subsequent chapters, my aim is the more general one of considering what contribution a school of thought offers towards understanding the workings of modern government and reforming its institutions. Therefore I cannot do justice to individual thinkers, or to significant differences among the public choice theorists, but must concentrate upon some key examples of the economic approach to politics.

POLITICAL AND ORGANIZATIONAL BEHAVIOUR

The public choice theorists build their world upon laws or tendencies of individual behaviour. As noted earlier, a problem for public choice theory, and one to which its early exponents gave far too little attention, is precisely how the postulated 'egoism' and (to a lesser extent) 'rationality' of the individual actor is to be defined. Different assumptions or suppositions about these matters yield different predictions. Consequently, while starting apparently from the same general standpoint of 'methodological individualism', one can model the policy process in different shades from a tolerable mutual adjustment to the blackest mutual frustration. As Chapter 1 suggested, the tendency of public choice writers has been to move towards the latter, highly pessimistic position.

The usual entry point for this discussion is Olson's (1965) well-known exposition of the 'free rider' problem. Why should a rational individual bother to support an organization formed to advance his interest? He will share automatically in any benefits which result without incurring the cost of participation, while if he invests enough time and energy to influence the outcome, his cost-benefit ratio will be a high one.

56

The individualist state

Olson's test of his hypothesis is the way that trade unions and other interest groups offer commercial services and employ individualized incentives and sanctions in order to recruit and keep members. Farmers' unions and labour unions (especially in their earlier years) offer many services of this kind, which entitle individuals to join for direct benefits; later, membership may be enforced by coercive agreements with employers or other sanctions. The same theory explains *failure* to organize large groups such as the unemployed, migrant workers, consumers, etc., because selective incentives are harder to offer in their cases (since Olson's book, consumer associations have grown with the help of selective services of information and advice).

Olson does not claim too much for his theory. He accepts that it works best where the interests engaged are economic and material, and would be less applicable to religious and charitable organizations. The need for incentives also applies more strongly to a large than a small group since in the latter case the individual has at least a closer interest in the outcome.

This theory undermines the frequent pluralist assumption that groups form and grow through a process of free association. Clearly, both material incentives and coercive sanctions (direct and indirect) play a central part in the growth of economic organizations. On the other hand, many voluntary and 'cause' groups involve personal sacrifices on the part of their founders and active members which clearly contradict the 'free rider' hypothesis. Free riding is *not* a universal human characteristic and indeed is qualified in economic organizations also by sentiments of group loyalty and shared goals.

One can also use the free rider hypothesis to inquire why anyone bothers to vote in an election, for while the cost of going to the polls may be small, the probability of one vote affecting the result is utterly minute. The fact that voting is significantly higher in marginal constituencies might lend support to this thesis. However, in a marginal constituency the probability of a single vote determining the outcome is still minutely small, so that the extra voters are not really being logical. An explanation both of this situation and of greater participation in successful organizations is that the rational calculations of individuals are not equal to statistical fine tuning. A probable explanation of voting behaviour generally, and especially in marginal constituencies, is that many voters reckon their costs as tiny or irrelevant in relation to almost *any* possibility of getting their preferred result, especially if it is a question of 'turning the rascals out'. The rationality postulated by the theorists is bounded in practice and is mixed with or overlain by motives of self-expression, civic duty, group loyalty, etc.

It is certainly true that political participation is less likely among individuals who are poor or ill informed, a situation which can be explained by a theory such as Maslow's (1954) 'hierarchy of needs'. No doubt the poor are too concerned with basic needs to feel the same intrinsic interest in participation as the middle class, but poor individuals will often work altruistically for a party in a most un-Olson-like way for basic goals of social justice. It is true enough that 'free riding' is a widespread feature of political and organizational behaviour, but as one factor in a complex set of motivations.

Interesting evidence that political behaviour has become more individualistic and in some ways 'rational' comes from Himmelweit *et al.*'s (1981) longitudinal study of a group of 459 male English voters over a sixteen-year period covering six elections (1959–74). Longitudinal studies of this kind are very few. Only 30 per cent of this group voted throughout for the same party. Voters were influenced both by party policies on a range of specific issues and also by their opinion about the probability of a party implementing a policy. It seems that many of these voters became increasingly sceptical over party promises about economic management, and consequently gave more weight to policies of less salience but more likelihood of implementation. The authors compare these voters to consumers struggling to make as rational a choice as possible between frequently changing party packages that have to be tested for both content and reliability. Moreover, the package has to be bought or rejected as a whole. The fact that rational judgements are attempted in this difficult situation need not imply that the judgement is wholly self-interested, since it also reflects what the individual considers will be best for society.

Anthony Downs' pioneering *An Economic Theory of Democracy* (1957) argues that since the cost of acquiring adequate information about public policies is high, it is rational for a voter to select a general policy preference and leave its detailed application to a political party. A party is supposed to consist of a team of politicians whose single objective and reward is to win office. If individual preferences are arrayed along a single continuum, and if further the electoral system structurally favours a two-party system, as in the USA or UK, then it will pay each party to pitch its appeal to the median voter. Consequently the two main parties will cluster close together in the middle of the public policy spectrum, and if the median voter's preference moves either way, it will pay both parties to do likewise.

The individualist state

These assumptions are bold and, as with all such theories, unlikely to be more than partly realized; but still Downs did give an intelligible account of one brand of democratic politics. British politics are his example and up to perhaps 1970 (well beyond the date of his book) a good one to take. After a leftward move by the electorate in wartime, Labour won the 1945 election handsomely, the Conservatives then moved to the left embracing much of the programme of the 'welfare state', Labour moved back somewhat to the right as normality returned, and both parties despite their rhetoric then followed very similar policies over economic management, employment, regional assistance, defence, the health service, town planning, the expansion of education, etc. Those issues over which the parties quarrelled loudly, such as the nationalization of steel, were really minor and even the eventually divisive issue of incomes policy was one on which both parties would have liked to reach a rather similar solution. It was the failure to reach *any* solution of this problem which ushered in the fiercer politics of the 1970s.

However, Downs' theory was time and space specific. Voters' preferences have decreasingly been arrayed along a single continuum in Britain and many other countries, for reasons to be explored in Chapter 7. This fact alone must make voting and party positions more erratic. Then Downs assumes unrealistically that voters' intensities of interest are equal whereas party activists care more about policies than do most people. Typically such activists also occupy more differentiated or extreme positions. The very fact that party extremists may find it difficult to exit to an alternative party will make them exercise their voice more vociferously (Hirschman, 1970). Their influence is likely to grow if median party policies seem to be failing and structural conflicts in society are growing. These circumstances explain why, contrary to Downs, the two main British parties have moved much further apart since 1970, to the point where a third party has entered to try and mop up the middle ground.

Downs assumed that party politicians, while only keen on winning, acted collectively and honestly over following the median voter's policy preferences. Naturally, public choice theorists need make no such assumption. They may argue that politicians will extract a surplus from the public with which to satisfy their own preferences. According to Breton (1974), the higher the costs of citizen participation and the longer the politicians' tenure of office, the bigger their surplus will be. Moreover, an individual politician will tend to act egoistically, which means that he is always liable to default on his promises or on party loyalty when that course is to his private advantage.

Similar theories have been advanced about bureaucrats. A bureaucrat will allegedly try always to maximize the size of his budget since to do so will increase his income, status, and influence (Niskanen, 1971). Once a bureau has started up, it is almost impossible to dismantle it (Downs, 1967). Bureaucrats will frequently distort public policy and evade political control for private gain (Tullock, 1965). Bureaucrats will wrest from politicians as much as they can of the surplus resources extracted from the electorate (Breton, 1974).

These dark predictions are instantly recognizable as possible and perhaps frequent forms of human behaviour. Perhaps that is why their presentation in scientific dress strikes so ready a chord among political cynics and bureaucrat-bashers. Yet as their exponents sometimes recognize, the egoistic assumption is qualified by the existence of counter-sanctions. For example, in countries like Britain and France, the tendency of bureaucrats to expand their budgets is constrained by the fact that the most prestigious jobs within the administrative elite belong to budgetary controllers (Self, 1977).

The theory that politicians or bureaucrats have no personal interest in the choice of public policies will hardly stand up to examination. Logically, the personal advantage to a politician from the policy that he prefers is much less than the benefit from supporting policies which help his re-election; but moral and emotional attachment to beliefs and policies are facts of normal human behaviour, and it would be strange indeed if politicians, who spend their lives dealing with policies, had no personal preferences for which they would make at least some effort and sacrifice. It is as if doctors were wholly indifferent to medicine. This kind of reasoning reflects on the intellectual climate of depersonalized specialization which has come under increasing criticism. This is perhaps a situation where the enunciation of a theory itself reinforces the behaviour which the theory predicts.

The public choice approach tends to dissolve all organizational life into the competing interests of individuals (Jackson, 1982). Every individual has an inducement-contribution balance; if the inducements are inadequate he will quit (if he has a better alternative), and in any case he will seek to change or evade organizational policy so as to suit his own interest. Thus an organization becomes an unstable coalition of individuals, and organizational goals cease to have any reality. Actually, this last proposition is not true. An organization normally possesses machinery for reaching authoritative decisions and committing resources in various ways. Provided its leaders can elicit compliance from members, they can pursue durable policies if they have sufficient joint interest to do so. Even if the leaders and other participants have differing goals, enduring features in the structure of the organization and in its environment can produce fairly durable patterns of behaviour. Admittedly, the 'goals' which might be inferred from an organization's behaviour patterns may only very partially have been 'willed'.

As Jackson points out, this type of analysis has implications not only for government but also for the theory of economic markets. Neo-classical economic theory ignored the internal organization of the firm, simply assuming that it would make an efficient response to market signals. But if an economic firm also is an unstable coalition of individuals, its response to the market cannot be taken for granted. This finding led to the analysis of X-efficiency (Leibenstein, 1966), viewed as the capacity of any organization (public or private) to elicit effective contributions from its members. An individual's contribution can be viewed as his APQT bundle (his activities, pace of work, quality of work, and time spent on work), and the problem for management is to elicit the optimum APQT from each member. However, it can still be argued that *external* competitive conditions are a factor making for greater X-efficiency. Thus the public choice approach leads to the conclusion that both external environment and the internal structure of public organizations should be made more competitive through a much stronger use of economic inducements and sanctions.

But is this restrictive view of individual motivation at all adequate? Etzioni (1961) gives a more plausible account of motives as being either utilitarian, normative, or coercive. He suggests that economic organizations draw primarily upon the first motive, cultural and educational bodies upon the second, penal institutions upon the third. In practice motivations are mixed, while the same organization may change its character over time. A revolutionary party draws initially upon moral and idealistic support, but once in power it is liable to switch, as the Bolsheviks did, to massive coercion. In democracies, a radical party will also (more moderately) change its behaviour in office, as utilitarian motives about jobs and discipline replace moral enthusiasm for policies and ideals. Disillusioning examples of this cycle are frequent, but the cycle still rolls on. Still more obviously, an army must concern itself in peacetime with utilitarian motives of pay and conditions, but in wartime relies upon a contradictory mixture of normative and coercive motives. Soldiers often fight idealistically for their country, but if they refuse they are liable to be shot. Public choice theory cannot deal with such stark situations.

Nor do these theories cover situations where idealistic or altruistic motivations really do predominate. Many cause groups, to some extent anyhow, contradict Olson's point about the need to offer utilitarian rewards so as to secure participation. As Goodin (1982, Ch. 6) says, members of such a group may actively dislike side-payments because it denigrates their moral purpose. Cynics may contend that only the relatively rich will afford this luxury, but in fact many humble people help cause groups without wish for reward.

Modern Western societies have moved away from reliance upon direct coercion, save in penal situations, and have placed an increasing weight upon economic incentives and sanctions. It may be questioned whether individual motivations vary much between the public and business sectors. In both cases, organizational loyalties and personal ideals have some relevance, and material inducements are very important. The special pride in 'public service duty' (which could also be a source of arrogance) has diminished as government and society have absorbed each other. However, government still provides a much more secure career structure and pension rights, together with weaker financial incentives and disciplines, than does business. This arrangement accords with intrinsic differences in the work of government, such as a greater need for attention to rules, procedures and equity rather than to speed of results, the strongly collective character of much bureaucratic work, and the greater difficulties of evaluating individual performance. Government needs to draw upon stronger social norms and sanctions than do business organizations. Public choice theories often fail to confront this issue, through their bias towards the economic market model. *

THE DEMAND AND SUPPLY OF PUBLIC GOODS

From a public choice perspective, political choice can be viewed as a demand for public goods rather than particular policies or some abstraction called the 'public interest'. To some extent a 'goods' approach and a 'policy' approach come to the same thing, because the definition of public goods can be made a wide one. The obvious examples are the direct supply of services, such as health, education, and public utilities; but 'public goods' can also refer to the products of regulatory activities such as maintenance of clean air and pure water, the upholding of honesty in commercial transactions, the prevention of crime, and so on. If government planning succeeds in improving economic stability or increasing employment, which is arguable, that too should be counted a public good. A more equal distribution of wealth, jobs or access to services may be reckoned a 'public good' if the sum total of individual satisfactions is thereby increased, or if violence or other threats to individual tranquillity are thereby reduced. Many public services or subsidies are also partly justified by indirect effects of a 'public goods' nature, such as the civic or democratic effect of public education and the effect of recreational and cultural activities upon individuals' health and mental development. But we need to recognize that government can also produce bad side-effects – for example, cause pollution – and that private organizations may produce desirable 'externalities'. It was an error of the older welfare economics to assume that government action would actually resolve the problem it was supposed to be tackling.

In principle the voter can be pictured as choosing (from the options available) that party programme which will provide him with his optimum package of public goods and taxes; but his information, patience, and mental skills are patently inadequate for making such a calculation. He will tend instead to be swayed by more limited considerations, such as the degree of his resistance to more taxation and the extent of his desire for particular public goods. Since the evidence is that often these contradictory desires are both strongly held, his choice may be somewhat ambivalent. Not only this, but in modern societies any tax/public goods package is much affected by the state of the economy, so that he will have to judge the probable impact of a party upon the economy, viewed both as a public good itself and for its effect upon other goods and taxes.

It is worth making these fairly familiar points since many public choice theorists assume an unrealistic procedure of logical choice, and forget the basic importance of how the political agenda is actually set up, and of the consequent degree of ambivalence or confusion in the minds of those voters attempting a rational choice. (The irrational ones need not bother anyhow.) These conditions are quite consistent, as I suggested earlier, with a growing amount of reasoned individual choice, and indeed with increased attention to the costs and benefits of specific public goods. Politicians find it increasingly necessary to put figures upon their proposals, although much of this is only presentational.

Political theories of modern government

Another problem is the disjunction between the demand and supply functions of public goods. If a public good is free, each consumer will tend to demand as much of it as he can personally utilize; but as a taxpayer he will be reluctant to vote an adequate supply for this purpose. James Buchanan (1965) gives a reasonable explanation in these terms for the delays and shortages of treatment in the British national health service. There are other at least partial explanations for this state of affairs, such as the high visibility of costs in a financially centralized system and the use of a complex planning system to aid public economy (Klein, 1980).

Buchanan does not question that the principle of a free or low-cost health service may be desirable for its efficiency in checking the spread of diseases or for other reasons. Equally a free service may be the most equitable arangement, as between both poor and rich, and sick and healthy. Buchanan does not discuss either the possible effects of an equitably designed service upon the willingness of patients to restrain their demands in the interests of more urgent cases, and upon the willingness of doctors to work harder and more selflessly than in commercial practice. Yet such normative ideals played a definite part in the creation of the British national health service and in its practices in its earlier years. As Titmuss (1971) points out, blood giving in Britain uses voluntary donors as opposed to the cash payments made in the USA, and gets better results from the arrangement. No doubt, as with the 'tragedy of the commons', these normative values are liable to successive erosion, and given the increasing costs of medical technology, they could hardly cope with the growing gap between demand and supply. Buchanan's analysis of the pressure upon free public goods is logically pertinent but assumes too complete a domination of economic motives.

What effects will the rational egoism of voters, politicians and bureaucrats have upon the actual supply and financing of public goods? Much of the analysis upon this subject has centred around the role either of the median voter or else of the pressures that can be exerted by favourably placed minorities.

Tullock in *The Vote Motive* (1976) claims that the median voter theorem establishes an *optimum* expenditure for each public service. He further contends that in the USA the median voter theory 'has been found of great value in predicting the size of school budgets, government policies on conservation, etc.' The school budget is Tullock's likeliest example, because in the USA this is set by a specially elected authority, but he produces little evidence. Curiously the same booklet includes a contradictory pluralist example from Morris Perlman. Perlman points out that median consumer preferences would strongly favour switching transportation subsidies from railways to buses, but that this course is barred by the much stronger organization of rail authorities and rail commuters. Perlman's example may support Tullock's case for the purpose of reform but not of explanation.

It sounds plausible to argue, as many besides Tullock have done, that the cost-benefit package of public goods will be skewed toward the preference of the median voter. There is little clear evidence that this is the case, although the hypothesis gets some small support from surveys of municipal budgets (Mueller, 1979, pp. 106–111). Associated with this belief is the idea that the mass of middle-income voters will be able to impose their tax and service preferences at the expense of both rich and poor. Wilensky's (1975) argument about the anti-welfare, anti-taxation bias of the 'middle mass' accords with this belief. So does the contention of Rowley and Peacock (1975, Ch. 7) that the interests of middle-income voters are clearly responsible for free or subsidized health care, education, and culture, and that this same group's prejudices explain why the poor are helped through services in kind rather than income redistribution. The influence of the median voter will also depend upon the nature of the dominant political majority or coalition. For example, the Roosevelt coalition which backed the 'New Deal' incorporated the poor and minority groups of that period, whereas postwar political majorities have increasingly been tilted 'upward' so as to exclude the poorer groups.

Olson and others argue that large and diffused groups will be too poorly organized to demand the public goods that they would like because of the free rider problem. Hence such public goods will be under-supplied. By contrast, minorities with an intense interest in extracting some subsidized good or other concession from the state can organize better, and their support will be worth more to politicians than the cost which will thereby be spread among a large, unaware majority. Hence public goods to these minority groups will be over-supplied. The actual minorities to benefit from this principle will depend upon the institutional rules and conventions of the political system; for example the US system makes Congressmen strongly beholden to the support of local economic interests, whereas in the UK local political control is much weaker and successful minority interests must use national or regional pull.

This analysis reveals 'distorted spending' in a familiar pluralist light. However, public choice theory does not necessarily endorse pluralism, because group interest dissolves into individual interests. For example, the Concorde aircraft case showed the amazing extravagance which can result from the combined influence of a large aircraft firm, enthusiastic experts and public servants, and politicians pipe-dreaming about national prestige. However, it is not a clear example of pluralism, because industrial pressure seems to have been less influential than the advocacy of individual bureaucrats and politicians (Bruce-Gardyne and Lawson, 1976). These various individuals seem to have been swayed not by direct career interests, but by their own policy preferences which they could indulge in at relatively little direct cost to themselves, e.g. at no more than their share of a national tax bill whose eventual size they did not anticipate. As the cost escalated, they could sustain their pride at the expense of all other taxpayers.

The 'business election cycle' represents an obvious way for governments to win popularity, or stave off unpopularity, before an election through inflating the economy. This gambit was sometimes but not always played under conditions of Keynesian demand management. However, the trick depends upon the electorate being gullible, and rational voters will progressively see through the device and discount its benefits. By contrast, an 'austerity' appeal to the electorate which calls upon sentiments of national unity can sometimes have some effect, not only through its ethical appeal (which public choice theorists will disbelieve), but because it suggests that an 'honest' government is more likely to deliver its promises. In post-1945 Britain, Conservative governments have been more disposed to inflate the economy before elections but to reduce public expenditure upon winning office, whereas Labour governments have tended toward the opposite behaviour. The popular associations between austerity, honesty and actual delivery are more emotional than closely reasoned, which follows from the difficulty of 'cost-benefit' voting once governments are held responsible for general economic conditions. Moreover, when these conditions deteriorate seriously, right-wing politicians have an incentive to pass much of the blame to impersonal market forces. This shifting of the agenda requires a rational voter to be able also to judge correctly the possible limits of government action.

Discussion about electoral tactics often assumes that politicians' only concern is to win or to keep office. This discounting of individual politicians' private interests or policy preferences is not realistic, but these factors cannot easily be the subject of a general theory. Breton's (1974) theory that politicians will maximize the surplus available for their private purposes, and that bureaucrats will in turn maximize the resources that they can extract from politicians, seems incapable of testing. He argues that the greater is the independence of politicians from the electorate, for example through longer intervals between elections, the larger this surplus will be. This conclusion does not seem to follow either; for example, if elections are frequent, the electorate's ability to assess the use of public resources by politicians becomes less.

Interestingly perhaps, it is the consequences of the rational egoism of bureaucrats, not politicians, which has most concerned public choice theorists. The best known theory is Niskanen's (1971), probably because it is logically and mathematically elegant, although empirically false on each main point. Niskanen argues that all the possible goals of a bureau chief, except ease in managing his bureau, are positively and monotonically related to the size of his budget. A larger budget will increase the bureaucrat's salary, status and power, and will also coincide with his own probably high evaluation of the bureau's work. The bureau is assumed to hold a monopoly of an unpriced public good whose output cannot be economically measured, and to have a bilateral monopoly relationship with its political sponsors. Given the bureau's control of information and the difficulties of judging its efficiency, Niskanen predicts that the bureau chief will be able to extract a substantial surplus from his political 'masters' for his own advantage. Niskanen's thesis is wrong on most facts:

(1) Bureau heads do not necessarily seek to expand their activities. Sometimes they prefer a quiet life, particularly when old. They may have some respect at least for the goal of public economy. Herbert Morrison reported that when he was Minister of Transport between 1929 and 1931, his chief engineer, Sir Henry Maybury, 'underestimated traffic needs, was sceptical about whether a big programme could be implemented and doubted if any major advantages would follow' (Donoughue and Jones, 1973, p. 156). If times have changed a lot since then, that only shows the culture-bound nature of Niskanen's theory.

(2) Bureau chiefs in the USA do not, as Niskanen implies, generally control a monopoly. Often there is competition for clientele between bureaux offering similar or comparable services. Thus the federal agencies offering more than 200 grant-in-aid programmes to state and local governments are said by a witness to 'duplicate each other and compete for clientele as if they were the corner grocer' (Self, 1977, p. 101).

Such a system may indeed be wasteful, but it is not monopolistic. By contrast in European states, government departments generally are monopolistic, but then the career structure of senior bureaucrats is more mobile than in the USA, so that there is not the same degree of egoistic interest in maximizing the department's expenditure.

(3) It is not true that political controllers are starved of information about bureaucratic activities. The extensive reports of parliamentary committees contain a mass of information if carefully used. But anyhow, it is a feature of almost all administrative systems to 'set bureaucrats to catch bureaucrats', e.g. to have highly paid and prestigious financial officials scrutinizing and checking the estimates of operating agencies. No doubt this financial control is limited and imperfect, but its significance cannot be defined away in the interest of a neat equation.

In brief then, theorists like Niskanen fail to analyse the various forms which self-interest can take in bureaucratic situations when linked with varied career patterns and normative constraints. Such works illustrate the barrenness of applying a general economic methodology to political behaviour. They get their persuasiveness from the circumstances that the expansion of government can be partly attributed to the self-interest or ambitions of bureaucrats; but deductions based upon this assumption go badly wrong through their neglect of administrative sociology and behaviour.

To summarize this section, a number of conclusions from public choice theory accord with those which can be drawn from pluralist political analysis (see Ch. 4). An economic analysis helps to explain the ability of interested minorities to exploit majorities, the possible influence of the median voter and the ambivalent attitudes towards the choice between more public goods and more taxation. The hypothesis of rational voting takes some hard knocks. There is certainly evidence that many individuals attempt to make rational political choices, but their ability to do so has become harder as governmental intervention in the economy and society has grown. Particularly when things go wrong, voters are liable to be swayed by emotional appeals to crude and often contradictory desires or fears. The place for hard-nosed rationalism seems to lie in narrower contexts than the polling station.

However, it would be mistaken to view public choice theories as simply confirming or modifying the findings of pluralist political analysis. They question the solidity of any group or organization through their assumption that the individual will withdraw his co-operation or obstruct and manipulate the implementation of policies in the interest of personal gain. Co-operation will also be lacking if the individual can expect to get the same benefit without personal trouble or cost. If these assumptions were actually true, social co-operation and trust would soon dissolve and one would enter a dark, Hobbesian world. The assumptions are widely invalidated because of the prevalence of group loyalties, sanctions and norms which deter the individual from taking too narrow or ruthless a view of his own interest. The problem then becomes one of discovering and analysing those situations in which 'rational egoism' gains leverage through the weakness of social restraints. Certainly the growth and complexity of government, and perhaps a decline in the force of social opinion and sanctions, has given increased opportunities for politicians and bureaucrats to pursue their own gain at the general expense; but the extent to which they actually do so is another matter which is unlikely to be settled by formal models of behaviour based upon simple assumptions.

On the other hand, the individualist assumption could be stated more broadly. The individual can be conceived as concerned not only with personal gain, but often with his own policy preferences or ideals for society. He may on occasion be altruistic as well as egoistical. Individualism in this reasoned or responsible sense makes rather a weak appearance in public choice theories, but it is of some importance in the real world. It also seems to offer an indispensable basis for any normative reforms of government which are rooted in liberal individualism.

THE INDIVIDUALIST REFORM OF THE STATE

The normative ideas of the public choice theorists are more interesting than their explanatory 'laws'. This is because their reform proposals are highly relevant to the modern political agenda, and in particular appeal to those many individuals who are disgruntled by the apparently endless expansion of modern government. However these reformist proposals are by no means consistent, but correspond to several different and now fairly familiar political positions. To investigate their nature, it will be convenient to divide the subject matter into two parts: first, into proposals for achieving a fairer or better political representation of individual preferences, and secondly, into ideas for restructuring the market in public goods. In each case, the reform proposals again divide between conservative and populist approaches, although the former approach is the more dominant.

A conservative position about collective action starts from the assumed interest of the individual over protecting his existing assets and freedom of action. The expression of this position in welfare economics is the absurdly revered 'Pareto principle' which, starting from the alleged non-comparability of individual utilities, contends that a 'welfare change' can be justified only when it makes some individual better off but none worse off. Any changes which satisfy this condition will be 'Pareto efficient', and it is often claimed by welfare economists that no-one should logically object to such a change, although they could logically object to being left worse off.

In politics, the unanimity rule is claimed to fulfil a comparable function. Political exchange is likened in principle to market exchange in the sense that it ought to leave no-one worse off. The lion in the path is, of course, the virtual impossibility save in trivial cases of getting unanimous agreement; and if agreement is possible at all, large (and surely ethically unjustified) side-payments must be made to all those who use their vote strategically. However, the achievement of any non-unanimous agreement entails coercion, and for Buchanan and Tullock (1962) the problem for any individual is to balance the costs of bargaining (which rise with the proportion of voters who must agree) against the costs of coercion (which rise with each reduction in that proportion). The trade-off between these two factors can be modelled as a graph, although nothing much seems to be gained thereby.

Buchanan and Tullock's analysis of how egoistic individuals try to reach a majority decision predicts an endless cycle of a variable majority trying to exploit a variable minority. An alternative result might be a more durable majority tyranny. In fact the former result would occur among a group of tolerably equal individuals, and the latter if there were some class or ethnic or other schism. That such morbid results do not more frequently occur in Western democracies is surely due to the role of disciplined competing groups like political parties and to the resolution of many minor conflicts through bureaucratic rules and routines. The egoistic farmers in Buchanan and Tullock's example (1962, Ch. 10) could not agree upon a road system to serve their farms, because a shifting majority would want to service their own farms at the expense of all, but in real life the farmers would quite likely agree to let the priorities be worked out on bureaucratic or technical criteria, provided that each farmer got his road within a reasonable time. The authors object that this administrative, or as they call it

70

Kantian (e.g. impartial), solution would ignore differences in the intensity with which individual farmers wanted roads; but the costs and delays of endless bargaining, and the inequity of numerous side-payments to those farmers who use their vote strategically, would surely be worse and help to explain the influential role of modern bureaucracies.

These authors' reponse to the drawbacks of coercion by majorities is to revert to social contract theory. They surmise that all citizens might agree to a basic constitution which guarantees them certain individual rights in return for them accepting less than unanimous decision rules (e.g. some element of coercion) over the provision of public goods. These protected rights should include some protection against the imposition of laws by bare majorities – for example, by giving reserve powers to an upper house of the legislature and by requiring a two-thirds or larger majority on some issues, such as the introduction of new taxes. Such an arrangement might appeal to all those who are reasonably content with the existing distribution of property rights, but it is hard to see how it could appeal to a rational egoist who is dissatisfied. A normative basis for this argument requires a prescriptive appeal to the sanctity of existing rights (Nozick, 1974); but it is hard to see why some redistribution of wealth by a democratic majority should be ethically more objectionable than are historical processes of appropriation and inheritance. The more valid point in Buchanan's arguments is the desirability of basing constitutional laws upon widely shared (but hardly unanimous) values, subject to the need to provide careful but reasonable scope for constitutional change.

An alternative remedy for the distortion of individual preferences is to bring politicians and bureaucrats under closer control of the electorate. This essentially is a populist prescription which was aired long ago by the Chartists and the Philosophical Radicals in the nineteenth century. Their solutions included adult suffrage (now realized), annual parliaments, referenda for deciding key issues, and powers to recall elected 'delegates' who exceeded their mandate. The same solutions would seem relevant for the Breton problem of political and bureaucratic appropriations of a private surplus. However, the solution runs at once into the problems of the voter's lack of information suggested by Downs, and Olson's 'free-rider' problem which would discourage any individual voter from the efforts needed to exercise his many choices rationally. In the real world, the populist solution also leaves considerable scope for manipulation of the electorate by political leaders, the media, business interests, etc.

Consequently the case for populism of this kind must depend upon the nature of the society, the constraints placed upon manipulation, and the duties (as well as rights) placed upon individuals to acquaint themselves with policy issues. Populism can reasonably be argued for, not in isolation but as one element within an egalitarian, educated polity. Thus the theory rests not upon the hypothesis that its results would better maximize the sum of individual utilities (which cannot be predicted), but upon the liberal principle of the intrinsic value of responsible individual choice.

Public choice theories strike a familiar, pragmatic note when one examines the second reform issue of how to restructure the market in public goods. Their usual principle is that the choice between economic and political markets ought to be based upon which system is more efficient for meeting consumers' preferences. Given the many distortions in the political process, the logical answer would often seem to be to revert to the economic market provided it is made competitive − a condition which requires anti-market legislation strong enough to overcome the apparently contrary logic of capitalist development. However, this answer has to be modified to cope with the many 'externalities' which only public action can resolve; and, as was noted earlier, the consequent list of public goods can be large or small, depending upon very arguable evaluations of the consequent effects, and their costs and benefits to individuals.

In any event, public choice theorists would favour remaking political markets according to economic tests wherever possible, and many proposals have been suggested toward this end. Competition could be introduced into the public goods market, for example by issuing vouchers which give clients a choice of services and by promoting competition for clientele among public agencies. More economic incentives could be introduced into the bureaucracy, for example by rewarding officials who reduced their budgets. The claimed tendency towards excessive public expenditure might be met by constitutional limits or other restraints upon the maximum level of taxation. Finally, where public regulation is essential, this could take the form of financial penalties and incentives, rather than administrative controls (Mueller, 1979, pp. 162–70).

This list of possible and now familiar 'economizing' reforms is not a monopoly of public choice theorists, but their elegant demonstrations of political distortions have helped to rationalize some widely held pragmatic opinions. There are indeed sound reasons for arguing that modern government is a self-exciting system with a strong tendency towards the proliferation of functions and agencies. Even if one believes that in some respects the future role of government will need to be still broader, it becomes that much more necessary to eliminate or to rationalize those public programmes which have outlived their original value or are not of great importance. Thus, one need not believe in the superiority of economic markets to be interested in 'economizing' proposals, but one must still consider carefully how far any such proposal would achieve its intended objective and what unwanted effects it might produce.

For example, the idea of fostering competition between public agencies may sound helpful for the welfare of clients, and sometimes may be so, but experience with 'bureaucratic free enterprise' in the USA does not seem to be a good advertisement (Self, 1977, Ch. 3). In a genuinely competitive market, there is a turnover of firms as new ones start up and inefficient ones get absorbed; but within government, commercial competition of this type is difficult or artificial while the allocation of jurisdictions and resources has to be politically determined and policed. The competition between agencies may thus be symbolic and presentational, while the costs of duplication are real. Public functions of regulation, control and enforcement are not suitable subjects for administrative competition, and historical experiences with competitive tax farming hardly endorse that particular procedure. A competitive allocation of government subsidies through different public agencies may be beneficial sometimes, but not if it reaches the enormous complexity and duplication of federal grants-in-aid in the USA.

The main scope for administrative competition occurs with direct services such as education and housing, where voucher schemes would in principle widen the clients' freedom of choice between public and also private suppliers, but the common value of citizenship would thereby be reduced. It can be counter-argued that this value has *already* withered because of the big differences in the quality of public education between rich and poor areas. In that sense, public choice theory might be only making explicit and possibly more equitable a switch in values (e.g. from shared citizenship to individual choice and ability to pay) which has already politically happened. Others, however, will contend that a better harmonization of individual interests *depends upon* the reassertion of the values of common citizenship.

Greater use of economic incentives within the bureaucracy could lead to some perverse results. For example, a head whose salary goes up when he reduces his budget will be getting a higher proportion of public expenditure for himself. Since some services must necessarily expand sometimes through a growing clientele, bureaucrats could collude together to share the profits from periodic cuts in an expanding budget. Indeed, if one is dealing with an absolute egoist, it is not clear what controls can be effective.

The concept of 'privatization' digs deeper than any reform of the bureaucracy because it can provide a platform for drastically curtailing the scope of public goods. If individuals purchase their own requirements, their private tastes will be more efficiently met. If public property is privately appropriated, the scope of bureaucracy is reduced. None the less many frustrating 'externalities' of private acts will remain, and new ones will be added by private appropriation, like the further congestion effects of 'positional goods' such as cars, yachts, second homes, private beaches, etc. (Hirsch, 1976).

A privatization philosophy is liable to produce a more unequal, divided and perhaps violent society. To meet this problem, some liberals are willing to contemplate a redistribution of wealth through taxation and subsidies so that economic markets will operate more equitably. It would then be possible to follow more comprehensively the logic of consumers' choice without the injustice or distortions caused by large differences in consumers' ability to pay for all kinds of goods. The redistribution of wealth would need to be considerable, if a tolerably equal society is to be created within a primarily market context. This issue is taken further in Chapter 7.

The concept of economizing has most potential significance in relation to the design of public policies. It can be argued that economic incentives (taxes and subsidies) could often be utilized with advantage in place of administrative regulations (Schultze, 1977). These methods would harness the economic motivations of rational egoism to the pursuit of public policy goals, while they would simultaneously reduce the size of bureaucracy and its expansionist tendencies. However, this recipe need not imply any curtailment of the role or tasks of government, since its main effect would be to transfer the incentives for achieving desired results *from* bureaucracy to other actors. Hence this policy is consistent with a quite different and radical approach towards restructuring the market in public goods.

Instead of concluding that political markets are intrinsically inferior to economic ones for meeting individual preferences, it can be argued that welfare economics properly applied could convert this inferiority into a definite superiority. The tool for this purpose would be social cost-benefit analysis, which by putting appropriate shadow prices upon the effects of public decisions, and the side effects of private ones, could establish a truer calculus of social value than economic markets, with their many imperfections and unpriced side-effects, can possibly manage.

As the most fervid welfare economist recognizes, this cost-benefit utopia is a long way off. In an earlier work (Self, 1975), I criticized this goal as being quite unattainable even in principle and often perverse in its actual applications. There is no need here to repeat this critique, which centred around the inconsistency of the techniques available, the lack of data for their application, the existence of 'horse and rabbit stew' where some items are quantified and others are not, the illogicalities over reckoning of 'costs' and 'benefits' and the dependence of all these techniques upon prior social decision rules about property, compensation, etc. Moreover, actual uses of cost-benefit analysis often (although not always) ignore distributive effects, and stick to narrow, quasi-market criteria.

Despite these strong criticisms, I would accept (more definitely than in my earlier book) that social cost-benefit analysis *can* be a helpful aid to public policy. Used with caution and understanding, it can provide a very useful check upon the claims of interest group leaders about the likely effects of a public decision upon their members. Used within a framework of social decision-rules and general policy goals, social cost-benefit analysis can help with the formulation and evaluation of policies, and in particular with the design of appropriate taxes or subsidies for treating harmful and beneficial externalities. A modest use of cost-benefit analysis might therefore at least help to improve the market in public goods.

Let us try to summarize this complex discussion. Economists who analyse the nature of politics often claim to be 'value-neutral'. As individuals they may hold any of a number of ethical views about society, but as economists they seek neutrality. The main exception to this conclusion is the widespread endorsement among economists of the Pareto principle. Of course Paretianism is *not* actually value-free, but the usual view is that it is a 'weak' value judgement; in other words, it states merely that a welfare change ought not to leave any individual worse off. Since Paretianism also asserts that individual utilities are not comparable − I cannot measure my satisfactions against yours − it follows that only the affected individual can accurately judge how far his welfare is reduced by some policy measure. This simple concept is held to accord with some minimal notion of distributive justice; Mishan (1971, pp. 310–15), for example, holds that a qualified version of Paretianism is inscribed in the hearts of men.

The history of this curious belief is interesting. Its origins lie in the subjectivist philosophy of Berkeley and Hume, who were sceptical about an individual's capacity to experience anything at all beyond his own sensations. By contrast, the implications of welfare economics seemed to be quite strongly redistributive, since if each individual is to count equally, the total sum of utilities will be increased by transfers of wealth from the rich who have many satisfactions to the poor who have few. The Pareto concept draws upon the counter-argument that the satisfactions of individuals cannot be compared. Within the study of welfare economics, the victory of the ordinalists, who contended that welfare could not be measured but only ranked in ascending states, strengthened the position of the Paretians (Cooter and Rapport, 1984). Thus, the humanist and egalitarian implications of earlier welfare economics disappeared – except for the Pareto principle.

However, this 'weak' sacred cow of a principle actually represents a strong conservative position. Logically it would rule out any policy change if anyone objects. Its assumption of the 'non-comparability of utilities', if taken literally, virtually excludes any policy making at all, since someone is likely to claim that his 'welfare loss' is enormous or even infinite (as happened with the Roskill survey of householders affected by an airport; Self, 1975, p. 83). To make the principle more realistic, the Kaldor-Hicks amendment argued that full compensation to those affected need not actually be paid provided that the total 'welfare gain' would in principle suffice for this purpose. This revision makes nonsense of the Pareto conception of justice; but to pay out large sums in compensation to objectors who use their rights strategically also seems ethically dubious and objectionable. Thus the Pareto principle is unlikely to be applied in practice, but it casts a long shadow over economic thought about policies.

In other respects Paretian welfare economics accepts no goal beyond the maximization of individual utilities or welfare. This exaltation of welfare over other values has been strongly criticised by some liberals (Rowley and Peacock, 1975). While all the theories in this chapter can be described as individualist, the concept of rational egoism itself is devoid of any ethical content. Some theorists meet this problem by arguing that an understanding of the logic of self-interest is essential to the maintenance of a realistic social ethic, which is seen as occupying a limited but separate sphere. Others appeal to the old Utilitarian principle of 'enlightened self-interest', which commends the utility of some concern for others as well as oneself, but the logic of 'free riding' – the notion that it is more rational to leave altruism to others – stands in the way of this conclusion. Building upon the 'prisoners' dilemma' and the tragedy of the commons, it can be shown that it may pay an individual to behave less selfishly if he can be sure that all others will do the same; but this conclusion requires the support of an ethic of individual responsibility toward the rights of other members of society. It is sometimes claimed that rational egoists will learn by small steps to take some risk or sacrifice which will build up mutual trust and co-operation; but it is not clear that this can come about without the acceptance of principles beyond those of 'rational egoism'.

These normative issues are confronted in this book's conclusions. We can conclude here by listing three political positions which draw in various ways upon the theories which we have discussed.

The first position is 'new right' conservatism. This position clings to a very old belief about the inability of governments to make men better or more equal, or to solve other problems of the basic 'human condition'. The old biblical curse of original sin is given its modern version in the political consequences of rational egoism. Property rights are re-defended against an encroaching state through appeals to the Pareto principle, to the unstable or tyrannical tendencies of majorities, and to the reinvocation of an implied social contract.

For writers like Buchanan and Tullock, this position assumes a society of free individuals who will accept the constraints of government only on condition that adequate protection is given to their existing rights. Their appeal is to enlightened self-interest in the form of the advantage to each individual of an agreed constitution, but there seem to be no adequate reasons of either interest or ethics to make this appeal successful. The maxim of rational self-interest can equally lead, under harsher assumptions, to a Hobbesian position which urges the surrender of all political rights to a sovereign in the hope of protecting one's person and property. In political argument a position of extreme individualism seems often to be combined with an appeal to a strong or aggressive nationalism, which offers a foil or support for the defence of existing entitlements. Such a confused position is not, of course, taken by public choice thinkers themselves.

A second position concerns itself with the goal of welfare

maximization. Besides the familiar Arrow problem, this goal entails close attention to the problems of agenda setting and political manipulation, and to the respective roles of voters, politicians and bureaucrats. A negative and cynical conclusion about this process can lead back to 'new right' conservatism. A conclusion that individual preferences could be better articulated, conveyed and implemented leads to a reformist position in favour of more direct democracy, which might be assisted by the use of social cost-benefit analysis.

There may be and usually is an ethical assumption that each individual should count equally; hence the position is strongly democratic, its basic problem being the familiar one of how to elicit and combine individual 'utilities' in an equitable way. Thus this position contains no ethical concept of a good or desirable society beyond procedural principles for articulating and aggregating individual preferences.

A third position, which has fallen somewhat outside this discussion, is that of liberal individualism. This position supports competitive markets and private property as essential elements in individual freedom of choice. Thus it accepts many modern criticisms of political markets and supports an economizing approach towards the reform of government. However, this liberal position is more prepared than the first position to contemplate some reduction of inequalities of wealth, and is not committed like the second one to welfare maximization as the supreme goal.

The ethical basis of this third position is the value of responsible individual choice which takes account of the needs of other members of society, together with personal development and self-realization. Thus this position contains some view of the desirable nature of society, and is not neutral about the content of individual preferences. The ethical problem of such a theory is to work out the role of government, and the distribution of rights and duties, in terms of its rather hazy ideals. Essentially this position restates the values of J. S. Mill and T. H. Green as against the felicific calculus of Bentham or the Lockean or Hobbesian implications of the first position.

4

THE PLURALIST STATE

MODERN PLURALISM

Modern pluralism started out as a reaction to the concentration of sovereignty in the nation state. Its exponents argued that 'intermediate institutions' such as churches, universities and professional or economic organizations ought not to be regarded as dependent upon the will of a sovereign authority, but should enjoy a degree of rightful autonomy.

Pluralists believed that a rich variety of self-governing associations represented bulwarks of liberty, democracy and meaningful social life. De Tocqueville argued that the absence of such intermediate bodies (intermediate, that is, between the state and the family or other primary groups) was a prime cause of the French Revolution, just as their presence in America was a vital prop of democracy in that country. In England, Figgis' defence of the autonomy of the Church, G. D. H. Cole's guild socialism and Laski's support for an independent trade unionism derived from the same arguments.

Within governmental systems the theories of the separation of powers and of federalism represented clear applications of pluralist thought. By parcelling out the powers of government, the tyranny of any group or majority would be prevented, the value of political compromise would be promoted and (in theory at least) opportunities for political participation would be maximized. If anyone could not get satisfaction from one type of government, he could turn to another or remove himself to a different jurisdiction. The structure of American government was created and remains extraordinarily pluralistic by comparison with all other systems.

The unitary states of Europe offered no such shield against the assertion of a centralized sovereignty, which explains the strong interest in the decentralization of power of English and some continental pluralists. The value of local self-government appealed to a long line of English thinkers, including J. S. Mill, Toulmin Smith, Maitland, G. D. H. Cole and W. A. Robson. However, local government structure and powers can be and frequently are varied by parliamentary acts, which makes its autonomy precarious if central government becomes authoritarian, as has recently happened in Britain.

While these earlier theories of pluralism retain their relevance, more recent versions concentrate upon the policy process and are both empirical and prescriptive. Pluralism suggests how the policy process *should* work and also provides a framework for empirical analysis. Pluralist political science is primarily American and was at its peak during the 1950s and 1960s, since when the gap between the ideal model and the reality has grown wider and pluralism has come under attack by counter-theories of corporatism and neo-Marxism.

As a form of positive analysis, pluralism views political action as a process which, in Lasswell's phrase, settles who gets what, when, how (1950). It assumes a multiplicity of actors competing for 'stakes' (such as influence, money, jobs) in a variety of political arenas. It tends to minimize the connections between the different arenas, to maximize the openness of the contests, and to assume a wide spread of influence and power, although all these assumptions may be changed by investigation. Pluralism in this sense, like public choice theory, views politics as competitive rather than consensual and is pragmatically focused upon the 'here and now' of political action rather than upon basic properties of the political system.

Pluralist analysis has provided a flexible framework for much excellent research by American political scientists. For example, Wildavsky's *Politics of the Budgetary Process* (1964) shows the wide diffusion of influence among bureaux, departmental heads, Presidential agencies and Congressional committees over the making of the Federal budget, and the calculated strategies which the various actors employ. Sayre and Kaufman's finely researched *Governing New York City* (1960) reveals an enormously intricate set of internal agencies and groups interacting with each other and with agencies in both State and Federal government. Both these studies commend the wide diffusion of influence and bargaining which they unravel, although Sayre and Kaufman admit that this has a deterrent effect upon change or innovation. Numerous volumes of the American inter-university casebooks from Stein (1952) onwards have revealed a rich variety of pluralist behaviour, so rich that the cases read like novels and resist absorption into general theories.

Pluralist political analysis concentrated initially upon the role of organized groups. A. F. Bentley (1949), its founding father,

80

The pluralist state

regarded group interests as objective facts of the political system in much the same way as Marxism identified class interest. This methodology is not tenable since group interests even more than class interests have to be mobilized and interpreted. Groups are also unstable coalitions of individuals, as the public choice theorists stress, and individuals may identify their interests with a variety of groups. Later pluralists stress this very point and see competing group organizations as the vehicles for reconciling the diverse interests of the individual as taxpayer, motorist, homeowner, etc.

Empirical studies soon revealed the very unequal influence of interest groups due to such factors as: (1) ease of group mobilization, e.g. concentrated mineworkers are much easier to recruit than are scattered farmworkers; (2) intensity of group interests, e.g. producers have a stronger stake in policies affecting them than do taxpayers or consumers; (3) financial resources and information, which explains the middle-class character of environmental groups and the strength of business organizations; (4) availability of sanctions, e.g. a strike at a power plant or the collapse of a major firm is much more threatening to government than is a strike at a doll factory or the disappearance of a small business.

From a pluralist perspective, political parties perform the function of 'aggregating' group interests, rather than of subordinating these interests to the party's goals or ideology. Parties will therefore bid competitively for the support of groups in their efforts to win elections. One can make some predictions as to how their policies will be affected by the consequent distribution of costs and benefits. If the benefits are concentrated upon a visible group (say, a subsidy to wheat farmers) but the costs are widely diffused (say among taxpayers), the farmers have a strategic advantage over the taxpayers; and the converse relationship will also hold, as when a concentrated local group holds up some facility that is needed by a large but diffused number of consumers (Wilson, 1973, pp. 332–7). These demonstrations of the weight of specific group interests have become a little less convincing with the emergence of taxpayers' revolts and other mass movements, but they do explain quite well the influence which a strategically placed group can exert upon party policies, especially in marginal constituencies and closely fought elections.

A basic weakness of early pluralist analysis was its assumption that government itself is simply a transmission belt for registering and implementing political demands. This assumption is quite unrealistic. In the first place, administrative rules can be

81

manipulated to some extent by groups; but further, government is not a passive transmitter of external pressures but itself a generator of specific interests. For example, a government may promote home ownership for many reasons including its political ideology; but once substantial tax and other concessions have been granted to a growing class of owner occupiers, this group becomes a more potent political force. Thus 'policies make politics' and do not simply reflect them.

Interests are also generated inside government, so that government can be assimilated in principle to a pluralist analysis. Bureaucratic agencies and groups can be seen as participants within the various pluralist arenas. This point is fully recognized in a number of studies, for example those by Wildavsky and by Sayre and Kaufman. Indeed in the New York study, the bureaucratic agencies and groups seem to be more influential than the outside pressure groups or the parties and their leaders.

Normative theories of pluralism justified the dominance of group influences in modern democracies. The freedom of groups to organize and to try to influence government is a basic democratic right. The existence of a large number of such groups is proof of the health of the system. The overlapping membership of these groups helps to modify political conflicts and to promote reasonable compromises between conflicting interests. Political parties serve the useful function of integrating group demands into manageable programmes. Constitutional laws and conventions have the important function of refereeing group conflicts in a fairly impartial manner. A pluralist polity therefore may be highly competitive but should be fundamentally balanced and equitable (Dahl, 1967).

Of course no pluralist would pretend that these conditions have ever been fully satisfied. Empirical studies have in fact revealed the very disparate power of organized groups and the permeation of government by particular interests. These demonstrations do not necessarily invalidate the pluralist ideal, or show that it is not realized to some extent in modern democracies. For example, freedom to organize is an important right and a multiplicity of groups is evidence that the right is being exercised; and some important constitutional rules – such as the necessity for elections – do give some scope for the balance of group interests to be changed.

The extent to which a pluralist system actually exists is also a matter of judgement. This point is illustrated by the American debate over local community power. Is power in American cities exercised by a ruling elite or is it dispersed between different policy arenas and a variety of groups and individuals? The answer given will depend partly upon the methodology employed – for example, whether one asks people *who* is influential in the city (the reputational approach) which may point to an elite, or analyses separate policy issues which may point to pluralism. These problems apart, the answer is very likely a mixed one. American cities seem to have both pluralist and elitist characteristics and to vary quite a lot – which is of course useful to know (Self, 1982, pp. 35–7).

Normative pluralism also concentrates, like public choice theory, upon the 'demand' side of the political system. A pluralist government system was held to be desirable because it should be more responsive to a diversity of group interests. However, a difficulty emerges when pluralist analysis reveals the influence of organizational interests within government. Will these interests pervert the wants of the ultimate clients or beneficiaries? The diffusion of power within government may simply confirm or augment the influence of the strongest political pressure groups; and decentralized bureaucracies can act selfishly or inefficiently. The usual pluralist answer is to argue that a balance between competing organizational interests is at least preferable to a strong, centralized bureaucracy.

A contemporary defence of pluralism encounters another objection. The earlier pluralist thinkers like de Tocqueville had a *defensive* view of 'intermediate institutions', which was that bodies like churches or universities should be protected against interventions by government. But modern pluralism is much more concerned with the *assertive* claims of private organizations for a share of governmental resources and coercive authority. On what basis and conditions are such claims to be granted? An appeal to the value of 'intermediate institutions' will not suffice unless one is prepared to unscramble and divide up the power of government according to some coherent and defensible plan. Otherwise one is merely conceding power to the strongest interests and pressures. Earlier pluralist thinkers were not very successful over specifying the rules for the division of public authority, but this problem has become more acute under modern conditions.

Linked with this issue is the difficulty presented for pluralists by the idea of general or public interest. They usually confine this concept to rules for conflict management and dissolve its substantive meanings into the interests of actual or latent groups. This treatment does help to throw out much mystical or self-interested argument about 'public interest'. It is true that 'public interest' often refers to latent or diffused interests such as those of taxpayers or consumers who rely upon the political leadership for protection.

This interpretation is not fully adequate, however. If organized groups have meaningful common interests, so surely does an organized community constituted as a national or local government. 'Interest' is a way of referring to the common concerns of a given community or reference group. A farmers' union derives the specificity of its interests (which are still always debatable) from its relations with government or with farm workers – particularly its interest as a supplicant for public favours. 'National interest' similarly becomes clearer, although still controversial, in the context of international competition, but an organized national community can also be said to have an interest in the prosperity, welfare and safety of its members, however much disagreement may exist over the means. The issue which pluralists must face is whether group competition is actually a satisfactory and sufficient means for realizing the common concerns of a national or institutional community.

Following the general approach of this book, the next two sections will reverse the priority which pluralists usually give to interest groups and concentrate upon the workings of pluralism inside government. Interest groups are of course still present in their capacities as supplicants, supporters, or indirect controllers of public agencies. Our aim in the next section, therefore, is to take a 'micro-view' of the behaviour of administrative agencies and groups, as opposed to the 'macro-view' associated with theories of corporatism.

PLURALISM WITHIN GOVERNMENT

A pluralist analysis has to reckon with the fact that the governmental system is in important respects integrated and unified as well as fragmented. Political networks, especially where the same parties function locally, link together the various levels of government. Administrative networks of control and co-ordination extend vertically and horizontally throughout the system. The bureaucracy is sometimes integrated through the pervasive activity of a broad-based administrative cadre as in the UK, or through traditional habits of conformity and co-operation as in Germany. Most centralized of all is finance since a high and increasing proportion of all public revenues is paid into a central Treasury, whence money flows out through an elaborate conduit of pipes to central departments, public boards, local governments, etc. Finance is the main lever of centralized control, especially in federations.

The demand and supply sides of a political system are roughly symmetrical and are joined together by an apex consisting of the political executive and its advisors. The generalized role of parties is matched by that of general administrators and staff aides working at the centre of government. The specialized role of interest groups is matched by that of operating agencies. The policy process can be roughly divided between the continuous flux of issues and priorities being handled at the centre of government, and the operations of specialized and partly self-contained sub-systems such as education, trade, agriculture, etc. A Minister or other political chief and his immediate staff provide the linkage between general policy goals and those of a policy sub-system like agriculture or education whose boundaries can only be roughly defined and frequently shift, but whose politics have a recognizable character which produces similar policy agendas, interest groups, professional skills, specialized press, etc., in different countries.

The polities of the Western world vary considerably in their degree of integration or fragmentation. The main factors here are the constitutional system; the relative importance of specialized organs (interest groups and individual public agencies) as against generalized organs (parties and a centralized bureaucracy); and the nature of political and organizational culture. On all these counts the US system is much the most fragmented and pluralized. Other federations share some of the same features, particularly the reliance of national governments upon 'fiscal federalism' (the power of the purse) as the main instrument of influence over other governments. However, the German and Swiss federations possess more integrated and co-operative bureaucracies than does the USA with its divided organizational loyalties. There is argument as to which West European government is the most centralized and unified. This title traditionally went to France, although Ashford (1982) has recently argued that in some respects the French system is more decentralized than the British.

In general, all Western governments have been becoming increasingly fragmented through the multiplication of specialized departments and agencies, many of a semi-autonomous character. There have been some counter-trends, such as attempts to rationalize local government systems in many European countries and various experiments with 'giant departments' as devices for policy and resource co-ordination. These counter-trends have had very limited effect, since new metropolitan or regional governments have also been created and big departments often prove ineffective or are disbanded for political reasons. A more significant counter-trend has been the growth of elaborate mechanisms of policy co-ordination through the use of specialized agencies and staffs. Whether or not effective, the stress widely placed upon the *need* for better co-ordination is itself witness to the partition of administrative authority.

This brief analysis of the structure of modern governments will enable us to tackle some questions about the meanings of pluralism. What are the relationships between governments and interest groups? What determines the behaviour of government departments, boards and other agencies? What is the meaning and extent of the concept of organizational autonomy? No adequate theoretical framework exists for considering these issues because of the diversity of systems and arrangements; but a brief review will at least assist the understanding and evaluation of pluralist theories.

Peters (1978, Ch. 6) suggests a number of models for the relationship between government and interest groups. A *parentela* relationship arises where a political party requires the bureaucracy to favour the interests of the sector of society which is linked with or dependent upon the party. This situation is quite frequent in Third World countries, but in Western societies it usually occurs in only a limited and conditional form. The obvious examples are the linkages between trade unions and Labour parties in many European countries, and the less formal linkages between business interests and Conservative or right-wing parties. These linkages influence party policies, but government relations with interest groups are to a considerable extent independent of party politics and the interest groups often act independently and not as the clients of a party. Corporatism introduces a more *integrated* relationship between government and economic interest groups, but the integration is not closely dependent upon party politics.

In contrast, a *clientela* relationship develops where one interest group is accepted or singled out by a department as the legitimate spokesman for some section of society. This situation needs to be contrasted with the proper pluralist model, which is one of equal access to the department on the part of all relevant interest groups. 'Equal access' is always a myth, but it is true that competition among groups for the attention of government often develops into a monopolistic relation. This result may occur through the dominance of an interest group or through departmental interest and convenience, and often leads to 'corporate pluralism', meaning an arrangement whereby some economic or professional group achieves official recognition and the right to regulate its members' affairs in exchange for accepting some responsibility for public policy. This recognition in turn strengthens the membership of the group and its monopoly status. Its policy also gets changed as a result of its 'partnership' with the government, and the question of who co-opts whom becomes an open question in theory. The evidence suggests that the stronger group organizations have often been successful in getting government support and recognition on favourable terms.

Cause groups are in a weaker position because they lack recourse to economic sanctions. They can sometimes establish influential relations with a public agency through their ability to speak for a dependent clientele or through their usefulness over promoting some respectable cause. Otherwise, they must have recourse to the party and political arena rather than the administrative one and try to exert electoral leverage. Even successful action of this kind may later encounter obstacles to implementation by interest groups which have stabler contacts with government departments. Finally, there are 'illegitimate' groups which are unable to attract political attention and are administratively excluded, and which consequently resort to obstructive action or violence.

The influence of interest groups varies with both the political system and the type of agency. The USA is the supreme example of what Lowi describes as 'interest group liberalism'. The decentralization of discretionary power favours the growth of bilateral links between specialized agencies and sectional interests. The agency and interest group develop a mutual interest in a particular programme and, by forming an 'iron triangle' with the relevant Congressional sub-committee, they can fend off attempts by the political executive to change policies or jurisdictions. A well-known example of this institutionalized pluralism are the ten autonomous agricultural sub-systems, each performing a narrow programme and serving a different constituency, which have managed to resist the reform efforts of successive Secretaries of Agriculture (Lowi, 1979, pp. 68–77). Grant McConnell (1966, p. 162) views this system as 'the conquest of segments of formal State power by private groups and associations'. Equally, government bureaux often initiate or strengthen sectional interests groups for their own ends.

However, this American system is not typical of Western

governments. More usually, it is not so much departmental politics or convenience (although these play a part) as national policy goals which bring about *clientela* relationships. Powerful bureaucratic groups, as in France, may also play an important part over the treatment and recognition of interest groups. Under these conditions, the monopoly position of a recognized interest group becomes stronger and it becomes harder for smaller groups to receive recognition. The question of 'who wins' turns partly upon whether the bureaucracy treats private interests defensively or assertively, a question taken up in Chapter 6.

We can turn next to the question of organizational behaviour within the government system. This behaviour is dependent upon many variables such as the nature of the organization's task or function, its internal resources, its clientele, its external environment, etc. It is the aim of 'contingency theory' to try to plot the impact of these variables, but the task is complex and bedevilled by the elusiveness of organizational boundaries and the openness of most organizations to external influences or control.

Here our particular interest is the influence of the *political environment* upon the behaviour of public agencies. Every such agency, be it a department or a public board, is located between its political controllers and its clients. The clients vary. Thus the clients of finance, personnel and co-ordinating agencies are other government departments. The immediate clients of many line departments are local governments or public corporations. The whole governmental system is knit together by complex networks of financial and administrative controls. These controls do not work in a political vacuum. They get strengthened whenever an issue is successfully transferred to a broader political arena and leads to intervention by national politicians and controllers (Schnattschneider, 1960). They have also been strengthened by the growing centralization of public finance which has come about through the superior flexibility and efficiency of national forms of taxation.

Almost every agency works within an environment of both latent and direct interests. The direct interests are present in day to day relations with clients and suppliers and sometimes objectors to particular projects. The latent interests of consumers, taxpayers, unemployed or other diffused groups are largely interpreted by political controllers since their direct representation is often weak or non-existent. Thus some tragedy or scandal or movement of public opinion will periodically bring about political intervention into the operating routines of public agencies. A disastrous fire may lead to a strengthening of the technical standards of the fire authority or the removal of the fire chief for incompetence, or both results. Widespread protests by employers and parents may cause politicians to try to influence teaching methods so as to secure a more useful or utilitarian basic curriculum. If regional unemployment increases, politicians may insist upon a tougher use of controls and incentives for steering industries to depressed areas. Such interventions will not be necessary to the extent that the public agency is anyhow sensitive to a political balance of interests. However, its continual involvement with clients whom it is helping or controlling can easily lead to neglect of these wider interests and to reliance upon its own established methods and standards.

The relationship of a public agency with interest groups also depends upon the *type* of function. Thus agencies concerned with the support or regulation of particular industries usually encounter strong interest groups, which they may further strengthen by their own policies. On the other hand, agencies which provide personal social services deal with dependent clienteles whose direct representation is usually weak and who must rely upon political parties and controllers to speak up for their interests. In such cases public agencies are largely guided by their own professional or technical standards. Professional bodies will exert significant influence from within government as well as from outside it, according to the status and leverage of the profession; doctors have more weight than teachers and teachers more than social workers.

The most interesting cases of organizational autonomy are those where political controllers *deliberately* abnegate their formal authority by creating an 'independent' board or corporation. These cases are often regarded as exceptional by politicians themselves because of the loss of political and parliamentary accountability. Actually, these actions are taken for several reasons of growing significance. Hence the political campaigns to abolish QUANGOS (the popular misnomer for appointed boards), such as that launched by the Thatcher Government in Britain, are largely ineffective. Equally, the 'independence' enjoyed by these public boards is often rather limited and precarious. It may in practice be less than that of a government department, since the members of an appointed board may be more open to informal pressure than are permanent bureaucrats.

Table 4.1 shows four motives for devolving power upon public boards, with examples drawn mainly from Britain. The managerial motive is the best known and is most acceptable where

Table 4.1 *Political devolution to appointed boards*

Motive for devolution	Examples	Contraints upon devolution	Effects of devolution
Managerial or commerical efficiency	Nationalized industries; some public utilities	Financial dependence of industry or utility; macro-economic problems/ policies; social impacts of economic change	Formal autonomy mixed with informal pressures; search for strategic frameworks of control; intervention increases with subsidization
Arbitrative			
Need for political neutrality	British Broadcasting Corporation	Sensitivity of issues	Organizational caution and ortho-doxy or elitism
Need to balance interests	Independent regulatory commissions	Limits of judicial approach: interests appeal to wider constituencies	Internal policy conflicts or sub-servience to regulated interests
Need to protect individual rights	Compensation tribunals; public inquiries	Political salience of some issues	Most effective in routine cases; tendencies to legitimize public decisions
Professional co-option	Regional hospital boards (UK)	Strong financial control; consumers' complaints	Professional control of service delivery; sporadic political interventions; internal rationing of limited resources
Political co-option			
To invest private interests with powers of self-regulation	Agricultural marketing boards (UK)	Complaints from other interests and consumers; financial costs or trade policy constraints	Autonomy hinges upon favourable political environment and organizational conditions
To secure co-operation of affected interests	National Economic Development Council (UK)	Policy ineffective-ness or dependence upon interests	Organization has fragile or cautious role
To placate opposition to government initiative	Land Commission (UK)	Policy ineffective-ness or perversion	Tendencies to political instability or short life

users are expected to pay all or most of the cost of some service. The arbitrative motive is also familiar and takes several forms. The motive of professional co-option is more unusual, but essentially it follows the same logic as that of corporate pluralism. A strong professional group, such as the British medical profession, is given a central place in the management of a public service in exchange for accepting some responsibility for the rationing of scarce financial resources (Klein, 1975). Political co-option is a means for securing the co-operation of various important interests or of disarming potentially hostile ones, by taking the function away from the bureaucracy and handing it to a board comprising representative individuals or professional experts.

The prospect of political interventions (formal or more often, informal) limits the autonomy of each public board in a different way. Public enterprises are most vulnerable when they become very dependent upon subsidies, but they are also subject to many economic and social reasons for political intervention. Arbitrative bodies typically adopt a quasi-judicial approach to individual cases but may be undercut by appeals to the political arena or by becoming subservient to regulated interests. Professional-type boards follow their own expert standards, but frustrated consumers can prompt political controllers into imposing new policies. Boards reflecting political co-option may not achieve their intended goal or may fail to placate hostile interests and thus be liable to abolition when a different party gets office. They survive best when they have broad-based political support or can establish a form of economic or professional self-regulation which is not costly to government. To take the British examples in the chart, the Land Commission was abolished, the National Economic Development Council has been cautious but has rested upon a broad political consensus, while the agricultural marketing boards have proved a cheap way of supporting British agriculture.

What factors will maximize the autonomy of a public board? The most obvious factor is a favourable political environment consisting of strong backing or voluntary abnegation on the part of political controllers and the existence of acquiescent or dependent clients. Other important factors are strong internal resources and financial viability. A favourable public 'image' is also very desirable. Some examples of successful public corporations will show how necessary – and how precarious – are these various factors.

After 1945 British governments gave strong and consistent support to the development of domestic nuclear reactors, and the know-how for this task was concentrated almost exclusively in the Atomic Energy Authority (AEA). For a time the AEA had a free hand to determine policies. However, a growing belief among its principal clients in the British electricity industry that American reactors might be commercially preferable, a belief muted for some time by the fact that electricity generation was nationalized, eventually opened up the performance of the AEA to critical scrutiny. Environmental opposition heightened the controversy. The AEA's policies became subject to political scrutiny and strong opposition at local public inquiries.

The British Broadcasting Corporation (BBC) is an interesting example of deliberate political abnegation plus monopoly powers. For many years the BBC had a free hand to purvey its own special brand of cultural uplift and wholesome popular entertainment. Eventually governments became more critical or paranoid about 'Auntie's' political impartiality, and the introduction of commercial television compelled the BBC to compete in the quasi-market of viewing ratings. Its freedom of action became more restricted and its financial dependence upon authorized licence fees more precarious.

In the USA, the Tennessee Valley Authority (TVA) initially obtained powerful Presidential backing for a multi-purpose programme of resource management and development. Its large investment and job-creating activities in a very depressed region helped to overcome the resistance of numerous other public agencies and interest groups, and gave it a fairly free hand with a novel experiment in multi-purpose regional planning and development, never since fully matched. None the less the TVA gradually found it expedient to co-opt and placate local interests, while the rapid growth of its electricity supply function dwarfed its many other activities which also came to seem less essential as prosperity grew. The TVA has survived primarily as a public utility, not a uniquely independent agency for regional development, although a few elements of the latter role remain.

Probably the best example in the world of a financially very successful (and hence very independent) public agency is the Port of New York Authority (PNYA). Appointed under an inter-state compact by the governors of New York and New Jersey, it never achieved its intended task of rationalizing port facilities but instead found openings to construct and to manage a growing empire of bridges, tunnels, terminal buildings and airports. By using public powers of acquisition and by charging tolls for its facilities, the PNYA built up a strong financial position and high credit ratings on Wall Street, and thus stood ready to take over facilities like Kennedy International Airport which the financially hard-pressed city government reluctantly handed over. The PNYA's successful business image, always an asset in the USA, has strengthened the autonomy conferred by its politically detached, bi-state status.

These are all cases of public corporations operating within favourable political environments. In two cases (AEA, TVA) there was strong political support and in the other two (BBC, PNYA) deliberate political disengagement. Opposition from other interests could be countered by the use of the ample resources (PNYA, TVA) or the absence of any blocking competition (AEA, BBC). However, in each case save the PNYA the political environment deteriorated and in each case save perhaps the AEA a succession of goals occurred. The TVA cut down its functions and changed its structure, the PNYA expanded into new arenas, the BBC became more commercially sensitive and defensive.

A full pluralist analysis would give as much attention to the roles and interests of bureaucratic groups as to those of public agencies. Like the agencies these groups variously compete and co-operate with each other, seek to protect their turf and stabilize their environment, and try sometimes to innovate. Powerful groups like the French *grands corps* and *polytechniciens* colonize and dominate particular departments and public corporations. This does not imply that in France the policies of a department are subordinate to the 'philosophy' of some *corps*, because departmental policy is shaped by its particular task and clientele, and because some departments contain competing adminstrative groups. Departmental behaviour is therefore a complex product of organizational interests and group influences (Suleiman, 1974).

In many cases there is close identification between a public agency and a professional *cadre*. In the USA this occurs in bureaux such as the Forestry Service, the Soil Conservation Agency, and the Army Corps of Engineers (Self, 1977, pp. 208–9). The influence and ethos of the professional *cadre*, especially if this is strong, will shape and strengthen the agency's goals and independence of action.

Departmental independence is much modified by the influence of service-wide administrators like the British administrative class, who are centrally recruited and move frequently between sections of a department and at senior levels between departments. The most prestigious *grands corps* in France play a similar role, despite their rivalries, in respect of financial control, administrative regulation and the co-ordination of field services. When such groups are weakly established, as in the USA, the various co-ordinating agencies operate along more limited, specialized lines, and public agencies act more independently.

The behaviour of a public organization is also much affected by how its head officials are recruited. In many cases an organization is effectively controlled from a different, usually higher level. Political controllers such as ministers have an ambivalent role, since they are both the conveyors of Cabinet and party policies and also spokesmen for their department. How they influence or control their department depends a lot upon whether they are primarily assisted by a politically selected staff, by a group of generalists, or by officials steeped in departmental lore and tradition. The degree of independence of a public board depends a great deal upon appointments. A chairman who is a successful businessman or has independent resources can afford to snap his fingers at the Minister on occasion; a general administrator will be more disposed to align the board with general public policies; an outside expert may limit his independent stance to his own knowledge; an internally promoted official will be more disposed to uphold the agency's traditional interests and policies but perhaps be wary of innovation. There are of course many personal exceptions to such tendencies.

The interaction between the internal and external politics of a public agency is a complex business. A well integrated and assertive internal staff such as a professional *cadre* will strengthen the agency's ability to control its environment and to innovate, whereas internal conflicts expose an agency to stronger external influences. A change in the external environment affects internal behaviour; if political criticism grows, more authority will accrue to internal controllers. If functions change, so will organizational balance and structure.

The behaviour of public agencies is often explained by the concept of 'organizational interest'. However, the meaning of this concept is variable. In the hands of the public choice school, it usually means the wish of controllers or other staff to further their careers and ambitions by a policy of expansion. While this is a frequent tendency, it is not a universal one as the previous chapter suggested; much depends upon career structures and training and upon the strength of external constraints. Again, organizations frequently try to stabilize their environment so as to simplify their tasks, but some must necessarily 'live dangerously' and adapt their policies to the uncertainty of their environment. Even the most basic organizational interest, that of securing adequate finance, offers a useful but limited insight. For example, Peterson (1981) argues that local governments which are heavily dependent upon local property tax must above all protect their financial base by respecting the interests of business and wealthy residents. The policies of American cities often reflect Peterson's dictum, but New York City was not unique in acting otherwise, even up to bankruptcy, under a set of pluralist pressures which showed little respect for 'organizational interest'.

None the less, the managers of a large organization do control vast resources of money, staff, legal powers and political influence which they will usually want to use to advance their view of the organization's functions and purpose. Banfield (1961) has described how in Chicago most policy issues arise out of the drive of large public and private organizations (such as a hospital, a newspaper, a public housing authority) towards 'goal effectiveness and enhancement'. The policies of such bodies vary within limits according to internal politics and personalities, but they can also be mapped as responses to external opportunities and constraints affecting the organization's work. The political system of Chicago may be unique, but the dominant role of big organizations is more general.

This discussion of pluralism within modern government has mapped a complex arena which largely resists generalization. There are certainly multiple centres of decision making, but their nature varies from the 'narrow interest-centred structures of US administration' (McConnell, 1966, p. 339) to the 'authoritarian anarchy' which is said to characterize the mobile interplay of French departments and *cadres*. Strong and partly independent organizations play an active part in the policy process, but (especially outside the USA) their behaviour is increasingly modified by the growth of 'organizational systems' − families of organizations which are held together by networks of co-ordination and mutual adjustment (Hanf and Sharpf, 1978). Put more simply, pluralism has been giving way in some arenas to a form of 'corporatism'.

PLURALISM AND PLANNING

The pluralist policy process has been described as one of 'disjointed incrementalism' (Braybrooke and Lindblom, 1963). This theory assumes that functional tasks are divided among a variety of specialized agencies, each of which attends to its own specific goal and adapts its behaviour to environmental changes or the policies of other organizations (public or private) which affect the efficient performance of its duties. These policy adjustments have an incremental nature, because they are constrained both by opposing interests and also by the tendency of the agency itself to choose policies as close as possible to its established routines (March and Simon, 1958). The process is disjointed, because it works through agencies meeting their problems step by step and not through any form of comprehensive or centralized decision making.

This account is a recognizable description of much policy making in Western societies, but does it achieve the optimum policy results claimed by pluralists? There are strong reasons for saying it often will not do so. The side-effects or 'externalities' of the decision of a public agency will often be considerable, especially under modern conditions of rapid technological and economic change. In theory these side-effects will be taken care of by the intervention of other agencies speaking for the interests which will be affected. But the initiating agency, especially if it is a strong one, will have an advantage over other agencies whose concerns are less directly or immediately engaged. Moreover, pluralist analysis reveals that latent or weak interests are unlikely to be effectively represented. Once again, the pluralist solution is for those affected to take action to ensure that their interests are not permanently ignored. Such corrective action may and does occur if the injury is considerable enough, but at the best it will take time to be effective. *Disjointed* incrementalism recognizes the fact of delayed responses by other agencies or interests, but it offers no solution for the damage which can occur in the meantime.

To give an example, an airports authority will locate a new airport, if allowed to do so, on the site most convenient for airlines and their passengers. The effects of this decision will include new demands upon public transport for access to the airport, noise and environmental effects upon the locality, and the creation (directly and by inducement) of a large volume of employment which will put pressure upon the supply of housing and other services. If all these effects were fully considered, instead of primary attention being given to the much narrower criteria of the airports authority, a preferable alternative site – less satisfactory to the authority perhaps but producing better overall results – could very likely be found.

If the pluralist policy process is working properly, the various interests affected by the airport decision will be represented by bodies such as a public transport agency, a local planning authority (for environmental matters), a regional development agency (for employment creation), etc. These various agencies will bargain with the airports authority, state conditions for their co-operation, and perhaps force it to change its decision. Affected interests may also organize to put their case. If the result of these multiple pressures is deadlock, then ultimate political arbitration cannot be avoided – but such arbitration need not (on a pluralist view) involve a full reassessment of the situation (which would be 'planning'), but could select an incremental solution which balances the weight of contending interests. Pluralists often argue that the test of a good solution is not its comprehensiveness but its ability to command agreement.

One problem with this analysis is the far-reaching and delayed impact of big decisions. In this example, the effects of a large airport upon employment and upon the local and regional environment will take a long time to materialize. Those who will eventually be affected (either negatively or positively) are usually not alert to these effects. The agencies which might in theory articulate their interests have a less compelling stake in the decision than does the airports authority which needs to act now. Experience shows that it often takes a large-scale, independent inquiry to open up an issue and to activate relevant but latent interests; for example this was the case with the history of the third London airport (Self, 1975, Ch. 7).

The rational pursuit by an organization of its own goals, which is what pluralism recommends, often produces results which from a broader social standpoint seem irrational. Where this result takes the form of an obvious mutual frustration of goals, the organizations concerned may get together and agree upon some compromise, but this is unlikely to occur if organizations are very differentially affected, or are bound by rules which they cannot or do not question. For example, a highway authority will go on building roads in a vain attempt to overcome traffic congestion, and a public transport agency will go on cutting services in a vain attempt to break even, unless an overall transportation policy is introduced which modifies their respective goals and constraints.

This drawback to incrementalism arises also in any situation where there is an interchangeability between the inputs or outputs of separate programmes, which cannot be resolved satisfactorily through market allocations. One well-known example is the competition between armed services over the procurement and use of expensive multi-purpose weapon systems, so that letting each service choose its own weapon requirements becomes very wasteful. The case for a co-ordinated energy policy is less obvious because the allocation of resources can be settled by the market even if the suppliers are public agencies. However, the erratic nature of energy markets and the large environmental and employment impacts of energy decisions combine to make a strong case for the introduction of overall policy guidelines or an energy plan.

Advocates of incrementalism often point to the drawbacks of the presumed alternative of 'rational decision making' or 'planning'. Planning, it is said, involves both an impossible intellectual feat of synthesizing complex and uncertain factors, and a centralization of decision making which is authoritarian, not democratic. By contrast, incrementalism utilizes 'mutual partisan adjustment', meaning competition between pragmatically rooted and informed viewpoints. Thereby a diversity of admittedly partisan opinions get fed into the policy process and produce a greater 'collective wisdom' than can a more comprehensive but remote approach. Lindblom (1965) contends that the decisions of a cabinet of ministers, each responsible for a particular function, will usually be more intelligent and more democratic than will those of a president supposedly taking an overall viewpoint.

Lindblom may be right about the best form of the political executive, but only if the cabinet ministers are not too bound by departmental viewpoints and if some of them at least have broader responsibilities. In general, however, the textbook comparisons between incrementalism and planning are a debate between straw men. 'Incrementalism' is in practice strongly qualified by concentrations of organizational power, and its exponents have never explained how far its recommended fragmentation of decision making is supposed to go. In practice, policy making follows adminstrative divisions which result in a form of 'sectoral politics'. Those interests outside the administrative space of the relevant department find great difficulty over breaking into its closed circle. On the other hand, 'planning' in Western societies is too limited in practice to depend upon impossible intellectual feats or to become authoritarian. Authoritarianism seems much more likely to result from the imposition of dogmatic policies by political leaders than from attempts at 'rational decision making'.

It is therefore desirable to consider further the ability of planning to overcome the failures of incrementalism. In theory, planning is concerned with some concept of the general or community interest. In practice, planning agencies function in a great variety of ways. This fact makes it much harder to develop a *normative* theory of planning than one of incrementalism, since the latter can draw upon helpful but misleading analogies of spontaneous equilibrium. We can, however, list some of the functions which planners perform.

(1) They may provide support for clarifying and applying the priorities of political leaders.
(2) They may speak on behalf of an important but latent interest, e.g. a budget office can be viewed as an 'efficiency advocate' on behalf of taxpayers (Schultze, 1968).
(3) They may speak on behalf of weak interests, e.g. town planning departments often stress aesthetic values, and sometimes speak up for cyclists and pedestrians.
(4) They may produce a synoptic plan or policy guidelines for co-ordinating the activities of other organizations, or they may review and evaluate major decisions from a synoptic viewpoint.

A planning agency may perform all of these functions in differing degrees. For example, a budget office will be at least as concerned with the first task (political priorities) as with the second (efficiency advocate). It may occasionally take a protective view of weak interests (the British Treasury took the arts and even universities under its wing until these became expensive), but more often a hard one when it is trying to cut expenditure. It may also attempt some synoptic plan for redirecting the flow of public expenditure although this is less likely.

The fourth function will be attempted by agencies concerned with policy co-ordination in particular fields (e.g. energy, transportation, defence) or for the whole economy or a particular region (economic or regional planning). Such activities involve a high professional input and are intellectually difficult or ambitious, as incrementalists say. However, it does not follow that the value of such planning depends upon its intellectual quality. Its value also turns upon the possession of a broader and less biased policy viewpoint than is to be found within existing organizations. Such a viewpoint has two advantages. First, it may enable policy problems to be redefined and resolved upon a scale which better matches their actual social complexity. Secondly, it may enable a more effective and balanced synthesis of interests to be achieved than would occur through organizational competition which is one-sided or mutually frustrating.

Of course, any such advantages for planning are conditional and may not be realized in practice. Effective planning requires political, organizational and professional support and resources. It hinges upon some synthesis of political interests, administrative reorganization and an integration of professional skills, if the planning agency is not to fail (Self, 1974). Often it does fail. Moreover, planning of this type is not wholly *contradictory* to pluralism. It will maintain features of incrementalism and mutual partisan adjustment, but it will shift their operations on to a broader political and organizational stage.

The modern pluralist state is marked by an extensive representation of multiple interests within the framework of government. The interests represented are both private and public ones. The private interests utilize lobbying (political or administrative) as well as direct representation on joint bodies (advisory or executive) and incorporation within the decision premises of some public departments; for example, the Treasurer's department of a local government will be aware of the financial benefits which private development may bring. Public agencies for housing, highways, parks, etc., will speak with varying effectiveness for the needs of their clients. Other public agencies speak for more latent interests, such as the consumers of food or drugs. This kaleidoscopic scene often produces complex alliances which cut across the public–private dichotomy. For example, at a British public inquiry into some development project, a public corporation may be allied with business interests against local governments and environmental objectors. The distinctions between 'public' and 'private' interests become blurred, and replaced by a different distinction between stronger and weaker ones.

Planning or co-ordinating agencies may speak up for missing interests, but equally they may simply confirm or rationalize the power of the strongest interests. However, they may possess some capacity to counter organizational bias, to anticipate significant side-effects of public decisions and to develop a superior policy framework for solving complex issues. In these ways, planning may act as a partial corrective to the limitations of disjointed incrementalism. Planning is closely linked with the development of the more integrated decision frameworks which accompany the emergence of corporatism and will be returned to in that context. To conclude this section, pluralism is surely right to recognize the complexity of society and the difficulties of finding overall solutions to complex problems; but it does not follow that the maximum fragmentation and diffusion of decision making is the best answer to this situation. A balance has to be struck between spontaneous adjustments and integrated plans, and if the complex interdependencies of modern societies make the latter course harder they also make it more necessary.

THE DILEMMAS OF PLURALIST VALUES

Up to a point, pluralism has an obvious value and appeal to believers in liberty and political democracy. Anyone who abhors tyranny will favour a considerable dispersion and balance of power within government and society. 'Intermediate institutions', as the earlier pluralists claimed, are essential elements of a free society and are more necessary than ever today as defences against the erratic movements of mass opinion and its manipulation by elites (Kornhauser, 1959). The theme of a spontaneous mutual adjustment of interests is also instinctively attractive through its promise of defining organizational responsibilities and facilitating compromises. These values, however, are not unconditional or unqualified. They all require judgements of degree and application – of the balances to be struck between private and public power, between narrower and broader interests, between the freedom of 'intermediate institutions' and their accountability for grants of privileged status or coercive power. Any evaluation must also take account of how the pluralist policy process works in practice.

The normative claims of pluralism have come under strong attack in the country where the system is most entrenched and was once so widely praised. McConnell (1966) contends that American distrust of the uses of public power has led to its widespread fragmentation and appropriation by private interests. Lowi (1979) argues that the same process has eroded the rule of law, undermined the principle of equal rights, and ended in 'a hell of administrative boredom'. Kariel (1961) concludes that the ethical appeal of pluralism has collapsed and that the 'public interest' needs to be vigorously reasserted. Dahl (1982), perhaps the most influential exponent of American pluralism, now believes that the system can only be rescued by basic changes in political and economic institutions.

Before accepting these criticisms, it is best to consider the remedies which pluralism itself might offer.

As noted earlier, pluralist analysis concentrated initially (like public choice theory) upon demand-side politics. Initially government was seen as responding adequately, if not always perfectly, to the balance of demands generated by interest groups, parties and political leaders. Bureaucracy was seen as a neutral conductor for the implementation of public policies. The public

101

interest consisted in procedural 'rules of the game' which would ensure open access to the policy process and maintain tolerably fair or anyhow acceptable outcomes. If the rules were bent by the pressure of organized interests, then (it could be argued) there was a generalized interest in restoring the system to an acceptable equilibrium. This would be a collective task for political leadership, resting ultimately upon the shared ethics and majority voting power of a democratic polity.

Clearly, as this chapter has amply demonstrated, these assumptions about the behaviour of government are false. Public agencies and bureaucratic groups are active participants in the policy process. Even so their activities might still be accommodated, up to a point anyhow, within a normative theory of pluralism. Thus public agencies are still responding to their perceptions of client needs or are balancing a wider interest (say of consumers) against a specific one (say of a regulated industry). Overhead units such as a budget office are usually expressing some broad interest, in this case that of taxpayers. Co-ordinating agencies are vehicles for political 'climate setting' whereby operating agencies are made aware of the general directions and priorities of political leadership. Bureaucratic pressure groups can be said to be no more self-interested than comparable groups in the private sector, and to have an equal right to press for their material interests or professional goals.

If then there are undesirable outcomes of governmental activity, the pluralist answer will be to strengthen the political inputs into the system and to sensitize bureaucracies to their political environments. Thus if clients are being roughly treated, they (or political leaders on their behalf) should organize and act to get better treatment. If party policies are resisted by the bureaucracy, the answer is to strengthen the agencies for political control and co-ordination and/or to politicize key branches of the bureaucracy. If bureaucratic pressure groups are too greedy, they can be reined back with the help of a taxpayers' revolt.

An alternative defence of pluralism is to argue that the system in practice works better than its critics allege. Some tests of this hypothesis can be considered. First, has the policy process in Western states in fact showed the qualities of stability and compromise promised by the concept of incrementalism? A fair case for an affirmative answer can be made in respect of the quarter century of rising affluence which followed World War II. In more recent times, hasty reversals of policy throw this contention into doubt. For example, the steady expansion of education, health and other social services in Western societies was thrown into reverse, with highly wasteful effects upon capital investment, career structures and opportunities, and the diffusion of knowledge. If such sudden policy changes are blamed upon 'inescapable' economic conditions, it is still clear that pluralism has failed to stabilize the economic system.

Secondly, how far have the interests of all those affected by environmental degradation and the wastage of natural and indeed social resources been inserted into the policy process? Certainly environmental agencies of various kinds have been set up, although few have attempted the 'synoptic vision' of some older agencies like the National Resources Planning Board – a product of the Roosevelt 'New Deal' (Lepawsky, 1978). Generally these environmental agencies, whatever their formal powers, have performed rather weakly when faced with the pressure of industrial or financial interests. However, the political difficulty of responding adequately to environmental problems has to be recognized. Communist systems have produced as much environmental degradation as Western societies. To tackle such issues effectively, one would require either an enlightened despotism or an egalitarian democracy with a widely shared concern about the future.

Thirdly, and perhaps the most important as an empirical test, how far has pluralism protected the interests of the weaker groups in society? Truman's (1951) now classic defence of pluralism argued that political entrepreneurs could be expected to espouse the cause of weak or minority groups in exchange for their votes. His example was the way in which F. D. Roosevelt mobilized the support of disadvantaged groups such as small farmers, the unemployed, and poor immigrants through his 'New Deal' measures of support and assistance. Roosevelt's initiatives did not break with the American model of 'representative bureaucracy'. Special agencies were set up to help groups such as small farmers and the unemployed. The same approach was later used by Kennedy and Johnson in their equal opportunity programmes, which assigned special aid for the poor through local representative agencies. However, the special agencies created to help weak groups are themselves weaker and less durable than those helping strong groups. This kind of 'representative bureaucracy' is better at co-opting the leaders of weak groups into the system than at ensuring them equal attention or support.

None the less the Roosevelt 'New Deal' was an important example of 'countervailing power' exercised on behalf of weaker

103

groups. Why has such action become rarer? The answer seems to lie in the fragmentation of the economic and social structure produced by changes in the economy and the workforce. The earlier industrial proletariat had at least the advantages of great numbers and common work experiences and meeting places. Modern deprived groups are smaller, less cohesive, and more isolated, while successful groups (including the more skilled industrial workers) have grown in strength. Political pluralism may have reflected these trends and thereby reduced strong class conflicts, but it has also diminished the effective representation of the unfortunate.

The difficulty with these defences is that political pluralism as it works in practice is not a self-corrective system, but is completely pragmatic and open-ended. It has no way of specifying a desirable equilibrium point of political pressures. Despite frequent use of market analogies, the pluralist policy process cannot mirror the theoretical model of perfect competition. The ground rules of 'equal access' are even harder to establish and to maintain than in the case of the market, and the distribution of organizational power is at least as unequal and resistant to change as are market monopolies.

Theories of organizational leadership often adopt a pluralist perspective. Selznick (1957) argues that the task of leadership is to uphold the special competence of an organization. This theory calls attention to the ethical responsibilities of organizational leadership and rejects the theories which treat organizational policy making in instrumental terms.

All the same, the 'distinctive competence' of an organization still needs to be judged by wider standards than its own efficiency or effectiveness. The worth of the 'autonomy' of a successful public organization will usually be judged by the purposes for which it is exercised. For example, the idealism which for some time surrounded the TVA was a tribute to the breadth and humanism of its goals which contrasted with the narrow criteria of technical specialization. When the TVA evolved into being on the whole just another large public utility, it lost these favourable evaluations.

Specialization of roles can have a dehumanizing effect upon individual behaviour and responsibility. If the politician's function is interpreted as one of maximizing votes and support, he will have no personal concern with the public welfare. The most efficient politician will be the most dehumanized one (as is indeed sometimes recommended). The same point applies to the bureaucrat if his standard is to be simply efficient policy execution. Many writers have argued persuasively (Thomas, 1977; Hodgkinson, 1978) that career officials have a legitimate as well as a *de facto* interest in the content of public policies. No doubt their personal judgements should be kept within limits and matched by some form of accountability, but it is another matter to regard these judgements as invalid.

Normative pluralism need not take a narrow view of role specialization, but it does rely upon the mutual competition and adjustment of interests for reaching satisfactory outcomes. An organizational leader would not last long if he failed to give priority to his own tasks and goals, but the social responsibility of leadership consists precisely in recognizing the relevance of broader evaluations. Otherwise the paradox of organizational rationality producing social irrationality goes unchecked.

Thus one returns to the old pluralist riddle of the 'general interest'. The general interest can be understood defensively as a critical scrutiny of the biases of particular organizations, and positively as an attempt to resolve societal problems upon the scale and at the level where they are most soluble. Such evaluations are ultimately a political function but they will be badly made unless there is a wide sharing of social perceptions and values which transcend organizational and group boundaries. As was said before, the case for 'planning' as a corrective to pluralism is not based upon the intellectual superiority of planners but upon their broader vantage point and hopefully upon their generalist skills and values. However, the quality of planning still turns upon the goals and quality of political leadership.

Throughout this chapter, we have been dealing primarily with modern American-style pluralism rather than with the earlier English or European variety. This earlier pluralism stressed the value of self-governing 'intermediate institutions' for their own sake and as a bulwark against centralized power. The pluralist ideal is the cultivation of a great variety of such institutions, which might take the forms both of self-governing local communities and of self-governing associations for purposes of religion, culture, trade and the professions. As Eckstein (1973) argues in the case of Norway, democracy proves most stable when its practices pervade a wide range of social institutions.

This pluralist ideal is severely compromised by the growth of concentrations of economic and professional power which receive governmental recognition and support. Government is responding to group pressures which go contrary to the older pluralist ideals. The conferment of coercive power upon any organization should at the very least entail tests of its representative character and of its accountability to some broader forum for the use of its powers. Tests of this kind are largely lacking in Western societies.

A basic problem with modern pluralism is the range and complexity of the tentacles of government which embrace all intermediate institutions within their grasp. No longer is there a clear distance between central government and other institutions, so that in each case policy can be made and accountability can be established within a defined and intelligible framework. Instead, the policy process works through a complex web of administrative and political networks. It thus becomes hard, if not sometimes impossible, to apportion responsibility for the exercise of power or to establish the accountability of decision makers. Consequently, political elections and party policies also lose a large part of their significance. Democracy may be destroyed by over-centralization of power, but it may also wither on the vine of excessive fragmentation and complexity.

These developments have destroyed much of the traditional association between pluralism and liberalism. Shils (1956, p. 154) argued that: 'Liberalism is a system of pluralism. It is a system of many centres of power, many areas of privacy and a strong internal impulse towards the mutual adaption of the spheres, rather than the dominance or submission of any one to the others.'

But modern political pluralism confuses the location of power, invades traditional areas of privacy and does not comply too well with the idea of mutual balance. Hence it is open to Kariel's gloomy conclusion that political pluralism 'only lingers quietly as a submerged, inarticulate ingredient of Western liberalism' (1961, p. 168).

It does not follow that pluralist ideals are irrelevant to or unrealizable in a modern democracy. Rather would it seem that their interpretation and realization should be seen as dependent upon the basic institutions and social values of a democracy. Thus the decentralization of power needs to be grounded in a system which avoids large and disparate concentrations of wealth and influence; the power and rhetoric of private interests needs to be matched by an equivalent weight of civic goals and values. Pluralism has to be encompassed within an institutional and value system which prevents it from becoming cumulatively less equal and less open.

More radical cures for the failures of pluralism would move the political system either backwards or forwards. Lowi's remedy of 'juridical democracy' would entail a return to the authority of general laws made openly in the legislature. Group pressures would continue to operate fully at this level, but they could no longer latch on to the 'arbitrary' power of administrative agencies which would be revoked. Lowi's approach therefore involves reversing modern developments in the functioning of government. On the other hand, Dahl's prescriptions seem to accept the evolution of pluralism into some form of corporatism and are better considered later. Is it possible for Western societies to revert to some simpler and more accountable political system of limited and diversified pluralism? Or is some form of corporatism compatible with democratic pluralist ideals?

5

THE CORPORATIST STATE

Corporatism is an even more slippery concept than pluralism. As an expression of the values of social order, balance and harmony, corporatism has roots stretching back to an idealized conception of the medieval polity and to the writings of Catholic theologians. In principle, corporatist values are opposed to those of liberal individualism and pluralism. Corporatism stresses the social nature of men and their need for a systematic and stable social order, rather than opportunities for the competitive pursuit of individual freedom and happiness.

Corporatism as an ideal has always had more appeal in many continental European countries, especially those with Catholic traditions, than in the English-speaking world where the doctrines of individualism and of 'man making his own world' (and not accepting it as an ordained or necessary social order) had their strongest impact. However, as Beer (1965) pointed out, there are strong elements of corporatism in both the Disraelian 'paternalist' version of English conservatism, and in the equally paternalist stream of Fabian socialism. It was in the USA that *laissez-faire* liberalism and individualism reached their apogee and still dominate at least the ideological stage.

As a prescription for modern societies, corporatist values must be articulated through the directive or co-ordinating role of modern states. (It is as natural for a corporatist to talk of 'state', meaning some kind of organic system, as for a liberal to talk of 'government', meaning a collection of public institutions.) The most potent version of modern corporatism, which provided the philosophy for Italian and to a rather lesser extent for German fascism, conceived the state under a strong leader as the creator of a disciplined and hierarchical economic and social order. Individuals were supposed to participate in government through their membership of occupationally differentiated groups working under state supervision, although in practice this participation was largely sham. The tyrannical practices of fascism negated the rhetoric of social harmony and gave to corporatism a definition and reputation from which it has hardly as yet recovered.

Modern theories of corporatism differ according to whether they stress the directive and unifying role of government for which fascism would represent the extreme example, or the substantially autonomous character of the various functional bodies. On this basis a distinction is sometimes drawn between 'pure' or 'state' corporatism, and 'social' or 'liberal' corporatism.

As an ideology the former concept is linked with values of order and discipline, the latter with those of spontaneous harmony and adaptation. Thus 'social corporatism' may seem to come close to the pluralist ideal of self-governing intermediate institutions, but modern functional organizations are not in any meaningful way *detached from* the state (as, for example, churches normally still are), but instead share in the exercise of governmental powers. Thus the question of autonomy becomes the more limited one of *how far* such organizations are responsive to and representative of their members, or have been co-opted into serving the interests of government; and of *how far* the articulation of group interests remains open-ended and flexible, or has become closed and restricted. Because of the entanglement of functional groups with government, 'liberal corporatism' is a better description than 'social corporatism' for a relatively autonomous conception of their role.

What causes confusion in debates about corporatism are the different explanations which can be offered for its development. Thus corporatism may be explained in at least three principal ways: as a development of pluralism; as a product of the requirements of advanced capitalism; and as a feature of modern economic nationalism. These explanations are not exclusive. They may all be (and in my view *are*) at least partly true. However, the choice of principal explanation affects the selection of the phenomena to be explained. In so far as these explanations differ, it is to some extent because they are concentrating upon rather different empirical developments. It certainly does not follow that all the explanations are *equally* true because they entail some sharp divergences in their understanding of modern government which cannot be defined away by the use of the term 'corporatism'.

Let us consider first the proposition that modern 'corporatism' represents a development of modern 'pluralism'. Schmitter gives a well-known definition of an ideal type of corporatism, used in the Weberian sense of explicating the fully realized tendencies of a system of organization:

Corporatism can be defined as a system of interest representation in which the constituent units are organised into a limited number of singular, compulsory, non-competitive, hierarchically ordered and functionally differentiated categories, recognised or licensed (if not created) by the state and granted a deliberate representational monopoly within their respective categories in exchange for observing certain controls on their selection of leaders and articulation of demands and supports. [Schmitter, 1979, p. 13.]

Schmitter's definition describes a *comprehensive incorporation of interest groups within the framework of government*. It does not say *why* this development is occurring nor *how* and in whose interest the system will work. Thus the description applies (according to its author) to a diversity of regimes, ranging from the Scandinavian countries, the Netherlands and Austria to Spain (anyhow under Franco), Portugal, Brazil and Greece. The difference between these two groups of countries corresponds to the issue of who controls the system. In Sweden, etc., the system remains democratic in as much as interest groups are responsive to their members, have independent influence within government, and are linked with competitive party politics. In the Iberian peninsula, etc., the system is or was authoritarian and linked with single-party regimes and bureaucratic control of interest representation.

Thus it might seem that the anatomy of corporatism is consistent with very different types of internal dynamic. Schmitter's analysis reverts to the distinction between 'pure' or state-imposed corporatism and 'liberal corporatism', and the latter form is the more relevant one for modern Western democracies. However, even in the Scandinavian countries, Schmitter's description is only partly realized. The systems are 'functionally differentiated', 'state recognised', and 'representationally monopolistic' (subject to the competing influence or back-up of political parties), but are sometimes only weakly 'hierarchically ordered'.

In other Western democracies, interest group integration is a lot weaker and peak organizations do not exist or have very limited influence. But some features of this description remain true in a more fragmented way. Interest groups in particular policy fields like agriculture often participate closely in public policy making and achieve a virtual monopoly of representation. Many professional and also technical bodies are licensed by governments to control the admission and behaviour of members and to give expert policy advice. Many industries are subject to corporate regulatory bodies.

The corporatist state

These activities also mean that membership of a professional or economic organization is often *de facto* essential even if not legally compulsory, and that organization leaders are under some pressure to 'act responsibly' if they are to retain their privileged public status.

Corporatism can be viewed as an evolution from pluralism for three reasons.

(a) *Policy co-operation*

It may pay both government and the interest group to co-operate closely in policy making and enforcement. This process is a familiar development or distortion of pluralism which arises because (1) both government agency and interest group are strengthened in their external relations and budgetary requests by close mutual co-operation; and/or (2) where economic change or restructuring is necessary, some or much of the responsibility for consequent regulation and the allocation of costs and benefits can be passed to the interest group (or a special body controlled by it) in exchange for government economic support. The first cause is more significant in the pluralist government system of the USA than elsewhere, but the second cause is widely prevalent. As the number of 'problem' industries increase, so does the pervasiveness of this 'corporate pluralism'.

An early example of this process in action is the 'partnership' over agricultural policy making in Britain between the government and the National Farmers' Union which began (as other similar developments did) as long ago as the 1930s (Self and Storing, 1962). A partial answer to the unstable and low level of farm prices was found in the creation of producer-elected marketing monopolies for certain products (milk, potatoes, hops) which, through their coercive powers to control distribution and sometimes to fix production quotas, raised the collective bargaining power of farmers over the marketing of these products.

Subsequently, under wartime and postwar pressures, the Ministry of Agriculture and the Union agreed to a system of annual price reviews which settled price guarantees and for a time production targets. The Union got in on the ground floor of the policy process, and knew that its assent to (or anyhow absence of dissent from) the price settlement was politically valued; conversely the Ministry could concentrate upon the goals of limiting the farm subsidy and trying to steer production in the most economic direction, while allowing the Union to propose and to take some responsibility for the distribution of support between different

111

sectors of farming. The licensed monopolistic status of the Farmers' Union became entrenched by the ability of its candidates to dominate the statutory marketing boards which it had promoted, and by the inability of any breakaway or rival union to get recognition from Whitehall and their consequent collapse.

This is an early example of 'corporate pluralism' which could be matched, often less completely, by many other cases. Thus in many countries declining industries such as coal, shipbuilding, steel and textiles have been the subject of rationalization schemes worked out by administrative agencies representative of government and industry (steel is also the one industry to be reorganized internationally under the aegis of the EEC). In the USA, neither employer nor Union organizations can achieve anything like a monopoly position, but a fragmented 'corporate pluralism' can be said to exist, most notably in the shared administration of agricultural support and regulation schemes between the main farm organizations and the various bureaux in the Department of Agriculture. As the number of such cases grows, the scope of corporate pluralism expands and leads on to attempts at overall policy co-ordination.

A different situation occurs where a government deliberately sets out to promote economic growth, as in France and Japan, rather than responding to the distress signals of an affected interest group. In such cases, government more actively sets the policy goals and its interventions stimulate the emergence of monopolistic interest groups. In these cases corporatism can hardly be seen as growing out of pluralism, although the resultant policy partnership may have similar features.

b) *Organizational sociology*

The evolution of pluralism into corporatism can be partly explained by organizational sociology. In government as well as in business, there has been a steady move towards larger organizations; for example, the experiments with 'giant departments' in UK, France, etc. As large organizations gobble up smaller ones, they become better able to stabilize their environment. The larger they get and the more they concert their policies, the more stabilized the total system becomes, at least in an organizational sense. The system will still be buffeted by external forces which will sometimes lead the members of interest groups (and government officials too) to repudiate the disciplines of concerted action.

Organizations, both private and public, also become increasingly

The corporatist state

bureaucratic and similar in their structures, methods of working and style of decision making. This convergence of style and attitudes between government departments and major interest groups is very apparent in Germany and was noted still earlier in respect of the UK (Nettl, 1965), although Nettl commented that it was the attitudes of civil servants which dominated the interaction, a point which has often been made about France. Leaders of government and industry have increasingly stressed the virtue of 'social responsibility' and of a concerted approach towards difficult economic problems. Naturally the close involvement of interest group leaders in government tends to distance them from their members, a process which resembles the distancing of ministers from their parliamentary followers by pressures within their departments.

The convergence of leadership in government and industry tends towards oligarchy and elitism. While career opportunities within large organizations do ensure some 'circulation of elites', new leaders will get selected for their ability to work the established system of organizational networks or will probably be soon socialized into its values.

c) *Rationing of political demands*
According to this theory, pluralism leads to excessive demands being placed upon the political system. Interest groups expect more than government is able to supply. Consequently, insoluble conflicts are engendered, particularly between the pressures for full employment and the pressures to control inflation. If political parties are unable to solve these economic problems, and if in the face of a dominant pluralism they cannot perform their function of disciplining and controlling the articulation of interests, the only alternative left becomes the incorporation of interests within government so as to limit and ration the satisfaction of their demands. Government is here seen as reacting to the problem in a non-ideological way through internalized rationing, because the economy cannot take any further pressures for public spending.

This thesis is ambivalent as to whether it is the excessive claims of interest groups which cause the trouble, or the inability of capitalist societies to meet social demands. Claus Offe (1983) argues that capitalism was reconciled with democracy only under two special conditions. These were the existence of a Keynesian welfare state, which provided full employment and social security, and a party political system whose leaders were continually pushed into the middle ground by electoral competition and by the mass

113

character of their parties. These conditions cease to apply once full employment is severely breached and political parties are pushed toward extremism. On this view, once economic growth ceases, group demands have to be controlled by a process of incorporation and rationing in the interests of capitalism.

On the other hand, the 'overload' thesis of excessive group demands was put forward when Western governments seemed to many observers (Brittan, 1975; King, 1975) to be locked within a 'revolution of rising expectations'. But what has happened to those expectations? The evidence is that, as economic conditions worsen, peoples' expectations of government fall (Alt, 1979). Time was when the difference between 3 and 4 per cent unemployment was believed to mean the difference between electoral success and disaster, but in 1983 the Thatcher government in the UK could get re-elected with unemployment above 12 per cent and rising.

Another interpretation of these lowered expectations is disillusionment with the promises of party leaders. Political parties have come to fight elections primarily over their ability to manage the economy and to solve economic problems; but their repeated failure to deliver the goods from the mid-1960s onwards has increased political cynicism and apathy (as shown by voting figures) and consequently undermined the idea that governments *can* solve problems such as unemployment. A beneficiary of this movement of opinion (at least for a time) is right-wing parties who believe in 'market forces'. Then again, although Beer (1982) claims that deferential voting is dead, it may be that economic recession produces 'deferential anxiety' – a clinging to what is supposedly the most orthodox and 'authoritative' party leadership lest worse befall.

The argument that rising expectations among the masses force interest groups to make excessive demands which cannot be ignored is therefore doubtful, but it could still be the case that the incorporation and rationing of some group demands are ways of helping a capitalist economy.

This analysis has not dealt with the tricky question of 'who wins' from the co-operation or collusion between government and interest groups. A possible definition of corporatism is the exercise of public authority by organized group interests. This definition suggests that corporatism may represent a fuller development of the appropriation of public power for private gain which McConnell saw as characteristic of American pluralism in practice. This conclusion would be misleading because corporatism involves organized groups in accepting a greater degree of disciplined and co-operative behaviour than in the more free-wheeling conditions of pluralist bargaining. In West Germany, for example, some measures of public regulation have been applied to the internal procedures and external relations of organized interests (Offe, 1981). Alternatively, corporatism may be seen as a system whereby government acts to give differential support to some interests while trying to neutralize the demands of others.

Thus there are several reasons why pluralism may tend to evolve toward some form of corporatism, although the above explanations are unclear about who benefits from the process. It should also be stressed that conditions of pluralism and corporatism can co-exist within the same political system. The complex picture of organizational and bureaucratic pluralism described in the previous chapter has not evaporated. Authoritative studies stress that considerable flux and instability still exist in relations between governments and interest groups (Berger, 1981). Moreover, there are also sources of pluralism within the administrative system itself. These reservations conceded, 'corporatism' does describe an axis of development in the evolution of capitalist societies.

CAPITALISM, NATIONALISM AND CORPORATISM

We need to consider deeper explanations for the rise of corporatism. Foremost here is the Marxist critique which views state corporatism as the product of the 'structural' requirements of advanced capitalism. Modern Marxist literature is too extensive, diverse and subtle to be analysed fully within the context of this book. Many writers within this tradition concede a 'relative autonomy' to the state, whose exact dimensions are the subject of much discussion, but none the less this autonomy is usually argued to be very restricted and partly presentational, so that it cannot interfere seriously with the 'imperative' of capital accumulation (Miliband, 1977; Poulantzas, 1978).

For our purposes, the first question to ask is how and why the growth of the state is necessary to capitalism. On the Marxist view, all surplus value over and above the socially necessary costs of labour accrues to the owners of capital, and the internal dynamics of capitalism (irrespective of what any capitalist may wish or intend) requires a maximization of surplus value through capital accumulation. Marx himself thought that taxation for public purposes represented a deduction from the surplus value which the owners of capital would otherwise receive, but modern Marxists contend that high levels of public taxation and expenditure are necessary to maintain capitalism in three main ways (O'Connor, 1973; Gough, 1979).

(1) *Social investment* A diminishing scope for markets and profits requires advanced capitalism to be 'baled out' by the state through the nationalization of unprofitable industries ('ash-can socialism'), government contracts and public subsidies. Additionally, public investment in unprofitable infrastructure is seen as aiding private capital accumulation.

(2) *Social consumption* Expenditure upon social services such as health, education, etc., aids capitalism by reducing the 'socially necessary' costs of reproducing the labour force. It also, as do (1) and (3), absorbs labour which with advancing technology becomes superfluous for the requirement of capital accumulation.

(3) *Social expenses* Spending to relieve poverty and unemployment, or to clear up the urban and industrial mess made by capitalism, is required to maintain the legitimacy of the state (and hence of the capitalist system), and to ward off the danger of revolt.

These arguments are certainly suggestive about the ways in which increasing state activities are made *consistent with* the needs of capitalism; but it is another thing to claim that all or almost all of these activities have been developed *in order to satisfy* the 'structural needs' of capitalism. The latter argument easily becomes closed and circular, and rests ultimately upon two assumptions which require empirical demonstration: (a) that the capitalist system is necessarily shrinking in terms of opportunities for profit and employment, and (b) that capitalism can somehow force the state to take over all those burdens which it cannot manage and to perform a dutiful supporting role.

Each Marxist contention about the role of the state is empirically open to counter-explanations. Nationalization removes at least some opportunities for private profit, as campaigns for 'privatization' demonstrate. State aid to capitalism has to be paid for, either by taxation of profits or by reduction of consumers' spending power, and if some capitalists gain thereby, others will surely lose. This point is often met by showing that it is large firms which primarily benefit from state aid, which is thereby directed towards the promotion of monopoly capitalism. State promotion of monopoly can best be understood in the context of international trade competition, which means that governments may be pursuing a nationalist goal but under conditions of international capitalism. At the same time, the bailing out of large firms can also be explained politically by the volume of jobs and investment at stake, and by the blow to national prestige which the collapse of a famous firm would entail. Expensive rescues of lame ducks hardly help the general prosperity of capitalism, but they can be explained by pressures of international competition as well as by domestic political pressures.

It is difficult to argue that the big post-1945 increase in public social services was essential for the reproduction of the labour force, unless one takes a very flexible view of the 'socially necessary costs' of labour. Curiously, Marx himself opens the door to such a viewpoint when he says:

> The number and extent of so-called necessary wants, as also the means of satisfying them, are themselves the product of historical development, and *depend therefore to a great extent on the degree of civilization of a country*, more particularly on the conditions under which, and consequently on the *habits and degree of comfort* in which the class of free labourers has been formed. [Marx, 1962, p. 171, my italics.]

Taken on its own, this passage suggests that in a 'civilized' country, surplus value might be indefinitely squeezed to provide a rising standard of living for the labour force − which of course is contrary to the usual Marxist thesis. One wonders how some developments in public education, such as the growth of subjects like sociology which offer a platform for radical critiques, have anything to do with the reproduction of the labour force. In any event, it is hard to attribute the growth of the welfare state simply to an 'imperative' of capital accumulation, although it is plausible that cuts in social services are due to the capitalist conditions of international competition.

To view many welfare services as a prop of state legitimacy (an argument which overlaps with the last one) raises the issue of what 'legitimacy' requires. Sharp increases in unemployment and cuts in welfare benefits suggest that 'legitimacy' may be a very flexible requirement. While welfare may have to be limited to what capitalism can afford, this is not the same thing as saying that capitalism 'requires' any particular level of welfare to be provided to sustain the state's legitimacy. Moreover, there is some limit to the welfare services that can be provided under any economic system, so that it is necessary to ask how far the limits to welfare

are imposed by 'structural' limits of capitalism itself, or result from a more complex balance of forces. Again, the need for public expenditure to cope with the urban problems of capitalist development is a leaky bucket, unless one differentiates between specific dysfunctions of capitalism (such as the effects of speculative land markets) and general social trends which also occur in non-capitalist countries (such as the fragmentation of families and suburbanization). Marxist critics of capitalism often fail to investigate this distinction (e.g. Gough, 1979, p. 92).

A more empirical explanation of the general relationship between capitalism and political democracy is advanced by Lindblom (1977, Part 5). Lindblom sees political leadership in Western governments as subject to two opposing types of pressure. The leadership is formally accountable to the electorate who demand employment policies, social services, consumer protection, pollution controls and other social measures whose achievement variously constrains the workings of capitalism. But conversely the leadership cannot avoid dependence upon the interests of capitalism, because effective capitalism is essential for national prosperity and hence also for the ability of politicians to deliver their promises. Hence political leaders' ability to satisfy the former pressure is strongly constrained by the latter.

This type of analysis does not depend upon any invisible 'structural' imperative. It views government as operating under a realistic mixture of political pressures and economic constraints. It can also allow for governments to have a considerable margin of discretion whose possible limits are not accurately known. For example, business men often argue that new taxes or controls will jeopardize the efficiency and prosperity of the economic system. It is improbably artificial to suppose that (without perhaps knowing it) the business men really 'want' the controls in the interest of capitalism itself. A good example is the debate about the weight of anti-pollution controls imposed by a number of US Federal agencies (Goldstein, 1978). While big companies can doubtless 'absorb' the consequent costs, the scope for rapid technological development and capital accumulation is also reduced. But equally, government might often act *more* radically without killing the chipped golden egg of capitalism, particularly of course if its actions could cumulatively reduce the nation's dependence upon the capitalist system. That, however, is an enormously difficult task.

Any governmental freedom of action will also be coterminous with the scope for overt political pressures. The influence of

118

capitalism does not just depend upon politicians' recognition of underlying constraints but upon the direct influence of business lobbies which, as Lindblom recognizes, is very considerable, particularly in the USA. These lobbies operate both as pressure groups and through their leverage within political parties, particularly but not exclusively right-wing ones. In the USA, the Republicans are the traditional party of business, but Democrats are certainly not immune from business pressures. Even Labour parties are open to some permeation by business interests. However, it would be wrong to regard *any* major party as simply a captive of business interests, because of its need to win votes and the internal dynamic of party policy making. It can be argued, for example, that business is more dependent upon the Republican party than Republicans upon business (Schattschneider, 1960).

As Marxists recognize, the interests of capitalism are not homogeneous and can internally conflict. None the less the general impact of business lobbies is to augment the underlying constraints placed upon political leadership by the capitalist economic system.

This general analysis must now be related to the specific phenomena of corporatism. One school of thought identifies corporatism with national economic planning, and more specifically with the existence of a corporate bargaining system over incomes and prices involving government together with peak organizations of employers and workers (Panitch, 1976; Jessop, 1979). However, this description would confine corporatism unrealistically to a few small Western democracies. It would not apply to the USA, Britain would rank as a corporatist failure, and France would present the curious mixture of an elaborate planning system without corporate bargaining over incomes.

Corporate bargaining by peak bodies has primarily developed in countries with a strong industrial and political labour movement, such as Sweden and Norway. In these countries, over 90 per cent of industrial workers and junior clerical staff are unionized, and employers also are highly organized and act collectively through peak organizations, with government playing a steering and mediating role. However, the interest groups themselves are not state-controlled and are only partly 'hierarchical', since in Norway for example grass-roots revolts occur against wage settlements, and corporate bargaining goes on also at the local government level (Schwerin, 1980). Thus Schmitter's concept of 'liberal corporatism', with a strong measure of 'partnership' between government and economic interests, seems a reasonable description of these countries.

Political theories of modern government

The problem is how to explain this phenomenon. A Marxist analysis views corporate bargaining of this kind as a defence of capitalist interests, but a truer explanation seems to be that the system has worked in the interests of both capital and labour. Castles (1978) makes the valid point that industrial settlements cannot be separated from the social gains realized simultaneously by strong left-wing parties. Thus, the distribution of market incomes in Sweden appears to be no more equal than in other capitalist systems, but social services are uniquely good, redundancy payments are generous, and the handicapped and aged get more sensitive attention than elsewhere. These welfare gains make Sweden overall a more egalitarian and humane society than most capitalist countries.

Castles gives a plausible Lindblom-type explanation of Swedish history. After a period of intensive conflict and heavy unemployment the *political* dominance of the Social Democrats from the 1930s onwards provided a balance to the *economic* power of capitalism. The result was a concordance to make capitalism work more efficiently and equitably – for example, through strong policies for assisting labour mobility and retraining – and to devote a large portion of the consequent economic growth to welfare goals. The same policy goals have had a strong appeal to left-wing politicians elsewhere (Crosland, 1956), but outside some of the smaller democracies they have not so far been achieved. Even in Sweden and Norway, the workers' gains remain to some extent vulnerable to the competitive pressures of international capitalism.

Panitch (1976) views the political attempts to forge a statutory incomes policy in Britain as attributable to the problems of capitalism under conditions of full employment. International competitiveness was being damaged and profits squeezed by a wages spiral. Although the Conservatives first set up the National Economic Development Council (NEDC) as a peak co-ordinating agency in 1962, it was Labour governments which made the strongest efforts for an incomes policy. Panitch attributes this fact to the greater ability of Labour to co-opt workers into support for national economic goals, which they would otherwise resist as being against their sectional interest. The condition of this co-option was that Labour would also control prices, keep down the cost of living, and pursue goals of economic growth and full employment. Panitch argues that while Labour failed to achieve these other goals, mainly because of international financial pressures, it did impose wage restraint over two separate periods until the unions revolted.

The corporatist state

Panitch's account is only partly accurate. The Labour Government did try hard to implement its other policies, especially during the 'social contract' period with the unions, while it scrapped its one really serious attempt to get an incomes policy in 1968 under union and party pressures. The difference with Sweden was that, failing to achieve economic growth, British Labour Governments could not achieve the successful mixture of social and economic policies, which together might make an incomes policy consistent with the interests of labour. Labour having failed, the Conservatives had little hope of success, so that both parties were forced to vacate the middle ground of a corporate bargaining system which actually had the support of a strong majority of the public (Alt, 1979, pp. 204–207).

At this point an alternative explanation of corporatism needs to be introduced. Winkler views corporatism as:

> an economic system in which the state directs and controls predominantly privately-owned business according to four principles: unity, order, nationalism, and success. [Winkler, 1976, pp. 100–136.]

Winkler's theory accords to government a significant autonomy from the influence of economic interests. He contends that the substance of property relations can be changed while their form is kept intact. In other words, corporatism is a mixture of private ownership and public control, which uses central economic management to advance nationalist goals by pragmatic means, e.g. through specific measures and incentives rather than traditional administrative rules (i.e. it follows the 'success' principle).

Winkler's example of the 'planning agreements' reached with firms by the British Labour Government in the 1970s does not support his case at all well, because these agreements had rather little effect upon the economy. A much better example would be the post-1945 activities of French economic planners, who used the economic incentives of 'quasi-contracts' (investment finance, subsidies and tax rebates) to promote and steer industrial investment, increase productivity, and create mergers between firms in the interests of efficiency (Shonfield, 1965, Ch. 7). In France, as in Japan, one can certainly observe a significant mixture of public control and private capital ownership since 1945. In Britain, attempts in this direction have been made, but have proved weaker and less effective.

A good case can therefore be made out for viewing nationalism

121

as the primary cause of corporatism. The fascist states which gave corporatism its ugly name were of course strongly nationalistic. They were prepared, ideologically and cumulatively in practice too, to subordinate the economy to the pursuit of military might. An equivalent explanation for the milder versions of modern corporatism can be sought in the growth of international economic competition. Thus governments seek by various devices to promote exports, to develop advanced technologies (for military as well as economic uses), to step up industrial investment and productivity and to fashion, through mergers and economic aid, 'chosen instruments' in the form of large firms or monopolies which are expected (often wrongly) to compete more effectively in the international arena.

This version of corporatism is well caught by a notion such as 'Great Britain, Limited' (the title of a lecture by Lord Beeching at the London School of Economics). The nation is viewed as a large firm, which must be strongly integrated to compete effectively in the international arena. The USA, as much the largest economy and the main headquarters of international firms, has much less need of corporatism than smaller states – although the US Government too has stepped in to rescue large firms like Lockheed and Chrysler. As suggested earlier, the pressures of international competition explain the effective victory of monopolistic industrial policies over anti-monopoly measures in many countries.

It would be wrong to view international competitiveness as the only goal or explanation of national economic planning. On the contrary, full employment was the principal post-1945 goal of economic planning and was primarily pursued for social and political reasons. One aspect of this goal was the strong and complex regional policies developed after 1945 by many West European governments. These policies were concerned with bringing jobs to the workers and with improving the physical equipment and amenities of depressed regions, and they were often criticized for harming international competitiveness (although the criticism may also have been mistaken).

The international competitive motive became more important as world trade became larger, firms became bigger and more mobile, and eventually economies became depressed. Regional policies again provide a good barometer of these conditions. In the Western European countries, regional aid has been much modified and scaled down since the mid-1970s, and has been increasingly switched into capital restructuring and modernization, which aids competitiveness but reduces employment.

The corporatist state

A Lindblom type of explanation seems fairly satisfactory for public policies in the 1950s and 1960s. In this period governments could successfully meet political demands for full employment, regional development, social services, etc., without basically injuring the interests of capitalism, although there were many conflicts on particular issues. Governments also might independently promote public social investment, as the French planners did in the Fourth Plan. Simultaneously, governments got drawn into close co-operation with interest groups through rapid changes in the economy, featuring the collapse of old industries and the development of new ones requiring large investments and long lead-times. Defensive measures of government aid and industrial self-regulation (or else nationalization) were the easiest political way to aid social and economic transition in countries like Britain. In other countries like Japan and France, government resources and initiative provided an effective and probably essential lever for enabling capitalism to take advantage of new economic and technological opportunities.

Thus one need not take a deterministic view of capitalist domination to explain many features of modern corporatism. When Shonfield (1965, p. 128) described French planning in the 1950s as a 'conspiracy in the public interest between big business and big officialdom', he was not being ironic. It was a reasonable claim that government could steer and control the development of capitalism, so as to promote both economic growth and social policies. The weak representation of labour interests in French planning, compared with Scandinavia, benefited big business but did not prevent a widespread diffusion of prosperity through paternalist measures.

However, domestic social and economic goals seem increasingly to be in conflict with the conditions of international capitalism. As capitalism has become more international in scope, nation states have been decreasingly able to plan their own economies, or to shield them from the destabilizing impact of world trade. As a consequence, economic planning has been trimmed down and corporatism has changed its character.

A Marxist analysis views corporatism in this context as a defensive shield for capitalist interests, which may take a more moderate or extreme form. If labour interests can be co-opted, as in Scandinavia, corporatism will be more liberal and consequently more stable; otherwise the state will take on a more repressive character as an alliance between right-wing governments and dominant capitalist elements. Jessop (1979) argues that capitalism

123

is in fact best protected by a Labour government and a corporate bargaining system, since the alternative will involve greater industrial unrest and instability.

The extent of the dominance of international capitalism must remain an open question; however, accepting that it infuses strong constraints upon national policy makers, it is still possible, as Scandinavia shows, to move towards a more egalitarian society. Moreover, nationalism may in various ways confront capitalism. If there is enough national integration and consensus, government policies may be forged to limit the impact of capitalism upon the national economy and society – perhaps by transforming the structure of capitalism itself. In any event, there is an obvious conflict between the interests of international business and finance and the claims of domestic investment and job maintenance. The latter interests, which include of course some capitalist elements, may successfully initiate strong protectionist measures or the conflict of interests may possibly lead back to the fascist movements of the 1930s.

To summarize this section, corporatism appears to be a product of diverse pressures, and to shift its character in different countries and conditions. In some countries, corporate bargaining appears to be a fairly successful way of promoting and sharing economic growth to the advantage of labour interests while retaining a capitalist system and its international constraints. In other cases corporatism takes the form of a partnership between government and capitalist interests, either to promote growth or to cope with problems of economic change in the politically most acceptable way. Corporatism also can be identified with economic nationalism, but such nationalism is increasingly in conflict with the international interests of capitalism, which may possibly lead to a recurrence of 'pure' or state-imposed corporatism. Crouch (1979, p. 188) argues that 'a distinct pattern is developing in the modern world of domestic corporatism disciplined by international monetarism'. However, the further evolution of the relations between capitalism, nationalism, and corporatism must remain for later consideration.

CORPORATISM AND PLANNING

The previous chapter compared the pluralist policy process with various concepts of planning. Now it is necessary to discuss the relationship between corporatism and planning. This is not an easy task, because much will depend upon how these two terms are defined.

The corporatist state

A movement from pluralism towards corporatism will change the nature of the policy process. The process will become less flexible and open, and more routinized, established and closed, as a result of the incorporation of interest groups, and the bilateral monopoly relationships between government departments and interest groups. The concentration of organizational power, and the wish of large organizations to stabilize their environment, will also impede the entry of new or dissenting interests.

However, we are dealing in practice not with any absolute contrast between pluralism and corporatism but with partial changes. Pluralism never lived up to its ideals of flexible group formation and easy access to decision makers, while corporatism as defined by Schmitter is only partially operative in most Western societies. But still more significantly, corporatism adds substantially to the systematic organization of interests.

The ideal model of corporatism points towards the representation within the policy process of *all* significant economic, professional and social interests, but requires or prefers this to be done upon an integrated, non-competitive basis. Thus corporatism in principle both activates missing interests and rejects competitive ones. Although this model is far from being realized in most Western societies, the incorporation of interest groups does stimulate further interest formation, both as a defensive reaction by the groups concerned and as a convenience to public decision makers. In these ways pluralism develops towards corporatism, and complex universes of organizational families (both public and private) develop within each policy field.

In the very complex world of inter-organizational networks in Western societies (Hanf and Sharpf, 1978), there are elements of both corporatism and pluralism. Corporatism is found in the ever-present drives towards the systematic representation and co-ordination of interests, both public and private. Pluralism continues to exist in the shifting alliances between the members of an organizational family, and in the independent options open to bodies with a strong organizational or political base. Inter-governmental relations, not only in federations but in supposedly unitary states like France (Ashford, 1982), constitute an especially rich field of balancing political and administrative interests, linked by various alliances and co-ordinating mechanisms. A particular policy system, such as the promotion of industrial development, is inhabited by a great number of public and private agencies, co-ordinated through representative bodies who may compete with each other or be themselves co-ordinated by some central government department or by a 'peak' representative agency (Grant and McKay, 1983).

Such a system has not got the hierarchical unified character of a corporatist model. It is too varied and decentralized for that. Equally, it has not got the spontaneity of organization, mobility of alliances and separation of issues which are said to characterize pluralism. But policy systems continually shift and change, becoming more hierarchical and unified or producing some degree of policy decentralization or disengagement on the part of government.

How then does a corporatist policy process work? One concept of corporatism is linked with the theme of comprehensive planning, which was contrasted with pluralism in the previous chapter. Normatively speaking, planning can be seen as the mechanism for realising Winkler's values of unity, order, nationalism and success. Of course, a statement of these values does not tell us how they will be applied through a planning process. The system may be variously democratic or authoritarian in its pursuit of 'unity' and 'order', it may be beneficial or not to particular interests, it may be strongly nationalistic or strongly constrained by international dependencies (or the first in form and the latter in substance), and it may be more or less successful in its goal achievement. Nor does the concept of planning tell us how much leverage it will actually get over existing institutions and interests.

One can get some insight into these issues by considering the specific case of French economic planning. This is because, save for the weak representation of labour interests (which on one view disqualifies it), the evolution of French planning fitted in quite closely with a number of corporatist prescriptions. It developed a special and elaborate set of institutions for the purposes of planning; it involved close co-operation and co-ordination between government and economic interests; it tried to build up a national consensus around the goals and purposes of planning; it successively broadened its scope, technically and institutionally and also in terms of the attempted representation of interests.

French experience also poses the familiar dilemma of how to reconcile government planning with democratic institutions. French planning was technocratic in leadership and inspiration and largely insulated from the normal political process, but this fact reflects more the traditional power of French executive government than the specific methods of modern planning. Within the governmental system, French planning was co-ordinative and persuasive rather than hierarchical, and it is arguable whether planning augmented or reduced the authoritarian use of public powers. The account which follows draws particularly upon Shonfield (1965), Ullmo (1975), Watson (1975), Cohen (1977) and Leruez (1980).

The integration of interests

French planning is based upon a small centre, the Commissariat General du Plan (CGP), containing only about fifty planners, with a semi-independent status under the general authority of the Prime Minister (at one time, the Minister for Finance). This body, the brainchild of Jean Monnet, started off after 1945 with plans for the modernization of French infrastructure, primarily provided by public enterprises. The first plan was technical, and politically uncontroversial.

Gradually, the CGP built up a large network of related institutions and linkages. Key instruments were the modernization commissions, which comprised 'vertical' groups dealing with the main sectors of economic production, and 'horizontal' groups making general plans for economic development, finance, manpower, social services and regional policy. The number and range of these commissions expanded in line with the scope and logic of the planning process itself. They comprised appointed representatives of business organizations, trade unions, relevant ministries and a sprinkling of experts, but it seems agreed that initiatives to action came from the bureaucracy, guided or stimulated by the CGP.

A main role of the commissions was to persuade industries to invest and modernize, by creating a climate of confidence in economic growth and by using the state's considerable command of financial resources via CGP membership of various investment funds. The 'quasi-contracts' with firms used to implement these goals were negotiated privately and entailed not so much *new* public powers as a specific concertation of existing ones over taxes, prices and subsidies. The co-ordinating commissions sought to establish positive and consistent but realistic targets for the economy generally and for its various sectors, and to allocate public resources between competing purposes and priorities on a medium-term basis.

The aims of French planning widened in the Fourth Plan from economic modernization to a new stress upon social development. With this development came the creation of a new institution, the Economic and Social Planning Council, designed to enlist the participation of rural, regional and social welfare organizations, although its membership and debates in practice often overlapped with those of the modernization commissions (Hayward, 1966). The creation in the 1960s of regional planning machinery, linked with the appointment of advisory regional councils drawn from industry, local government, the universities, etc., represented a further broadening of the scope of planning, and a new stress upon institutional and economic decentralization.

How did this history affect the balance and integration of interests? Labour representation was always much weaker than that of business, and was further weakened (as was planning generally) when the left-wing unions walked out in 1976. Thus planning did not lead to the incorporation of labour interests. Business interests were definitely less influential than civil servants over the making of plans, but planning favoured the growth and ascendency of big business, and led to a strengthened peak organization of employers. Finally, planning did activate to some extent latent social and regional interests, but their articulation remained very weak when compared with that of business.

Shonfield's 'conspiracy in the public interest' between senior civil servants and the senior managers of big business was so because it hinged upon *ad hoc* bargains largely reached outside the formal planning machinery, involving a discretionary manipulation of government powers. It could be claimed to be in the 'public interest', even though politicians and labour interests were largely excluded, because the consequent concentration of public and private decisions stimulated economic growth, and this growth was then used subsequently to develop public and social services. The planning machinery was also increasingly formalized and expanded and new interests were rather weakly introduced, but any consequent improvement in the workers' standard of living clearly owed much more to the paternalist attitudes of planners and bureaucrats than to direct political pressures or participation by affected interests.

Political priorities
One of the possible functions of planning units, which has become increasingly significant in Western societies, is to strengthen the ability of political leaders to clarify and implement their goals and priorities. However, French planning did not work in this manner. Politically responsive planning staff must immerse themselves in the immediate policy goals and problems of their political chiefs, whereas the systematic and rationalising processes of the French planners were possible only through a real measure of political

detachment and independence. French planning still required the general support of political leadership, which was forthcoming so long as planning seemed to work well. President Giscard d'Estaing in the 1970s was the first political head to be openly sceptical about the value of planning, although eventually he sanctioned the preparation of the Seventh Plan along more modest lines.

The involvement of Parliament in the planning process was very tardy, only reaching *post hoc* review and endorsement with the Fifth Plan and an initial review of guidelines with the Sixth. Members were quite unable to unravel and revise such a complex document, and concentrated instead upon airing particular views and interests. Parliament was eventually involved, not just from a wish to widen the arena of participation, but from a hope that it might assist the achievement of a prices and incomes policy. There is a curious reversal here of the development in other countries of corporate bargaining structures for the very reason that parliaments could not achieve the necessary concordat. But in France corporate planning was confined essentially to incentives for employers.

This democratic weakness might suggest that planning has been essentially authoritarian. However, French planning actually represented a complex mixture of values. The deliberate conjunction and manipulation of public powers can be claimed, as it has been in cases before the *Conseil d'Etat*, to be discriminatory and arbitrary. The only answer (good or bad) to this argument would be that in modern societies rules of law need to be replaced in some fields by flexible methods of public intervention made in conjunction with affected interests.

Such interventions are the reasons for saying that French planning has been as much coercive as 'indicative' although it has been both. Within the governmental system, however, planning can be seen more as an addition to the pluralism of competing power centres than as an instrument for centralized control. The plan's preparation and implementation depended upon networks of support in other ministries and which were always partial and limited by competing bureaucratic centres. The CGP and its network acted as a competitor for policy influence with its principal rival, the Ministry of Finance, and pressed the claims of a longer-term philosophy of economic and social development against the short-run exigencies of budgetary and financial mangement. This was the same kind of conflict as occurred in Britain in the 1960s when the Department of Economic Affairs conspicuously failed to uphold a longer-term developmental philosophy against the counter-pressure of the Treasury. In France, the planners also increasingly found specific decisions going against their goals, but they did successfully insert a new policy perspective into the complex governmental system. Thus they did widen the range of policy options available in principle to political leadership.

When planning's prestige was highest, a leading politician like Mendes-France could argue that it was the political system which should be brought into line with the needs of planning, not vice versa, through linking elections to the plan's timetable and fighting them over party versions of alternative plans. This suggestion clashed with the hopes of Lausanne school of economists that the planning system could grow its own informed and stable political institutions, which might gradually replace the ignorant sectional pressures within Parliament. For example, Oulés (1966) wanted plans to be judged by informed public juries who had attended classes in economics (presumably of a certain brand). Both these views wanted planning to be the centre of the governmental system whether it were politically or technocratically steered. Both theories fell foul of the incompatibilities between planning and politics, as well as the inequalities of functional representation within the planning system. But one can still detect in French planning the continuing appeal in modern dress of Rousseau's idea of a technical legislator capable of executing a 'general will' which ought to be differentiated from the 'will of all'.

The planners' efforts to build up a consensus about goals and methods largely failed as the goals became more complex and more subject to both market constraints and political pressures. Planning became increasingly controversial. Its concrete achievements after its early years got questioned. It can still be said (Leruez, 1980, p. 70) that, whatever its detailed impact, planning provided an essential catalyst for the nation's postwar will to regenerate and develop the economy. Although working mainly through bureaucratic channels, French planning could still present itself not wholly unsuccessfully as the embodiment of a corporatist 'general will'.

Professional synthesis

The French planners' use of economic techniques became increasingly sophisticated and elaborate, but decreasingly relevant because of the growing unpredictability of market forces. In any case, the techniques were only one input into the process of establishing normative goals which was done on the basis of information pooling and of successive adjustments or 'iterations' of the plans' targets so as to achieve more realism and consistency. As target setting became harder, the planners turned to a mixture of general guidelines and specific priorities.

But the intellectual interest of French planning lies less in its techniques than in its style and methods of working. It showed the intrinsic tendency of rationalist planning towards a continuous expansion of scope and horizons, as the interconnection of issues gets revealed by analysis. Moreover, the staff of the CGP was not confined to economists, but included engineers, sociologists and others. (Many technical services were provided from within the Ministry of Finance.) Planning moved from its initial concern with economic growth into the fields of social policy and regional development, for which new divisions were created in the CGP. For a time a lively debate went on about the meanings and relationships of 'economic' and 'social' policy, which has never been resolved.

French planning also reveals parallel tendencies towards more comprehensiveness and more decentralization. The complexity of French society and government joined with the planners' need to rely upon persuasion and infiltration to suggest that the methods and agenda of planning needed to be widely diffused. The regional economic planning machinery created in the 1960s made only a modest contribution towards the decentralization of planning, and has been partly superseded by the attempts to create new regional political institutions. Planning reinforced the often argued case for decentralization in France, although the logic of the planners pointed (as might be expected) towards the engagement or co-option of affected interests, rather than the creation of independent political institutions at regional level.

French planning is generally agreed to have had the educative effect of widening and lengthening the perspectives of policy makers, and getting them to pool information and to share problem solving. Planners repeatedly tried to stimulate debate about the choices for society, but without much effect beyond a small circle. It would be wrong to view these efforts as little more than a frothy legitimation of the consolidated power of government and business, since they penetrated, on the whole benignly, into public policy formation on a range of issues, such as budgeting methods and regional development; but the processes would have worked better within a more balanced arena of interests.

To sum up, French planning experience has considerable relevance to one concept of corporatism. This concept emphasizes the integration of interests through a process of institutional experiment and rational resolution of economic and social conflicts in society. In practice, French planning was faulted by its unequal treatment of interests and by its failure to bridge the gap between bureaucratic and political processes; but it remains informative about the possibilities of a co-ordinative, persuasive style of planning, which might correct some of the defects of incrementalism that were discussed in the previous chapter.

Corporatism is also linked with a different style of policy making, which can be termed 'managerialism'. The basic policy criterion used here is technical and economic efficiency, as determined by market tests under conditions of international capitalist competition. The corporatist element occurs through a coalescence of interests and attitudes between the managers of government and business organizations. In other respects, this type of system is not necessarily associated with corporatist ideas, since it may oppose any general incorporation of interests and be hostile or indifferent to overall planning.

French planning can of course partly be understood in managerial terms, since it fostered close co-operation between high officials and big business. In that case, however, government led and planned the processes of economic development. Under freer market conditions, government will limit its intervention to selective assistance for making industry more competitive without trying to follow any overall plan. Conversely, government economic activities, where they are not 'privatized', will be modelled in a commercial image and business managers will very likely by brought in to manage public corporations and to advise on government efficiency generally. Mobility between the top positions in government and business will very likely grow, but a business philosophy will tend to dominate both sectors.

These developments of 'managerialism' can be seen in Britain, especially since the advent of the Thatcher government in 1979. Over the years productive public functions, such as electricity distribution, water supply, and public transport have got transferred from democratic local governments to centrally appointed public corporations. 'Gas and water' municipal Fabianism has been ended. Since 1979 some public enterprises have been privatized and the others have been more clearly restricted to commercial criteria. Local social services have been cut and subjected to closer central control. Conservative governments have lost their interest in general economic and regional planning in favour of a doctrine of efficient management and maximum public economy.

These developments can be explained in Marxist terms. Under

conditions of economic growth, the 'relative autonomy' of the state viewed as a 'condensation' of class struggle comes to the fore (Poulantzas, 1978). The greater power of the working class under full employment, and the existence of a larger economic surplus, allowed the development of social and welfare policies. The planning of the 1960s, so admired by Shonfield, could for a time reconcile the interests of capitalism with social demands. But as capitalism became both less controllable and less capable of generating growth, governments had to abandon attempts at national planning and to restrict social demands which got in the way of capitalist enterprise. According to some theories of the 'relative autonomy' of the state, government activities divide into collective consumption (health, education, etc.) and productive investment (public utilities, etc.) (Castells, 1977). The former activities represent an arena of continuing class conflicts, which may be compressed within an increasingly supervised sphere of local government, while the latter activities (and perhaps some of the former too) get transferred to politically insulated public bodies modelled on the private corporation.

These Marxist explanations at least seem right in suggesting that 'corporatism' and 'corporatist planning' will be considerably affected by changes in international trade and capitalism. These changes cannot be adequately captured by a contrast between 'planning' and 'managerialism', because a coalescence of organizational power is a feature of all meanings of corporatism. The critical questions are who controls and constrains this power and in whose interests it operates. Planning at the nation state level can only be effective if the government has a fair capacity to manage its own economy, and planning can only be democratic if there is a balanced representation of interests. Thus some form of corporatism may be a necessary but not sufficient condition for democratic and effective national planning, and some aspects of corporatism are consistent with a largely unplanned economy.

THE VALUES OF CORPORATISM

In theory, the values of pluralism and corporatism are strongly opposed. Pluralism believes in the free association of individuals and the competition of groups within a framework of neutral laws, and its ideal result would be a largely self-governing system of decentralized institutions. Corporatism believes in a harmonious integration of social interests based upon consensus, and its ideal

133

result would be a society moving co-operatively towards collectively determined goals.

Enough has been said in the previous two chapters to suggest how remote Western societies are from realizing either set of values. Clearly too, the differences between pluralism and corporatism are a great deal narrower than the rhetoric of competing values would suggest. Given the very limited realization and ambiguities of both pluralist and corporatist systems, and the tendencies of the one to evolve into the other, it becomes clear that this statement of 'values' is really about ideological directions, whose function is to urge society backwards or onwards from its present condition, or to resist or rationalize developments which are currently occurring. Moreover, any simple statement about values misses out the complexity and contradictions of the institutional framework within which they have to be realized.

All this admitted, it remains the case that the same question – forwards or backwards? – which was asked about pluralism in the previous chapter, must now be addressed to the subject of corporatism. For there is a real difference between those who view corporatism as offering (at least potentially) a cure for the sectionalism and selfishness of pluralism, and those who see it as a further step along the road to the destruction of liberal democracy.

The first viewpoint is well represented by Dahl (1982) and Shonfield (1982). Dahl is an eminent theorist of pluralism, who has in no way abated his belief in freedom of organization for political, religious and cultural groups. But he now believes that liberal democracy cannot work equitably or effectively unless the economic system is reformed. 'Corporate pluralism' has virtues in this respect. This is because the leaders and members of a large, inclusive interest group cannot hope to realize gains at the community's expense to the same extent as smaller, narrower groups, but must accept that their own welfare is more closely linked to the general welfare. It is true that conflicts between large inclusive groups, if they do occur, will be more disruptive than are old-fashioned group conflicts. An example might be the 1980 general strike in Sweden, and still more the period of acute industrial unrest in Sweden which preceded the dominance of the Social Democrats (Castles, 1978). But once a satisfactory and equitable balance of interests within the economic system has been established, 'corporate pluralism' is likely to yield more generally beneficent outcomes than is unrestricted group competition. Dahl's rescue of pluralism also involves radical changes in the ownership of industry and the distribution of wealth, on the argument that wide inequalities of wealth and power produce large differences in political influence – hence undermine the ideals and workings of liberal democracy.

Shonfield's last, regrettably uncompleted book argues that corporatism is 'a means of preserving pluralism in a democracy' (1982, p. 110), because corporatist economic planning is the best way to achieve economic growth with high levels of employment, and thereby generate a surplus for welfare ends. Much of his last book concerns the failure of economic policy makers to sustain the promising performance of economic planning in some countries (particularly France) in the 1960s. He recognizes that national economic planning has been made harder by its much increased dependence upon international markets, but he argues that this dependence is essential to economic growth and has to be tackled by more effective international institutions of economic management. The remedy would apparently be international corporatism achieved by joint action of governments and financial institutions. Domestically, the legitimacy of corporate institutions would be recognized but made more politically accountable. While Dahl looks to drastic economic reforms to make pluralist democracy work, Shonfield more conventionally seeks changes in political institutions to make them compatible with an economic system of 'welfare capitalism'. But both end up recommending the corporate planning systems of Scandinavian democracies.

Those who want to put the corporatist clock back contend that it is more destructive of liberal democracy even than a free wheeling pluralism. This critique takes two forms. In the first place, corporatism piles up much stronger aggregations of economic power than the activities of smaller, sectional groups, however influential these may be. In principle, the activities of smaller pressure groups are open to stronger control by political parties and leaders, and competition between pressure groups should keep policy options open for political leadership. If, as the defenders of corporatism argue, inclusive and disciplined interest groups will show more concern for general interests, it is still the case that they acquire greater independence of the normal political process.

A second critique is that corporatism carries still further the highly discretionary and collusive type of policy making stigmatized by Lowi as 'interest group liberalism'. Government moves further down the road of reaching specific, discretionary bargains or accommodations with economic interests. The rule of general laws, and with it the doctrine of parliamentary control, gets further weakened. The control of bureaucracy by political leaders and (still more) of the executive by parliament or the judiciary becomes still harder to maintain.

The only effective answer to both these critiques would seem to be the creation of new channels of both economic and political accountability. In principle, corporatism much improves the scope for such accountability, since it replaces *ad hoc* bargaining between government and individual firms or narrow interest groups with more systematic and comprehensive forms of planning and bargaining. What is needed are mechanisms for making these processes accountable within the economic arena, while also making the ground rules and basic procedures of the system subject to parliamentary review and approval even if substantive decisions must to some extent be decided outside parliament.

This analysis reverts us again to the relationship between the political and economic systems. Classical liberal democracy was linked with conditions of economic competition which tended to prevent large concentrations of power, and which by leaving the workings of the economic system to the assumed beneficence of the market, made possible the rule of general laws and the control of parliament over the executive. Hayek (1944) argued that once general laws were breached in favour of discretionary and delegated uses of public power, a tyrannical socialism would result. But the result, as events have shown, could equally well be the rise of monopoly capitalism acting in a discretionary 'partnership' with government. The concentration of economic power in large firms or 'conglomerates' has been matched much more unevenly by the growth of consolidated union power. These changes in the economic system, and in the accompanying supportive and co-ordinative role of government, have undermined the classic conditions of liberal political democracy.

Those who want to put both corporatist and pluralist clocks back, in favour of the rule of general law, have therefore to unscramble the modern economic system. Olson (1982) for one does not shirk this task. Although his special interest is with the impediments to economic growth said to be caused by strong union monopolies, Olson is ready to outlaw monopolistic behaviour by the representatives of both workers and employers. But is such a drastic *bouleversement* at all realistic in a world of advanced technology and international capitalism? The history of anti-trust legislation, even under the favourable ideological climate of the USA, suggests that it is not, and the problems to be overcome by such legislation are not getting any easier. It seems all too likely that the actual impact of this policy would be mainly felt by the weaker side in industry, namely the unions (Crouch, 1983). This may be an acceptable result for the public choice theorists of property rights, but it would hardly help the values of either social justice or liberal democracy, or provide an ethically appealing alternative to corporatism.

A Marxist perspective views corporatism as an inevitable stage in the development of capitalism, either in the more restrictive and repressive form of a government–capitalist alliance dominated by the latter, or in the more accommodating and liberal form of tripartite corporate bargaining linked with a strong labour party. While the former type of corporatism is expected to be unstable and temporary, the latter form is sometimes supposed capable of a long or indefinite life. In ethical terms, this tripartite or labour-led version of corporatism has considerable normative appeal, since it achieves a fairer distribution of power and welfare than did earlier capitalism, while also retaining the main features of liberal democracy such as elections and party competition. However, if it be true (as Marxists say) that this system is necessarily dependent upon the 'logic' of international capitalism, its ability to retain these desirable features for long must be very doubtful. Thus Marxists usually conclude that the only ultimate normative solution to the problems of corporatism will lie with a socialist revolution of some kind, although the nature of that socialism is matter for much dispute.

An ethically appealing system of corporatism would have to resolve basic problems of social justice and individual liberty. Social justice is bound to be a central and highly controversial issue for any political system which tries to substitute collective allocations of costs and benefits in place of allocations through the market, individual competition or divine providence. Indeed the rise of corporatism is mirrored in the rise of economic and social movements seeking justice for particular groups. There can never be close agreement upon the principles of social justice, much less upon specific allocations over which partisan claims are quickly aroused, but at least a system is more likely to be viewed as fair if it gives effective and balanced representation to affected groups, and if it avoids large economic or political inequalities.

Secondly, there is the threat to individual liberties posed by corporatism. The coercive power of economic organizations over their members may be partly justified by the argument (if it is true) that this is a necessary price for reducing the coercive impact of market forces upon personal security and dignity. Yet liberty requires that any coercive organization be regulated in respect of its powers and procedures and be made in some form accountable to its members. The same requirements apply to the discretionary powers of bureaucracy. Thus a corporatist system normatively entails new systems of constitutional and administrative regulation.

Therefore, political systems evolving towards corporatism seem likely to require some quite basic changes in their economic systems and in their basic political rules, if they are to become normatively acceptable and democratic. Otherwise, corporatism quickly runs into its basic dilemma of 'coercion in the name of harmony' (Panitch, 1976, p. 247). What exactly these changes might be must be considered later.

6

THE BEHAVIOUR OF BUREAUCRACY

MODERN BUREAUCRACY

Previous chapters have all pointed to a growth in the size, influence and discretionary powers of bureaucracy. These developments can be seen as a necessary product of economic and social change (Ch. 2); as the outcome of the material ambitions of bureaucrats themselves (Ch. 3); as the result of alliances between interest groups and bureaucrats (Ch. 4); or as the outcome of international economic competition and the requirements of capitalism (Ch. 5). These explanations are not mutually consistent and do not have the same implications for bureaucratic behaviour, but they build upon the same perception of a bigger and stronger bureaucratic system carrying out an increased range of functions.

Modern theories of bureaucracy still stand in the giant shadow of Max Weber. Weber's famous theory viewed bureaucracy as being in a certain sense both 'rational' and 'efficient', but modern theories are largely concerned with demonstrating the inefficiencies or 'dysfunctions' which bureaucracy produces. This change of theoretical emphasis has a lot to do with changes in the role of government and unless the consequences of these changes for bureaucracy are appreciated, its operations can easily be judged by unrealistic standards.

Weber's theory was founded upon the ends–means distinction between politics and administration. Weber viewed bureaucracy as a highly efficient instrument for applying public policies with precision and consistency. Its 'rationality' consisted in the application of precise techniques of legal standards and financial accounting to the work of government, which was to be achieved organizationally through a hierarchy of offices and the detachment of bureaucrats from any personal interest in the results of their decisions (Gerth and Mills, 1948, pp. 196–244).

While Weber's 'ideal-typical' picture of bureaucracy was complex and had features which need not in practice go together, his general description did accord with the emerging characteristics of the modernization of government which was taking place in his time. Moreover, many of these features – the specialization of functions, the hierarchy of offices and public service as a guaranteed career based upon the 'merit principle' – have continued to mark the operation of bureaucracies.

However, Weber also argued that bureaucracy is essentially a directionless force which 'is easily made to work for anybody who knows how to gain control over it', through the device of changing the top officials (Gerth and Mills, 1948, p. 220). It is true that he doubted the capacity of political leaders for directing the bureaucratic experts, and became extremely pessimistic about the roles and responsibilities of democratic political leadership. His statement about the 'overtowering power' of the experts was partly an argument about the inevitable dominance of executive government over an elected legislature under modern conditions. Thus Weber voiced anxieties about the control of bureaucracy which strike a very modern note, but he did not envisage the growth of administrative pluralism. Bureaucracy was left by his theory as a juggernaut which, because it was technically competent but politically neutral, would necessarily be controlled from the top downwards.

Weber's theories raised the key issue of how bureaucratic 'efficiency' can be combined and reconciled with democratic 'accountability'. This issue was side-stepped in the influential doctrines of Woodrow Wilson and the 'scientific' school of administration, which followed the assumption that bureaucracy could be made to work for any political leadership and concentrated upon improving the organizational and instrumental efficiency of bureaucracy. The 'human relations' school of adminstration cast doubts upon the realism and efficacy of hierarchical systems, but did not question the role of political control. Thus bureaucracies have continued to be judged by the now unrealistic standard of an effective hierarchy.

The Weberian concept of bureaucracy has become outdated in two important respects. First, the bureaucratic exercise of discretionary powers has grown enormously. Weber thought of specialization primarily in terms of the precise use of legal and accounting skills and hardly reckoned (although his brother pointed the problem out) with the large influx of scientists, engineers, town planners, economists, etc., into government who exercise flexible forms of discretion. Still more significantly, bureaucracy has become increasingly involved with discretionary forms of intervention, arbitration and financial support, often carried out in close conjunction with interested parties.

Secondly, the political environment of modern bureaucracy has

The behaviour of bureaucracy

been transformed by the weakened capacity of political leadership to direct or control bureaucracy from the top down, and by the complex and variable political pressures which surround the work of bureaucratic agencies. The Weberian model does not allow for these developments or for the equally significant conflicts and alliances between bureaucratic groups and agencies. At the same time, the growth of more individualist or anti-authoritarian attitudes among officials themselves weakens the discipline of hierarchical systems.

If the Weberian concept of bureaucracy is in some (but not all) respects no longer applicable, how are we to understand and to judge the behaviour of modern bureaucracies? First, it is desirable to assess more carefully the nature and limits of the power of modern bureaucracies, drawing for this purpose on previous chapters. Then we can turn to an examination of the tests or criteria of efficient performance which are now relevant to bureaucrats. These two sections should reveal the nature of the tensions which exist between politicians and bureaucrats, and between the associated concepts of political control and administrative efficiency. The last section turns to ways of reforming the structure and changing the values of modern bureaucracies.

THE NATURE OF BUREAUCRATIC POWER

The control of bureaucracy by political leaders has inevitably receded and been modified because of the growth in the size and discretionary powers of bureaucracies. Political leadership, which works largely through 'conciliar' structures (such as legislatures and cabinets) cannot expand so easily as the 'pyramidal' structure of bureaucracies. Politicians are often reluctant to share their power and large cabinets and committees are inefficient. Conversely, bureaucracy can easily produce more and longer pyramids if the resources can be found.

To meet this problem, political leaders have expanded their personal staffs and advisers. The limitation of this process is the ability of one political chief to control and use a personal staff effectively, a fact that became very evident in the USA with the arrogations of Presidential power by members of the White House staff (Seidman, 1980).

Political leaders and the senior bureaucracy interact in a complex, symbiotic relationship in respect of both the formation and implementation of policies. Bureaucratic advice and support are indispensable to the leadership, and bureaucrats have many assets – their permanence, their freedom from electoral worries, their knowledge of the files, their control of communications – which they can use to get their way in encounters with politicians (Peters, 1978, Ch. 7). But it does not follow that they will want to frustrate Ministerial wishes. Their own career interests and professional ethos will often be better served by compliance, not opposition. However, these assets do give bureaucrats a considerable ability to block changes which they perceive as threatening to their status or convenience.

The greater reliance of politicians upon bureaucrats produces variable results. Where the bureaucrats are recruited and trained, as in Britain, to show political sensitivity, their influence will be essentially an interpretative one. Their skill lies in a subtle use of discretion which does not cross the rather uncertain parameters of Ministerial wishes. Their interpretative influence over relaying and condensing information, preparing policy options, and applying policies is considerable, and is guided by subtle social and cultural values as well as by considerations of administrative convenience and advantage; but this influence is also constrained by strong traditions of political detachment and neutrality which make the system (as its critics say) a rather 'bloodless' form of administration. The pathology of such a system is either *stasis* – the inability to get effective action because of political overload and indecision – or else a strong susceptibility to changing political fashions (Self, 1977, Ch. 5).

In France bureaucratic policy innovation has been much greater as a consequence of the instability of political leadership and of the stronger tradition of state authority. Bureaucratic power is concentrated in the two wings of the administrative *grands corps* and the *polytechniciens* (especially the engineers). The fact that their education is broad, highly elitist and specifically directed towards government service (unlike administrative education in English-speaking countries), equips these cadres for the exercise of power. The pathology of this system is 'technocracy', in the sense of an excessive or irrational use of expert authority (Meynaud, 1968).

In the USA, on the other hand, Presidential appointment of a large band of 'political executives' theoretically ensures political leadership and keeps the permanent bureaucracy in a subordinate position. In practice the ramshackle and hasty recruitment of the political executives, their short term of office and their lack of party discipline and programme make the power of the permanent bureaucracy greater than might appear. The bureaucrats, distanced from the political leadership, exercise a narrow but fairly independent type of managerial authority (Heclo, 1977).

These three contrasting systems of political–bureaucratic relationships alert us to the difficulties of generalizing about bureaucratic power. Power does not necessarily pass from politicians to bureaucrats. It may be spread among other political groups or be diffused widely throughout the system or become neutralized through a pattern of mutual frustration. *One* result of 'political overload' is certainly an increased absorption of bureaucratic resources into servicing the leadership. The existence of many competing programmes and priorities has increased the burden of administrative co-ordination, and there is always a long queue of disputed issues awaiting political resolution, which is only kept manageable by the tacit understanding of bureaucrats that they must compromise rather than load the system further. Politicians' ambitions prompt them to pursue specific goals but they often have to buy bureaucratic support by relinquishing other goals and limiting their ambitions, as the Crossman Diaries (1975) eloquently testified.

Ferrel Heady (1966) views power as the most significant bureaucratic variable in his study of many states. Western democracies do not produce 'bureaucratic polities' of either a Communist or Third World variety. Instead bureaucratic power varies with both the effectiveness of political control and the integration of the political system. These two tests are hard to apply; for example, even France, which is traditionally held up as a centralized system, is also decentralized in a complex way. However, Table 6.1 illustrates some possibilities about the nature of bureaucratic power, although the position of the three countries shown is more speculative.

Undoubtedly, the strongest use of bureaucratic power is the defence of its own status and privileges. This use has been entrenched by the growth of bureaucratic self-regulation and the difficulties of political intervention in this process (Chapman, 1959). Moreover, within the bureaucracy, there is a complex balance of power which cannot be easily changed. Suleiman (1974, p. 388) argues, rather too extremely, that the principal new power of administrators is 'their ability to resist reforms aimed at altering the distribution of power between various sectors of the administration'.

Two different accounts about the role of bureaucracy can be derived from earlier chapters. The pluralist account describes the division of bureaucracy into many groups and organizations which

Table 6.1   *The nature of bureaucratic power*

		Political Control	
		Strong	*Weak*
	Integrated	Defensive bureaucracy	Assertive bureaucracy
Political System			France
		UK	
	Fragmented	Political pluralism	Bureaucratic pluralism
		USA	

variously compete or co-operate. The power of these bureaucratic centres varies considerably with the pressure of client groups, the involvement of political leadership and the internal resources available. Thus, bureaucracy is not a homogeneous or cohesive force, except perhaps in defence of its career privileges. One possible conclusion from this pluralist picture is that only political parties can produce coherent policies, so that in this sense bureaucracy is not a threat to political leadership (Bottomore, 1964). However, it could be counter-argued that policy making is substantially decentralized to sub-centres where bureaucrats may exercise considerable influence. Moreover politicians are infected by the pluralism of the system. Under the pressure of competing departmental interests, a cohesive party strategy soon wears thin.

A corporatist account stresses by contrast the accumulation of power in key political and bureaucratic centres. Bureaucracy is hypothesized to act in a more uniform and integrated manner than under the pluralist analysis. However, this bureaucratic role can be conceived either dependently or assertively. The neo-Marxist view conceives bureaucracy as playing a supportive and controlling role on behalf of capitalist interests, but having little real discretion or initiative. The neo-Weberian view sees bureaucracy as playing a central role over the allocation of services and benefits in virtue of its institutional strength and its accumulated power of professional discretion.

The pluralist account, as Chapter 4 showed, has the advantage of plentiful empirical analysis and support. Up to a point too, pluralist analysis (although not pluralist ethics) is consistent with the existence of differentially strong interest groups and power centres. Beyond this point, a corporatist theory of bureaucracy must depend upon the argument that the uniformities of bureaucratic behaviour which a 'systems' view suggests are more significant than the pluralist variations to be perceived at a micro-level. In this context we can consider some more general arguments about the professional and managerial power of modern bureaucracies.

As Daniel Bell (1978) pointed out, the uses of theoretical knowledge have come to occupy a central place in modern societies. Scientists and technologists have transformed the world, and their contributions towards public programmes such as research and development, environmental and health regulations or military defence have become completely indispensable. Indeed the place of scientific knowledge is much greater in government than in business, because governments shoulder most of the risks of developing advanced technologies in both the military and civil spheres and of co-ordinating or providing much of the infrastructure for economic development.

However, the knowledge of scientists or engineers is rarely determinative of broader policy problems. For example, only very sophisticated technologists could say whether or not the Concorde supersonic aircraft would fly, but they could not say whether the results would be economically, environmentally or politically acceptable. Their actual influence is also small if it opposes political power. The fact that Oppenheimer in the USA and Sakharov in Russia made indispensable contributions to the manufacture of the hydrogen bomb did not enable them to have much influence over the uses of this invention, although one risked his career and the other was persecuted and exiled for attempting to wield political influence.

To rise to a position of policy influence, an expert must learn administrative and political skills, probably to the detriment of his own expert knowledge – although there are exceptional individuals who may advance on both fronts. The 'authority of knowledge' gets subordinated to that of hierarchy (Thompson, 1963) save in flexible units devoted to research and planning. The prestigious corps of French engineers owe their power to their organizational strength and broad based training, not to their engineering skills as such, which would hardly justify many of their decisions. As Bell (1978, p. 79) also says, despite the centrality of knowledge, 'the technocrat in power is simply one kind of politician, not a *technicien*, no matter how much he employs his technical knowledge'. He is so because he is dealing with conflicts of interests and values.

Governments employ increasing numbers of policy experts such as economists, town planners, lawyers and management consultants, but their advice is more malleable than that of scientists and will vary with the political or organizational needs of their client. Important professional groups enjoy a high status and prestige, but their diversity and mutual competition precludes them from exercising any consistent policy influence.

Despite these limitations, professional skills and communities offer an important political device for solving policy problems. Given the prestige of expert knowledge, a measure of professional consensus is one way of securing political consensus or of containing conflicts within technical limitations. This 'ideological corporatism' can also be seen as a way of balancing public and private interests through the advice of experts who work in both sectors (Dunleavy, 1981b). It is most prevalent when ideological conflict is low, as in the 1960s period of economic growth when the future was seen as basically 'more of the same' and hence as a proper subject for technical solutions. Subsequently, the 'politics of expertise' (Benveniste, 1973) has receded and remains most influential in the intermediate stages of the policy process. For example, the question of *how much* money to spend upon roads is essentially political but the allocation of this sum among possible projects is often done by sophisticated cost-benefit techniques, the issue becoming political again at the point of local allocations and objections. Technical solutions flourish inside bureaucracy and out of the political limelight but provide only partisan ammunition when political and organizational conflicts are strong.

The issue of bureaucratic power should also be considered within a broader social context. The 'bureaucratisation of the world', to use Jacoby's (1973) phrase, has piled up great concentrations of resources and power. The familiar thesis that the managers of capitalist enterprises have taken over control from their shareholders (Burnham, 1943) is paralleled by the claim that senior bureaucrats have acted likewise in respect of their nominal owners, the politicians. The parallel is not close since political control is a massively more elaborate affair than is shareholders' control and is exercised for a much broader range of purposes. As we have seen, however, the much stronger resources of political control are offset by the difficulty of pursuing a much more diverse and conflicting set of objectives.

In the case of both public and private sectors, the goals get changed as a consequence. The 'managers' are able to assert *their* interests in the security of their careers and the stability of their organizations, at the expense of either shareholders or politicians. Any thesis of a 'power elite' cannot realistically refer to a planned concertation of action by so diffuse a class of individuals as managers. More probable is the existence of shared interests and attitudes among 'managers' as a result of their common problems of controlling large organizations under modern conditions and of defending their own privileges. These shared attitudes will represent a conservative force against political and social change, and in particular will bolster the concertations of organizational power produced by corporatism.

In European countries, bureaucratic recruitment remains quite strongly elitist. The British administrative class is drawn mainly from Oxford and Cambridge graduates, and the French *grands corps* come mainly from the *Institut d'Etudes Politiques* in Paris. The structure and manning of public services reflects the hierarchical outputs of educational systems more closely than is the case with business. Elites are strongly socialized by processes of peer group identification which may start in the hothouse of private schools and persist emotionally throughout life (Guttsman, 1969).

European administrative elites were traditionally educated in 'gentlemanly' or aristocratic places and subjects, the emphasis being placed upon quality of mind rather than specificity of knowledge. The German legal tradition of administration was rooted in university fraternities and training in an abstruse and lengthy curriculum. The post-1945 stress upon social science training for French administrators, and the growth of economics as an acceptable administrative qualification have somewhat changed the qualifications of administrators, although not their elitist backgrounds (Armstrong, 1973). Armstrong suggests that the older adminstrative elites have a 'regressive patrimonial tradition' of neutrality or hostility toward economic development. This tradition is valued for impartial administration of laws and policies, but puts the bureaucrats in a dependent or defensive position in negotiations with business – except perhaps to the extent that business leaders share the same tradition. Elites trained in engineering and economics like the French *polytechniciens* will be more development-minded and more capable of intervention in the private sector.

147

This review still leaves a considerable validity to the pluralist analysis of bureaucracy. While bureaucratic groups vary a lot in their status and influence, they hardly constitute a homogeneous *bloc* or force over policy issues. Elitist recruitment patterns do not seem to negate the influence of competing organizational interests upon bureaucratic behaviour. We can surmise, however, that there has been some convergence of managerial attitudes among senior officials in both the public and private sectors. This development can be partly traced to general changes in social structure and organizational structure which have shifted power from 'owners' to paid managers. More specifically, however, this convergence of attitudes is related to the corporatist integration of public power and economic interests. In this context the role of bureaucracy might be seen as simply responding to capitalist pressures, but it seems more plausible that this role will vary with other factors such as historical development of government's role and the character and training of the senior bureaucracy.

THE POLITICS OF BUREAUCRATIC EFFICIENCY

Bureaucratic efficiency is a complex and slippery concept. Basically, efficiency is an instrumental value; it is dependent upon the goals or values to be realized. Hence in government it is often linked with the notion of 'effectiveness', meaning as a rule the accomplishment of policy goals, at minimum cost and with the least organizational delay, waste or obstruction.

This Weberian concept of efficiency was the father of 'scientific administration' theories. Although these theories may have been intellectually discredited, they still provide the basis for most pragmatic or managerial proposals for administrative reform. Essentially these are prescriptions for keeping viable the concepts of hierarchy and specialization under increasingly complex conditions. For this purpose, they still stress the need for clarification of policy goals, monitoring of their implementation, rational division of functions, strengthening the powers of line managers, etc.

Following this approach, it is still generally assumed that bureaucratic effectiveness consists in the realization of goals set by the political leaders. This theory is still very much alive and kicking among politicians and parliamentarians themselves. Any number of official reports have adopted the sort of definition chosen by the Australian Joint Committee of Public Accounts:

The behaviour of bureaucracy

Senior public service managers should see their mandate as attempting to achieve the policy objectives and priorities established by the political process, developing programs to implement these policies and seeking adequate resources to implement them *effectively* with due regard to *economy* and *efficiency*. [Australia, 1982, para. 1.28, my italics.]

The difficulty with this statement, as has already emerged, is that objectives and priorities set by the political process are often vague, fluctuating and conflicting, and their interpretation depends strongly upon the interface between politicians and bureaucrats and upon the operations of bureaucracy itself. Committees of parliamentarians are surely well aware of these facts, but they are often passed over because of the awkward implications for bureaucratic efficiency. It is in the interest of politicians to suppose that they solve the political problems, and of bureaucrats to suppose that they occupy a neutral world of administrative efficiency where their insulated prescriptions can hold uninterrupted sway. This conspiracy of interests and myths still blocks recognition of the political problems of bureaucratic effectiveness.

Some writers distinguish problems of 'pure administration' from those of administrative politics (Hood, 1976). Supposing a policy goal is clear and officials are keen to implement it, many problems must be solved. An effective administrative programme must be designed and adequate resources of money, skills and relevant legal powers must be assembled. Orders and information must be accurately transmitted down and up the organization and sideways with other departments, and the large scale of modern government makes this process increasingly slow and error-prone. However, these familiar organizational problems merge in practice with those of administrative politics.

Recent administrative literature has tended to list and emphasize the many 'obstacles' to effective policy implementation, thereby overlooking the extent to which this is actually a political problem. For example, an agency of the US Federal Government performed the fantastic task of putting a man on the moon within a short time period. Another agency of that Government absolutely failed to achieve a modest demonstration project of providing work for black unemployed in the city of Oakland (Pressman and Wildavsky, 1973). The successful case was helped by plentiful funding but the failure was not really due to shortage of money. The difference was that in the first case the goal was clear, had strong political backing and was fully within the jurisdiction of the agency in question; whereas in the second case, the goal in question depended upon the co-operation of many agencies and levels of government as well as private employers. The conclusion to be drawn from the second case is not (as the authors seem to think) that policy implementation is almost impossibly difficult, as how mistaken it was for a Federal agency to take on a task which is well beyond its jurisdictional and political capacity.

Any simple hierarchical model of policy implementation is plainly out of date, since the political leaders themselves often accept and even intend that their goals be modified or amended. The extensive political sponsorship of semi-independent public boards is a deliberate form of policy delegation (Ch. 4). Policy is very likely modified when it crosses departmental boundaries, as happens all the time within government. Relations between different levels of government involve co-operative policy making, and even when local government is treated primarily as an agent of the centre it is usually conceded some policy discretion. The success of a high proportion of departmental policies depends upon influencing rather than ordering the behaviour of other public bodies or private firms. Policies made at the top levels of government often look quite different when they are eventually 'implemented'.

These requirements for policy co-operation and adjustment are not inevitable (in terms of 'pure administration') but reflect conditions of political and administrative pluralism. They imply the legitimacy of policy delegation to individuals chosen for their representative qualities or their expert knowledge or their diplomatic skills, and they imply too the reasonableness of organizations adjusting higher-level policies in accordance with their own circumstances and interests. In practice the meaning of 'goal effectiveness' for each bureaucrat will therefore vary considerably with his status.

A converse concept of efficiency concentrates not upon the goals of the leadership but upon the net benefits of public services to their clients (Ostrom, 1973). This concept gets closer to the economic theory of allocative efficiency, which will be maximized when the marginal cost of each function of government equals its marginal benefit to the consumer. This is an abstract ideal since the benefits of a government function are frequently uncertain, and since equalizing the marginal benefits of such diverse public products as defence, education and health control is hardly practicable. This view of efficiency follows the public choice approach and has implications for bureaucratic reform (see later).

However, the problems of economic measurement are not fatal to Ostrom's efficiency criterion if the interests of government clients can be accurately identified. Often this will mean balancing the costs to some group who are being regulated against the benefits to the public at large. Sometimes the interests of the regulated group will seem completely inimical to the service providers. A medical officer or a police chief can hardly be expected to take his criterion of efficiency from the wishes of the bearers of infectious diseases or from the criminal community, although it may certainly be right in a democracy that the interests of any controlled group should also be considered. Many social services such as education, health and welfare are awkwardly poised between the implementation of professional judgements and attention to client wishes. This is a problem which occurs also with private professional services, but the monopoly character of public services creates stronger tendencies towards professional domination. Thus the concept of benefit to clients involves some complex policy judgements.

One pathology of public service delivery is professional and administrative domination of dependent client groups. This can combine with the strong influence of other clients of government to bring about a severe neglect or perversion of client needs. One can have the situation that a policy goal *is* effectively implemented, but that its effects are highly perverse in terms of the interests of its recipients. Whether these effects should then be viewed as the *intended* domination of a dependent group or as the *unintended* and unwanted outcome of a mistaken policy, becomes a question for political analysis and judgement.

A clear example is the massive construction of high-rise public housing which occurred in many Western countries during the 1950s and 1960s. The policy goal *was* effectively implemented; the housing was constructed upon a massive scale and allocated to families on the long waiting lists of public housing authorities (which were usually local governments). The clientele was strongly dependent, consisting of people who looked to government to solve their pressing housing problems. These people provided the democratic support for large public programmes in countries like Britain, Sweden and France; and where they did not do so, as in the USA, they were often faced with the worse alternative of being shifted into slums by public redevelopment projects of a commercial character. However, this general political support for public housing was not followed by much client involvement over its type and quality. Within a brief time, the high-rise blocks which had been expensively constructed were vandalized, demolished or reallocated cheaply to single persons and students, while even in continental countries like Sweden and France the *grands ensembles* became very unpopular (Self, 1982, Ch. 2). Drawing on Dunleavy's (1981a) study, we can suggest three reasons for this massive example of 'policy perversion' in Britain:

(1) *Strong interest groups* wanted this policy for their own benefit – in particular, developers who could utilize new techniques of mass construction, and the Farmers' Union who argued that good agricultural land should be protected from public development – although they minded much less about private development, partly because financial compensation was lower in the case of public acquisition.
(2) *Organizational irrationality* in the form of the wish of urban local governments to keep population within their administrative areas for financial and prestige reasons.
(3) *'Technocracy'* in the form of the wish of many architects and sometimes politicians to experiment with new housing styles and to construct massive monuments which they hardly ever lived in themselves.

The outcome of this particular policy turned upon the inability of its supposed 'beneficiaries' to prevent the manipulation of their needs by economic, organizational and professional interests. This case shows the narrowness of 'goal effectiveness' as a test of bureaucratic performance, but it does not prove that decentralization of power to the level of service delivery will necessarily improve results for clients, although it will spread the risks (some local governments and professionals in England resisted the dominant housing fashion). What this case does show is that tests of effectiveness cannot be just technical or instrumental, but turn upon some balance of interests and values. The interests and values neglected in this case were those of a captive clientele.

The 'access' literature pioneered by Bernard Schaffer (1975) maps the encounters of clients with the often elaborate rules of bureaucratic systems. These rules have to be surmounted by the client if he is to get service, and queuing is used as an administrative response to scarcity of resources. The rules may be biased by intervention of political groups, they may be perverted for bureaucratic convenience, or their complexity may produce the 'irony of equity' whereby the correction of one inequity produces another.

Much of this literature is concerned with developing countries, where bureaucratic intimidation and delay and the political manipulation of rules are often gross (Schaffer and Lamb, 1981). In Western countries the system usually works better, but poor and disadvantaged individuals are the principal sufferers from the complexities of bureaucratic encounters. The influence and knowledge of wealthier groups, linked often with the cultural attitudes of bureaucrats themselves, ensures them better and prompter attention. Moreover the rules themselves may have been much influenced by interest groups, although this is not the fault of the service deliverers.

The rule book is a bureaucratic defence weapon which can produce the dysfunction of 'ritualism'. But ritualism can also be the result of poor opportunities to exercise initiative or to move elsewhere, as with the relapse into ritualism of the managers of the tobacco monopoly studied by Crozier (1964). Equally, the bureaucrat may have a 'trained incapacity' to adjust to new tasks requiring a more flexible approach than the rule book. But at the opposite extreme comes the danger of 'technocracy', meaning the excessive exercise of professional discretion. Thus bureaucratic behaviour can apparently oscillate, depending upon various factors, between a ritualistic and defensive use of the rules and an unjustified use of administrative discretion.

Bureaucratic effectiveness can be judged within a narrow or a broad context. In the former case, the stress is laid upon what may be called mechanical efficiency – the treatment of administration as a transmission belt for realizing specified goals. The techniques for this purpose have often been stated: the conversion of policies into operational programmes, the setting of quantitative targets, the monitoring of results. Such techniques have their place but can easily turn into a form of administrative ritualism. The setting of targets is intrinsically arbitrary: they may be set high to encourage effort or low to demonstrate successful achievement. The monitoring of progress can turn into no more than a record of administrative routines – orders issued, returns received, etc. Ritualism and an obsession with the instruments of control are particularly likely in central government because the actual outcome of a policy depends so often upon actions taken by other people in other places. The 'impact' of a policy flows back slowly and uncertainly in such cases.

A broader view of effectiveness concentrates upon the social outcome or impact of a public policy. This criterion entails difficult and arguable judgements. In some cases – crime prevention, for example – the effects of public policy can hardly be isolated from those of changes in social behaviour. In cases where direct services are provided, as in the housing example, social surveys can be informative about client satisfaction. One of the aims of budgetary reform is to evaluate the outcome of programmes more systematically as a basis for spending decisions. The quantification of benefits is elusive and controversial, but can be helpful in conjunction with broader forms of policy analysis. A device such as the 'planning balance sheet' attempts to show the distribution between groups of the costs and benefits of a public decision, as an aid to equity. It is not the purpose here to analyse these techniques, but rather to suggest that policy outcomes constitute an essential, even if indirect and difficult, test of bureaucratic effectiveness.

Thus the concept of administrative efficiency becomes a battleground of contending values and interests. The value of 'economic rationality' is pitted against those of other professional standards or ideologies. The value of 'accountability' to political leaders or to parliaments is pitted against that of 'responsiveness' to the pressures or the needs of client groups. The value of active or positive intervention in the economy is pitted against that of a non-interventionist philosophy or the neutral administration of general laws. All these issues are linked to the interests and ambitions of bureaucratic groups or individual officials.

BUREAUCRATIC REFORM AND VALUES

Bureaucracy has always been the subject of fierce criticism. Sociologists have laboured hard but not successfully to purge the word of its pejorative meaning. As bureaucracy has got bigger and more complex, new 'dysfunctions' have been discovered and analysed. The fiercest critics and reformers are the adherents of a 'market philosophy' which seeks the privatization of many public services and the replication within bureaucracy itself of market-type incentives and tests of efficiency. The limitations of this approach were discussed in Chapter 3.

Modern bureaucracy also has its more moderate defenders (Goodsell, 1983). These argue quite rightly that bureaucratic values embrace more than a mere subservience to the hierarchical principle of central control. Modern bureaucracy grew up as an effective system for applying laws uniformly and precisely and for delivering standardized services to all eligible individuals. It also

154

incorporates the goal of official detachment from personal interest or favouritism. These values remain fundamental and their application does entail centralized and hierarchical controls. A framework of bureaucratic rules is important not only for setting limits to administrative discretion but for allowing that discretion to be used with confidence and security (Perrow, 1979).

However, bureaucracy has become locked in a conflict of values. Its traditional strength was its impartial administration of general laws. This role called for a certain distancing from political control and intervention, which could be said to be in the interests of democracy: politicians should lay down the laws but should not influence their individual application (Etzioni-Halevy, 1983). However, the increased politicization of the administrative process has made this division of responsibilities very vulnerable, while bureaucrats themselves have acquired a more political role through grants of administrative discretion. Hence the idea of bureaucratic impartiality becomes suspect and bureaucrats themselves tend to adopt a purely pragmatic philosophy of response to political pressures.

One possible answer to this problem is Lowi's (1979) concept of 'juridical democracy' − a return to general laws and a dismantling of discretionary powers. This prescription would return bureaucracy to simpler and more standardized and hence more accountable forms of organization. Up to a point it has considerable appeal, particularly as a recipe for reducing the more irresponsible bastions of detached administrative power. At the same time, it does not reckon adequately with the complexities of service delivery in modern societies, or with the need for officials to exercise greater managerial or professional initiative to match the functions of modern government.

Theories of bureaucratic reform must necessarily seek to shift the relationships between political control and administrative efficiency, and to view each of these concepts in a different light. One can identify two related approaches to administrative reform. The first approach seeks to establish more decentralized forms of political control and accountability, which take account of the size and complexity of bureaucracy and which are more closely and equitably related to the needs of clients and the problems of service delivery. The second approach is concerned with the recasting of administrative values, ethics and accountability so as to improve the performance and morale of the public service. Both these large subjects will now be briefly reviewed.

Political theories of modern government

Political devolution and bureaucracy

The most extreme advocate of political devolution as a cure for bureaucratic problems is Vincent Ostrom (1973). In his view, American public administration has been misled and driven into an 'intellectual crisis' by its espousal of the Weberian and Wilsonian concepts of bureaucratic efficiency. The consequence has been the growth of a massive Federal bureaucracy, supposedly (but actually ineffectively) organized along hierarchical lines, which has become insulated from the direct demands of clients or consumers.

On this view, an efficient bureaucracy is one that is immediately accountable to the relevant community of interest for whom it is acting (Ostrom, 1973, p. 65). The nearest examples in the USA might be the locally elected school boards, although they have lost some of their independence. The problems of applying this concept widely are of course considerable. How is the relevant clientele to be defined, especially since many public functions are intended to control one group on behalf of another? How is the necessary high volume of political participation to be generated, without turning the numerous elected bodies into narrow or self-serving oligarchies? How is equity to be protected, and the allocation of costs and benefits among many sectional interests to be managed? How are the numerous 'externalities' arising from separate agency decisions to be coped with?

All the same, Ostrom's thesis has some merit. Exaggerated beliefs about political control from the top have reduced the responsiveness of bureaucracy to the clients whom they are serving. The diversity of modern service needs strengthens this argument, as does the size of the bureaucratic superstructure which overlays the final work of service delivery. However, the 'relevant community of interest' is also often powerfully articulated in the form of successful economic interest groups and associations. It is the wants of dependent or captive clients of public services which most obviously lack adequate consideration.

Remedies for this omission might include a stronger requirement that bureaucracies act on adequate information about their clients' wants. This arrangement would not be sufficient on its own. It would be necessary to provide for some direct client representation upon the local agencies which are responsible for the direct delivery of personal social services. This representation could also be linked with the creation of local offices of consumer affairs, which would have the specific duty of investigating clients' needs and complaints and of reporting to the political authority. Finally, there would

156

need to be changes in bureaucratic values and attitudes – a subject to be returned to later.

Ostrom's remedies merge in practice with the more familiar concept of a geographic devolution of functions to lower levels of government. This offers a more practicable method of breaking up the centralized concentrations of bureaucracy and moving staffs to a local level where they can operate in closer contact with their clients and under the more direct supervision of a locally elected body. Political devolution of this kind needs to be distinguished from a purely administrative decentralization, which may also be desirable but which leaves local officials under the hierarchical control of headquarters and provides no local political base.

At the same time, political devolution in the modern world never brings anything like full independence of action to locally elected bodies. These continue to be subject to central controls which are exercised primarily through administrative and financial channels. Thus in practice the issues of political and administrative decentralization are very closely linked together. The locally elected body is advised and served by a local bureaucracy which is partially responsive to control from the centre; but equally the local bureaucracy achieves some independence from the centre through its accountability to a locally elected body. The goals of local political accountability and local bureaucratic flexibility can only be jointly pursued, and the balances struck between politics and administration and between centralized and localized power will turn upon the structure of the whole system.

Thus an effective devolution of government turns upon very complex considerations. How complex can be seen from Ashford's (1982) comparative study of French and British local government. Administratively speaking, the French system is much more centralized because elected local and regional bodies are strongly dependent upon services supplied by national *corps* of administrators and experts; by contrast in Britain, local councils appoint and employ large bureaucratic staffs which are formally under their full control. However, in France, political influence is decentralized through the practice of politicians holding both local and national offices, and through the sensitivity of the prefects to local politicians; whereas in Britain, administration is much more insulated from politics and local elections are largely fought along national party lines, so that local political influence at the centre is limited and local councils have less power than appears.

If there are large numbers and multiple levels of local governments, and also a plethora of locally elected or appointed agencies for particular purposes, as is the case in the USA, the system is highly fragmented both politically and administratively. Such a system suffers from political 'overload' and leads to considerable inequalities in the provision of services for political, financial and organizational reasons. By contrast the ability of bureaucracy to deliver uniform services (or services which vary within tolerable limits) is eroded, and the professional and technical assets of bureaucracy are possibly underused. In Australia, the state governments provide nearly all the many services provided by local governments in the USA, and do so in a more equitable and perhaps effective manner (Parkin, 1982). This conclusion does not imply that local government provision is undesirable, but that it will *lose* desirable bureaucratic values if it is too fragmented and unequal.

Weak and fragmented units of government are also open to permeation by economic interests and more exposed to the interventions of central government departments. The latter point is modified by the sheer difficulty of controlling from the centre a large number of local units. The probability is that small units will enjoy autonomy within a very limited sphere, and that many functions will gravitate or be shifted to higher levels for reasons of 'efficiency'. Within tiny governments, the scope for a professionalized bureaucracy is also very limited.

Conversely, it might be supposed that local governments should be as large and strong as possible in order to operate a wide range of services and resist central government encroachments. However, this recipe can easily shift the political – bureaucratic balance too far in the opposite direction. The elected authorities of a large, multi-purpose local government will have restricted control of its bureaucratic staff whose size will replicate problems of big government at the centre. The seepage of political power to bureaucratic groups in New York City illustrates this point (Sayre and Kaufman, 1960). The city of New York, with over 7 million people, is one of the largest public organizations in the USA. Moreover a large elected government will also be weak politically if it cannot create effective community support on the necessary scale. A vicious circle can exist here because time and effective performance are needed to build up this support, but time may not be given if the authority offends national politicians, as happened with the Greater London Council (Self, 1982, Ch. 5).

A well-balanced system of devolution is therefore needed if

bureaucracy is to be made more politically accountable for service delivery while also maintaining service standards of reasonable uniformity and professional quality. Political and bureaucratic values have to be mixed in the right proportions and shaken together so as to resist the excesses of central government control which easily occur. Despite the difficulties, pressures for a more effective devolution of power appear to be growing in Western democracies, as shown by their important place in the policies of President Mitterand in France; but the results there have been mixed for both politicians and bureaucracy (Keating, 1983).

Restructuring administrative responsibilities

One of the hardest problems of big bureaucracy is the fact that political control is formally almost absolute, yet in practice is uncertain and sporadic. The answerability of bureaucrats for their acts is obscure where the concept of ministerial responsibility gleams like a pale sun over the whole ramshackle edifice of central government. There is no adequate distinction made between those acts of government for which political responsibility can and ought to be enforced, and those acts which should necessarily be left to the discretion or initiative of bureaucrats subject to some form of ultimate accounting.

A number of theoretical remedies are available for this state of affairs. One is to try to clarify the conventional distinction within a department between responsibilities of its political head for policy and those of its 'permanent' or public service chief for administration; but the distinction cannot realistically be made and the attempt merely confuses hierarchical relations. A related idea is to establish professional standards of administrative efficiency for which bureaucrats can be made separately accountable (Friedrich, 1940). This approach points to the need for a stronger code of public service ethics, but falters over the difficulties of defining 'efficiency'. It is still a promising approach when linked with structural changes.

Any reasonably effective distinction between 'policy' and 'administration' would seem to require structural reform. One model here is the Swedish system where small ministries deal only with policy issues and all operational functions are handled by a number of administrative boards. The distinction is only a rough one because the boards also in effect make policies, but they do so within a framework of laws and guidelines laid down by the ministries and cemented by constitutional provisions about the

159

division of responsibilities and the rights of appeal against their decisions. Public servants are trained to work the system because able ones frequently start in a ministry and later move to an executive position in one of the boards (Elder, 1970).

To some extent a similar distinction exists in the US government between the functions of political heads and bureau chiefs, and between those of ministerial staffs and the directors of divisions in France. Millett (1966) among others has urged the value of building upon a distinction between policy supervision, which he views as a triple control by executive, legislative and judicial agencies, and operational management which should have its own sphere of professional autonomy and responsibility within this framework. However, division of tasks is much more confused in these countries than in Sweden, and is marred by adversarial relationships which distort the performance of both functions.

Another possible answer to these problems is the idea of a 'representative bureaucracy'. This idea can mean many things. Its most generalized version is that a bureaucracy should closely reflect the structure and composition of the whole population. If this means simply that bureaucracy should parallel social class structure, the criterion is largely met. As a rule senior bureaucrats share much the same class and educational backgrounds, and lead similar lifestyles, as senior managerial and professional groups in the private sector. (There are exceptions, in the directions both of greater and lesser bureaucratic exclusiveness [Self, 1977, pp. 237–45] which need not be considered here.) However, this kind of representativeness makes bureaucracy a conservative force which will support the existing power structure of society, even if it is 'neutral' enough to act more radically under orders.

The more radical meaning of 'representative bureaucracy', therefore, is to open up the system, including its upper ranks, to individuals drawn from poorer social groups as well as from ethnic and other minorities. Bureaucratic reforms in France (the post-1945 *Ecole National d'Administration*), in Britain (the Fulton reforms), and elsewhere have tried to move cautiously in this direction, but have failed pretty comprehensively, partly through the weaker access to education of poorer groups and partly through the entrenched resistance of the senior civil service. This goal requires the creation of new and special ladders of educational opportunity for entering and rising in the public service. Such reforms might make bureaucracy more sensitive to the needs of weak or dependent clients.

A different sense of 'representative bureaucracy' is that of group representation, meaning that for example farmers' leaders should head farm bureau so that the bureau will be fully responsive to the clients' needs. This theory is an extreme version of group pluralism, and is at least partly realized in some US government bureaux – especially those which have built up a strong and stable agency–interest group bilateral relationship. This version of the concept makes bureaucracy all too responsive to group interests, while minimizing its concern for more general ones. The idea has more virtue as a way of strengthening the position of weak groups of clients. For example, a public housing agency manned partly by clients would be less likely to produce projects which nobody wants to live in.

Any bureaucratic reform will raise the question of the value and nature of general administration. The need for administrators who have a broad view of policy objectives and who can integrate a variety of specialized inputs has often been voiced. General administration can be seen as an essential corrective to the fragmentation and specialization of modern bureaucracies. Unfortunately the exact qualities required of such administrators are much harder to specify.

Keeling (1972) argues that British general administrators perform a mixture of administrative, managerial and diplomatic tasks. The first task is concerned with rules, cases and equity – the traditional tasks of bureaucracy; the second task with the effective use of staff and resources; and the third one with the numerous relations of administrative politics. The importance of the managerial and perhaps the diplomatic functions have grown, while that of the administrative one has declined relatively. This view of the desirable qualities of the administrator moves him closer to private sector managers, but he is still differentiated by the broader and vaguer criteria which govern efficient management in the public sector (Keeling's own recipe is for more use of cost–benefit analysis). However, this description does not tell us how far these different qualities can be found or developed in the same individual. It seems probable that they are unevenly spread.

Don Price criticizes the political misuse of scientific advice in the USA which arises from the lack of an 'intervening layer of administration between science and politics' (Price, 1962, pp. 108–9). He does not regard British administrators as a desirable model because they are too concerned with policy consistency rather than policy innovation. Such criticisms as these have influenced the creation of a cadre of senior career administrators in the US government, but it is doubtful how far they have combated the defects of specialized advice and administrative fragmentation.

Thus it must be questioned whether an all-purpose prescription for general administration can possibly exist. It would seem more realistic to differentiate between two types of generalist, one being the policy adviser and co-ordinator, and the other being the manager of programmes, staff and resources. The former 'generalist' needs the intellectual and diplomatic skills to assess expert advice, to absorb political pressures, and to design feasible policies, all within a framework of quite close political control. He or she does not need the skills to manage large staffs or resources. The latter 'generalist' does need these skills and comes closer to the view of administration as being concerned with the harnessing and co-ordination of social energies.

No differentiation of administrative skills is very satisfactory but the above one does accord with the scope for introducing a structural differentiation between central ministries and administrative boards or agencies. The chief officials of these boards would become responsible to parliament for the exercise of their managerial powers within the policy rules and guidelines which ministers would publicly prescribe. The range of functions which could be treated in this way might prove to be less comprehensive than in Sweden. Some politically sensitive functions might need to be excluded, as well as the general supervision and support of local governments and private enterprise. It is bureaucratic responsibility for the management of large operations which most clearly needs to be separately fixed.

The reform proposals discussed in this section have been fairly specific but do not add up to either a general panacea or a precise programme. They will be followed up in Chapter 8 by a broader discussion of political reform. They illustrate the dependence of bureaucratic upon political change which constitutes one theme of this chapter. They have not considered the important issue of 'public service ethics' which is actually a central element in many theories of reform; but that subject arises more conveniently at the end of the book.

7

THE FUTURE ROLE OF GOVERNMENT

To date we have been concerned with various theories about how modern governments work. In these last chapters I turn to a more normative discussion of the future role of government and the prospects for institutional reforms. We must first return to the thesis with which this book started, namely the highly critical nature of most theories about the workings of modern government. Why has modern government acquired such a bad name? How far are the criticisms justified and what changes in the political system could improve matters? It may be helpful first to summarize some of the empirical conclusions which can be drawn from the previous four chapters.

Public choice theories model and predict the egoistic or self-regarding behaviour of voters, politicians and bureaucrats under various rules. They suffer from the narrowness of their assumptions but are plausible because politicians and bureaucrats frequently do behave in an egoistic manner, even if their egoism is more complex and qualified than the theorists allow. These theorists are effective critics of idealistic beliefs about the public service motivations of officials and politicians. While their critique is much too extreme, it does accord with the likely growth of more egoistic or individualistic forms of behaviour within government which might be deduced from the findings of the other theories.

Pluralism analyses the growth and influence of groups and organizations, both private and public. This growth has been accompanied by a decline of those bodies which might speak for more general interests such as political parties. Pluralist analysis reveals great inequalities of power between organized interests. It also reveals a considerable displacement of parliamentary into administrative politics, and the development of strong alliances between public organizations and political groups.

Corporatism analyses the growing integration of actions between the public and private sectors, mediated through high-level co-ordinating bodies. It plots the delegation of coercive powers to economic and professional organizations and the sharing of responsibilities and influence over the making of public policies. Corporatism reveals the increasing pressure upon governments to adjust their economies to a changing system of international capitalism. Under these conditions the attitudes and interests of public and private sector 'managers' seem increasingly to converge.

Bureaucratic theories deal with many tensions and inefficiencies which derive from the growth of government and from the reduced role of political leadership. They point to many problems of bureaucratic indifference to client wants, of policy perversion by bureaucratic and external interests, and of overload of administrative machinery. They reveal the ambiguity of concepts of efficiency and accountability under modern conditions and the tensions between them. They point to the need for decentralization and the application of revised standards and tests for the exercise of administrative discretion.

This summation of four complex groups of theories may at least help us to identify some major defects of modern governments:

(1) Governments are inadequately responsive to both the goals of political leaders and the need of disadvantaged groups. They are too responsive to the demands of strong private interests which they have helped to entrench.
(2) Political parties have inadequate leverage in the face of pluralist and corporatist influences, both within and without government.
(3) Bureaucracies have become in various degrees ineffective and irresponsible or too beholden to powerful interests. The articulation and application of distinctive public interests and of a public service ethos has become eroded.
(4) The capacity of governments to cope effectively with the many problems of modern societies has been weakened, by failings of both political consensus and bureaucratic organization and ethos.

The normative or ideological remedies for those problems which might be derived from the various theories fall essentially into two groups – those which would turn backwards into a supposedly simpler world of less government, and those which would look for ways to enable governments to discharge their widening responsibilities more democratically, equitably and effectively.

The former approach rests upon the superiority of markets over governments for meeting individual demands effectively, and upon the waste and excesses of administrative growth. Because egoistic behaviour is acceptable and indeed desirable in a competitive economic context through meeting consumer demands efficiently, such government as is needed should reflect this economic model whenever possible. Bureaucratic analysis suggests the need for both trimming and decentralizing large bureaucracies, and for privatizing many public services.

The latter approach might accept some part of this diagnosis and these remedies, but would claim that the role of governments must still be a very wide one so as to meet societal needs. For these purposes a considerable degree of central planning and concertation of interests is unavoidable. The problem becomes one of balancing governments' more comprehensive role against the desirability of more decentralization of public functions. Democracy needs to be reconstructed so as to measure up to the policy agenda of modern societies, and bureaucracy needs to be harnessed to new conceptions of public purpose. For these purposes, some basic reforms of political and economic institutions become necessary.

The first approach represents the orthodox wisdom of the 1980s. It is espoused by influential advocates who can utilize elegant theories of economic and social competition which have returned to fashion in new styles. Its dismissal of the pretensions of government can build upon an accumulation of recently disappointed expectations, whereas its own theories of competitive individualism appeal to an economic order which has the nostalgic advantage of having largely ceased to exist.

By contrast the advocates of a more positive role for government encounter not only the list of its actual malfunctions or inefficiencies, but a weakness in their theoretical armoury. Government planning as a theoretical subject, despite the efforts of Karl Mannheim (1951) and others, has never attained the coherence or elegance of neoclassical economics. Its normative base may actually be none the worse for resting upon a variety of arguments, to which different individuals will attach different weights, but its presentation suffers. For this and other reasons the second approach to reform does not as yet constitute a coherent paradigm, but a mixture of proposals which share only the basic objective of equipping government to take on a growing agenda of policy issues in a more democratic and effective manner.

For these reasons, the next section will make a brief excursion into considering the actual capacity of a 'market philosophy' to meet the problems of modern societies. Subsequently we return to the capacity of political systems to generate and support a changed role for government. Further questions about the normative basis of the arguments which follow and their realism will be raised in the final chapter.

In the early 1980s a dominant policy paradigm emerged in Western societies. In each country the goal was seen as the creation of a more efficient and competitive national economy. This would require the rapid introduction of new technologies and the phasing out of 'inefficient' industries which could not compete on the world scene. Public expenditure needed to be cut in order to free more resources for profitable investment and to lighten taxation. Welfare spending was a particular target in some countries. Military expenditure was different because another type of international competition – the arms race – was widely supposed to require its increase, not its reduction.

Our concern here cannot be to offer a full critique of these policy goals. Our primary interest lies in the implications of the re-emergence of a 'market philosophy' for the role of government. What are the likely effects upon societies of a stronger reliance upon economic markets? What necessary functions which only governments can perform get thereby neglected? To consider these questions, we will briefly consider three relevant issues: the character of modern economic growth, economic instability and economic inequalities. The relevance of this discussion to the future of the political system and government's role will emerge subsequently.

The ambivalence of economic growth
Economic growth has been the dominant goal of Western governments since World War II. Growth has been highly valued both as an end in itself and as the source of funds for improved welfare and other public services. Within the dominant orthodoxy this goal remains paramount and largely unquestioned, and governments have become increasingly ready to sacrifice other ends so as to assist processes of capital accumulation and international competitiveness which are intended to produce further growth or at least to stop its actual reversal.

There seems little doubt about the social value and political appeal of the earlier stages of economic growth, as shown by the steady rise of standards of food, clothing, household goods and leisure facilities in Western societies. But beyond some point the value of economic growth becomes more ambivalent. This is partly explicable by the economic law of diminishing returns. As one type of satisfaction gets more plentiful, the receiver places more value on other types.

Economic growth is not of course a homogeneous entity but refers to the whole bundle of goods and services which, if properly measured, would constitute an index of economic welfare. In practice there are severe problems over the treatment of uncounted costs and benefits. The family which grows and cooks its own vegetables contributes nil to economic growth, its members show up in the statistics if they buy the vegetables and cook them at home, and they score much higher if they eat the vegetables in a restaurant. If one takes 'economic welfare' to include health, leisure satisfactions, etc., it seems probable that the first family scores highest in a society where families can sometimes eat out anyhow. Economic growth becomes more complex and 'qualitative' as it expands – and government actions become more significant for these qualitative aspects.

Economic growth produces large side-effects upon communal goods and resources. These impacts are numerous and diverse, including air and water pollution, rapid consumption or erosion of natural resources and agricultural land, the effects upon community health of new drugs and technologies, etc. Of course the technological side effects can be beneficial, but this result is less likely where the criterion is profit or (in a non-capitalist society) higher output per worker. Moreover the side effects extend also to the quality of what is produced which again need not (if the deterioration is general) show up in the statistics of a rising value of output. There are many cases of deteriorating quality of agricultural produce, of which battery produced eggs are a familiar example.

These points raise the question of how economic growth is to be understood and pursued. The usual assumption in Western societies is that the pursuit of profit will stimulate economic growth through providing in increasing quantities the goods and services for which consumers are prepared to pay. However, the test of profit is much affected by the existence of monopoly and financial manipulation, and by the production of many external costs (and sometimes benefits) which are not counted. Thus profitability is an inadequate guide even to the more tangible forms of wealth creation. Despite the difficulties of social cost-benefit analysis discussed in Chapter 3, one is driven back upon the need for a broader framework of welfare evaluation which can be used to discipline and steer the profit motive.

Chapter 2 demonstrated the largely unavoidable increase in governmental functions that has been consequential upon technological and economic change. It seems hardly conceivable, short of disaster, that this policing role of government can be reversed and every reason to suppose that it would have to be stepped up under conditions of faster economic and technological change. But the deeper issue is whether government can confine itself to the role of a defensive technological policeman, trying to mop up the side-effects of innovations which it does not control (and indeed often stimulates), or whether it must accept a more positive managerial role over the directions and timing of technological and economic change.

The instability of market systems

Keynesian policies were primarily concerned with balancing the instabilities of market systems by government action. This balancing act has become progressively harder at the national level through developments in international capitalism. It now has to be performed through an unstable array of international monetary agencies and banking consortia.

Expanding world trade was a major factor in the post-1945 period of economic growth (Shonfield, 1982). Trade liberalization could build upon the familiar 'principle of comparative advantage' which should enable each nation to maximize its gains from trade through specialization of production. The price of these gains by consumers is great instability for producers, which has grown with the increasing number of participating countries and the stepping up of competition. Capital and short-term money moves freely around the world in a volatile manner, precipitating financial crises, but labour is relatively immobile through restrictions upon migration, thus producing large differences in labour costs.

The costs of trade instability have become enormous in terms of structural unemployment, rapid shifts in the location of work, redundant services in some places and inadequate ones elsewhere, and much human waste and suffering. Exponents of market theory treat rapid obsolescence of investment as 'creative destruction', but one effect is to waste much investment which could still have a useful life. The liberal trade theorists fail to deal adequately with these large economic and human costs, which either fall upon government budgets or go unrelieved. This analysis need not deny the value of international trade for reducing the prices of many commodities. A denial of trade advantages or recourse to domestic protection regardless of cost would be quite unrealistic. The problem rather is to balance the gains from trade against the instability, disruption and waste of assets caused by rapid change.

Chapter 5 showed how the corporatist state represents an attempt by governments and interested groups to modify and steer the process of economic change. But, as was also shown, these efforts are becoming increasingly ineffective and are locked in contradiction between international and domestic interests. In particular, the dominant position of international capitalism, and the openness of national economies to disruptive financial movements have caused each government to concentrate primarily upon strengthening the competitive performance of its economy at the expense of more balanced, stable and forward-looking programmes of development. Governments are thereby caught to some extent in a zero-sum game, from which they can only be rescued by resuming a broader role over planning the direction of the economy – a road they started on in the 1960s but have increasingly abandoned under external economic pressures. While it may indeed be impracticable now for any government to plan its economy in isolation, a possible solution may be the emergence of a consortium of like-minded states, formed to advance common goals and values.

The inequalities of market systems

We need not enter into the old discussion as to how far market systems provide just rewards for scarce or valuable skills. Clearly they often do so, although the growth of monopoly reduces the force of the argument. In any case, large differences of wealth also arise from differences in effective bargaining power, and from the inheritance or acquisition of large stocks of capital.

Once again a major reason for government intervention in market system has been political demands for greater equality of wealth and basic services. This was or was supposed to be a main reason for the growth of the 'welfare state'. With the coming of formal democracy, the weight of majority voting was expected by many to offset the weight of capitalist interests, and to bring about greater equality. To some extent this did occur where mass labour movements have been united and powerful, and imbued with a strong sense of collective injustice (sometimes shared by members of upper income groups). The triumph of the Social Democrats in Sweden was one example of this process (Ch. 5).

However, any egalitarian bias by modern governments has been

169

much twisted by the influences of unequal pluralism (Ch. 4) and the constraints and influence of international capitalism (Ch. 5). The impact of governments upon wealth distribution is complex but has often been limited and uneven, and sometimes perverse. One can no longer presume that even in genuinely free democracies the effects of an increase in government budgets will be effectively egalitarian.

But neither of course will the effects of market systems, and economic development is producing new inequalities. One such is the growing gap between the incomes of skilled workers and those of the unskilled, marginally employed and unemployed. This is backed up by differences in the organizational power of various groups. Organizational power, especially when sanctioned or supported by government, is itself an important factor over the distribution of wealth and marks off those who have access to organizational privileges and support from those who do not. Once again, government is (from an egalitarian standpoint) as much a cause as a cure of this problem.

International capitalist competition creates pressures for high economic rewards in order to keep or attract the skills necessary for technological and economic development. National governments have to woo capital and to keep interest rates high enough to maintain financial reserves, a condition which depends upon the rates set by the highest bidder (currently and for long the USA).

A stronger reason for expecting governments to intervene in wealth distribution lies in its connection with social and political values. To cope effectively with the many crises of modern societies, a stronger sense of shared citizenship may prove to be indispensable. It may also offer the only alternative to growing conflict and violence or a repressive totalitarian regime.

Some writers have mounted a more comprehensive attack upon the goal of economic growth, and have argued that the pursuit of this goal is destructive of family and community life as well as being the cause of much noise, pollution and other environmental ill effects (Mishan, 1967). There is no intention here of taking such an extreme position. Many people in rich countries as well as the populations of poor ones clearly want and need an increase in the material standards of their lives. Economic growth in this sense must remain a basic goal of modern societies.

The problems of economic growth lie in distinguishing between its beneficial and harmful effects and in combating its strong tendencies towards the production of economic instability and

170

inequality. A further consequence of these ill effects is indeed the erosion of community values to which Mishan refers, especially where private profit is relied upon as the engine and selector of the forms of economic growth to be followed. On all the three scores that have been discussed (the issues of growth, of instability and of inequality), a 'market philosophy' would seem to be incapable of coping with the resultant problems or of offering alternative remedies to the acceptance of a broader governmental role.

None the less we still have to recognize certain significant advantages of a market philosophy when compared with even a much improved performance on the part of governments. Two important points require attention.

(1) Competitive markets remain the most efficient mechanism for allocating resources according to individual preferences. There are limits to this proposition. It does not apply to services which are deemed to have a strong civic or social content, in the sense that all citizens should be entitled to the service whatever they can afford. Such public services can be justified not only by the criterion of equality, but also by that of solidarity or community – the value of sharing in a common heritage and way of life. Then again, the evolution of markets into oligopoly or worse, monopoly, needs to be policed even though it may sometimes have to be accepted in part because of the economies of scale and international trade pressures. In no event should such a development be accepted in activities having a strong political and cultural impact, such as newspapers and television. Finally, the acceptability of market allocations is subject to the equity consideration that the distribution of spending capacity be judged reasonably fair – a point taken up later.

Given these large provisos, the neutrality of market allocations has great advantages over politically determined ones. It relates consumption to the sensible test of personal willingness to pay instead of to a political and administrative trial of strength between competing pressures. Increased governmental allocation of resources only heightens social conflicts and hostilities, unless done for purposes which can be seen to be socially desirable. Even desirable policies (in principle), such as the substantial expansion of education and social services after 1950, still had the drawback that the professional and welfare lobbies were far from satisfied and called for more, producing a strong political reaction in the opposite direction. Market systems operate at arms length from such pressures and have an acceptable degree of neutrality, provided always that they operate within a political environment which can control and neutralize their adverse side-effects.

Political theories of modern government

(2) Economic growth, however it shows up in the statistics, is popularly and primarily identified with the personal acquisition of goods and services through the market. It has been shown that this is a narrow view of economic welfare, not only because some goods should be communally provided but because many aspects of welfare − such as an attractive living environment, access to facilities, conservation of resources and regulation of the quality and safety of marketed goods themselves − depend upon government action. These qualitative aspects of growth have become more important. Just the same, market systems appear to be a lot more efficient at producing their share of total wealth than government systems are at contributing their desirable inputs. Moreover, the market contribution to economic growth continues to be of great importance, not only for its own sake but for its potential ability to relieve the excessive demands of public bureaucracies upon available resources.

There is a striking difference in this respect between the performance of markets and governments over the last forty years. Market systems have seen ruthless changes in technology and working methods which in many industries have reduced the requisite labour force by 50 per cent or still more. Even so it is a continued complaint of employers, and one generally accepted by politicians and bureaucrats, that the pace of change is undesirably delayed by the opposition of trade unions. By contrast, government bureaucracies have grown substantially, largely through the expansion of public social services but also through the growth of the staffs needed for administrative regulation, enforcement and co-ordination. While this contrasting pattern may up to a point be justified by the labour-intensive requirements of government services plus their necessary expansion, it still does suggest an undesirable disparity of behaviour and sacrifice. From a humanist standpoint, pressures of capitalist competition enjoin an excessive pace of economic change, especially when one observes that the societies in question are already technologically advanced and productive; whereas bureaucratic change seems excessively slow, especially when administrators and professionals usually recommend a pace of industrial change which they would fiercely oppose in their own cases.

Moreover, even if government has needed these increased resources, it has not used them to good effect. Any close student of bureaucracy knows the extent to which rules and regulations have been elaborated in order to satisfy escalating professional standards, to provide for adjudication or compromise in 'hard' cases, to meet multiple political criteria, to protect accountability and so on; yet at the end of the day the actual enforcement of public regulations is frequently slipshod and ineffective through lack of competent staff to do this unpleasing task. Thus there is a serious mismatch (of resources and effort) between regulative standards and their application. Then there is the enormous absorption of bureaucratic resources into internal processes of control and co-ordination and the quagmire of intergovernmental relations. These situations suggest that if government is to take on a still broader role, its methods of operation will require some drastic surgery.

We can draw some conclusions. One is that government must be careful not to squeeze too far the share of private consumption within the national economy. This of course is the political lesson to be drawn from the attempts of right-wing parties to limit the size of government, although it certainly does not follow that these parties have pursued this objective in a desirable way. Their tactics have reduced the necessary responsibilities of government, have run down the provision made for public infrastructure and have tended to reduce the size of the national economy. These tactics show failure to resolve the conflicts between international capitalism and the desirable goals of national planning. For this purpose the relevant proportion of government expenditure should be that spent directly, excluding transfer payments since these are available for private consumption. All the same, it needs to be recognized that an enhanced government role need not and should not entail increased government expenditure. In some respects, it can be made consistent with a reduction of that expenditure.

This conclusion follows from a more fundamental one, which is that governments need to understand and to utilize the mechanisms of the market for desirable social goals. Schultze (1977) recognizes that growth and affluence throw up problems that call for intervention of a very complex order. As a consequence,

> the boundaries of the 'public administration' problem have kept far beyond the question of how to effectively organise and run a public institution and now encompass the far more vexing question of how to change some aspect of the behaviour of a whole society. [Schultze, 1977, p. 12.]

This situation makes the traditional nostrums of left-wing movements somewhat outdated. Appropriate mechanisms need to be found to encourage private enterprise to function efficiently in its own terms and to meet a wider range of social demands than is now the case. Simultaneously, appropriate incentives are needed to persuade individuals and firms and other organizations to comply with public policy goals, without incurring the heavy costs and frequent ineffectiveness of an elaborate paraphernalia of administrative regulation. This 'social market' approach is no panacea; it has its limitations and can be applied in a variety of ways. Market concepts of 'micro-efficiency' have lessons for government, but any idea that they work automatically and effectively under appropriate conditions seems also to be outdated in economic thought; but more attention to the rational use of taxes and incentives to advance public objectives is highly desirable, even if it can be mistaken in cases when basic standards should be set and be enforced. These considerations certainly point to the need for a more sensitive and sophisticated approach to the design of public policies than is now the case.

THE FUTURE OF POLITICS

Writing in 1984, it is obviously hard to predict the future of politics with any confidence. Not only is 'a week a long time in politics', but the political scene in Western societies is turbulent and confused. The theories which I have discussed offer limited insight into the future. Orthodox politics continues to revolve around parties, pressure groups and administrative politics. Its workings are constrained by the structural features of modern capitalist economies and political systems, which have created an apparent straitjacket of restrictive policy options and assumed 'imperatives'. Simultaneously the old dogmas or nostrums of left-wing parties have lost political appeal, while those of the 'new right' possess a precarious and still largely untested political vitality.

At the same time, political orthodoxy has been confronted with a political counter-culture and new social movements. Will these movements be assimilated within the political system or will they act as a catalyst to transform or destroy it? Political parties have been in decline as the source of new policies and as mobilizers of opinion. Will this decline continue or will it be reversed through the successful integration of new movements, interests and ideas into party policies? The responses and calculations of political leaders have got more directly linked with volatile currents of mass opinion. Will this trend further undermine the traditional role of parties and produce more demagogic and unstable forms of leadership, or will it remain as one strand within a complex web of political behaviour?

These questions are too large and speculative to be tackled fully within the framework of this book, but they are relevant to any theory about how governments will operate. Therefore I shall offer a brief prognosis of the future of new movements, parties and public opinion in order to assess better the future role of government.

There has emerged a rich variety of social and political movements which fundamentally question the values and policies of governments. Environmentalism, the peace movement and radical feminism can each be seen as a major case of 'single-issue politics'. The strength of these movements lies in their large numbers. Their weakness lies in their detachment from the mainstream of 'orthodox politics', and their difficulty in persuading enough supporters to vote on a single issue to have a real electoral impact. In the case of the peace movement, enormous numbers of fully committed supporters are needed to dent the weight and resources of entrenched interests, helped by an apathetic or dubious public opinion. Environmentalism faces somewhat less powerful obstacles, but greater internal differences of attitude and interest. Feminism is to some extent polarized between specific demands over career opportunities and more radical or diffuse goals.

There has also been a growth of radical urban movements, triggered off by destructive changes which are at work within old urban areas. These movements variously mobilize the poor, unemployed and ethnic minorities, although they are often led by middle-class professionals who have rediscovered the vitality of city life. Their typical goals are better public services, more employment, more control over property owners and land speculators, and more local autonomy or 'self-management'.

These movements are widespread enough to be seen as the crisis points of the corporate state. They have won successes for particular groups such as housing tenants, but they have rarely commanded the resources or cohesion for major victories. Indeed their goals are often limited and defensive, and concerned with procedural rights and immediate remedies rather than basic policy changes. Still they testify eloquently to mass frustration with political orthodoxy (Castells, 1983).

Finally there is the widespread search for alternative lifestyles. This movement embraces a rich variety of beliefs about the virtues of intermediate or small-scale technology, co-operative action, self-sufficiency and 'naturalism', many of which are shared with parts

175

of the environmental movement. This search has produced a diversity of small communes and some significant experimental centres and communities, although bureaucratic controls are a serious constraint upon such experiments.

These various social movements reveal a widespread frustration with the existing political system and search for new policy directions, but their political leverage has (up to now) been very limited. This situation reflects the limitations of both single-issue and 'life-style' politics. Urban and environmental social movements often have a defensive and territorial character, being concerned with the protection of a given living-space or the way of life of some community or ethnic group. Thus their relevance to wider policy issues is limited, while their leaders are often suspicious of party politics, fearing the corruption of their aims by the restrictions of political bargaining.

These movements also often have an ambivalent or negative attitude towards the role of government. Believers in a 'sane society' might be expected to assign a stronger role to government over the control of technological and economic change, and sometimes do so. Believers in social justice would seem to need government for their purposes too. But the strongest (although of course not universal) attitude of social movements is deep suspicion of national governments, which are associated with centralized bureaucracy, 'technocracy' and capitalism. The chief exceptions are environmental groups of the Right, who are less afraid of governmental power because their aims are more limited.

This situation also reflects the political conditions of a particular period. The Left in many nations has suffered an eclipse of confidence over its traditional support for government initiatives. In addition, the new movements tend to assume that 'small is beautiful' in government as elsewhere and to espouse political decentralization as a remedy for the bureaucratic and technocratic 'alienation' of modern life, or else to seek new ways to reassert the value of local community. These ideas also have a rather different appeal to the theorists of the 'New Right' as a way of dismantling big bureaucracy. As a result, a contradiction exists between demands for the decentralization or dismantling of government and demands for new policies of a type which could only be initiated from the centre.

The traditional engines of policy change in a democracy are political parties, but parties have become less well equipped to fulfil this role. Their membership generally has declined and the communication gap between party activists and their increasingly volatile mass support has widened. In a world of big professional organizations, party systems remain ramshackle and amateur, and their resources for research and policy analysis are miniscule when compared with those of government or big corporations. In some countries their dependence for funds upon rich patrons has also grown.

As Chapter 5 noted, the decline of effective party programmes was linked with the growth of political and administrative pluralism. Conversely these new social movements are in conflict with what may be called pluralist elitism – the dominance of entrenched interest groups and powerful organizations – although their emergence accords with the pluralist principle of free association.

Parties still reflect the historical importance of class divisions in their formation. The main substantive conflict between parties has concerned the role of government over economic and social services, but disillusionment with actual performance and the weakening of socialist ideology has undermined support on the Left for economic planning and nationalization as originally conceived. The class basis of parties, and their emphasis upon distributional issues, makes it harder for them to absorb new issues and to offer new remedies. The Downsian view of party policies as being geared towards electoral success, not programmatic goals, has become more true, but this development is at least partly due to the ideological sclerosis of party philosophies, particularly of the Left.

An issue like environmentalism, which now ranks quite high on the political agenda, runs up against the political priority still given to crude economic growth as well as the polarizing effects of class interests. Environmental groups are partly divided along class lines, those on the Right being keener on the protection of wild animals and population control, those on the Left being interested in wider access to resources as well as in their better use and control. However, a class treatment turns many issues into a zero-sum game. To put environmentalism strongly on the political agenda, one has both to establish the desirability of certain general goals and to show that the consequent burdens and benefits will be equitably shared.

The increased volatility of mass opinion in Western democracies can be seen as both cause and consequence of the policy failures of parties. While the public choice theorists may be right over postulating an increase of rational egoism in close organizational contexts, the larger issues of policy escape such calculations. Issues of military defence, foreign policy, welfare spending or general taxation seem open to emotional swings of opinion, possibly of a cyclical nature, which can be manipulated by charismatic politicians and by the owners or moulders of the mass media. Moreover these swings of opinion appear increasingly to be guided by symbolic factors. Thus, an American election can now be much influenced by the symbolic candidature of a woman or a black, but the consequent effect upon policies is uncertain and doubtful.

The scope for policy change within existing political systems is restricted by structural and sociological constraints. Economic dependence upon the complex mechanism of international capitalism means that any radical policy initiative must cope with high initial costs and the disturbance of interests. The primary concern of individuals and groups with the immediate prospects for their jobs and incomes makes politicians reluctant to risk such initiatives. This tendency is increased by the short time horizons produced through the logic of electoral competition.

Moreover any system can draw upon some stock of existing favourable valuations and compensations which are sources of its legitimacy. In modern Western societies there is still considerable belief in the virtues of existing institutions, and the beneficence of an expanding realm of private consumption. The beneficiaries of these beliefs – big business, the controllers of the media and political leaders – can draw on and reinforce these sources of support for their own ends.

In considering the future of politics, one might postulate pessimistic and optimistic scenarios. On the former view, existing political and economic institutions will continue to be largely insulated from new movements of opinion. They will continue to evolve in a corporatist direction which is responsive to capitalist and military pressures, and any consequent crisis of social disaffection will be met by repressive measures. Politics will become more demagogic in character and could even follow the Aristotelian cycle of regimes and move from democracy into tyranny under the pressure of external threats or internal conflicts.

On the optimistic scenario, politics will eventually be rejuvenated by a synthesis of new policy ideas and initiatives centred on some concept of the 'sane society'. Many relevant elements of such a synthesis can already be found among the prolific output of the political counterculture. A parallel can be drawn between the 1930s and the 1980s. That earlier decade witnessed economic depression, mass unemployment, preparations for war, fascism in some countries and political polarization in the democracies.

The future role of government

Governments of the day were mostly ineffective and backward-looking in their choice of policies, and scope for change within existing systems seemed so restrictive as to foster political extremism. None the less that decade saw an intellectual flowering of policy ideas which eventually laid the foundations of the post-1945 'welfare states'. The same process of subterranean policy development may again occur and have an eventual flowering, whether or not preceded by some world catastrophe.

SOCIAL VALUES AND THE FUTURE OF GOVERNMENT

It is impossible to view government simply within the context of desirable goals. It is essential to relate its role to social and political values. If the social and democratic support is lacking, then no set of necessary governmental functions will be adequately performed.

The theories in this book have touched in various ways upon the future of political democracy. The public choice theorists, with their stress upon individualist and egoistic values, offer no basis for the social cohesion and acceptance of common citizenship which are essential for a working democracy. They may explain how social norms get eroded by egoism, but not how they can be created and sustained. That fact explains the normative preference of many (but not all) public choice theorists for a market philosophy, whereby the egoism of individuals would in theory bring about an increase in total wealth; but this result would leave untouched the many pressing problems which grow rather than diminish with private wealth accumulation.

Pluralist values stress the desirability of maintaining a diversity of self-governing organizations as the basis of democratic life. Up to a point this is a desirable, indeed essential democratic prescription, but it fails to cope with the overall role and power of government and the appropriation of that power by lesser organizations. The pluralist remedy is to try to reduce the inequalities of group influence so as to secure a fairer system of political competition, but this recipe (however desirable) fails to provide an adequate democratic base for government itself.

Corporatism deals more realistically with the expanding role of government. Its development suggests the need for a strong democratic base to control the exercise of the powers concentrated in government and exercised in conjunction with representative private organizations. Mendes-France grasped this point in suggesting that general elections should revolve around the preparation of the French economic plan, although his approach proved too intellectual for his times. A positive and democratic form of corporatism could only work in a society of active and socially concerned citizens.

Bureaucratic values raise the problem of specifying the responsibilities and ethics of officials more effectively, and of developing more distinctive criteria of the 'public interest' than are yielded by a wholly pragmatic administrative politics. Such an aim clearly requires a greater *rapport* of values and goals between bureaucrats and citizens.

The analysis in this chapter has suggested that the role of government in the future will almost certainly expand rather than contract, even though a great variety of detailed tasks may be 'hived off' to local governments or to co-operative and private bodies. Moreover the expanded role of government, being concentrated upon what may be called 'strategic' policies and decisions, will also become much harder to perform. These requirements will call for the exercise of much more understanding, imagination and sense of public purpose on the part of politicians and bureaucrats alike. It follows that the citizens of democracies will need also to become more aware of the responsibilities and privileges of their common citizenship, and more concerned with the nature of the policy problems which they must jointly solve. Unless they do so, there would be little hope of eliciting the necessary levels of performance from politicians and officials. But such suggestions may be quickly dismissed by some as hopelessly unrealistic or even totalitarian. Not only is political indifference often seen as a right in Western societies, it is considered by some to be beneficial through reducing the amount of political conflict.

These criticisms should be dismissed, provided that the propositions about greater citizen responsibility and participation are viewed sensibly. No one except a Utopian will really expect the attitudes of citizens to be quickly or completely transformed. Such an expectation might indeed, as the critics would say, lead into the excessive politicization of society which accompanied the French and Russian revolutions. The requirement is to move political behaviour by stages in the right direction; and the process will depend upon difficult changes in the prevailing social ethos.

But is the existing ethos at all defensible or desirable? It reflects a gross mismatch between political demands and supports. The load of government may be rearranged, some of it may be shed and new tasks may be added, but (if the analysis of this book is at all correct) the load will not go away. All expectations that this 'load' might be drastically reduced as a result of market or other expedients run into hard facts about the nature of modern economic and social development. Yet the role of government is only spasmodically viewed as positive and constructive by the media and public opinion, being seen rather as a sort of unsatisfactory dumping ground for all sorts of problems with which the private sector cannot cope. Social values are strongly oriented towards the goals of private acquisition and consumption, backed up by advertising and the media. Too rarely is citizenship itself seen as a valued source of both privileges and responsibilities, and politicians minimize the responsibilities which those policies entail, thus adding to government's bad name.

At the heart of democracy there is − or rather there must be if democracy is to survive in the modern world − some acceptance of equality in rights and responsibilities, some belief in shared citizenship. For long the question has been debated as to whether the formal equality of citizens is meaningful under conditions of large economic and organizational inequalities. Increasingly it is becoming apparent that this contradiction of status is real and could be mortal for political democracy. In part this is because wealth provides a strong and inequitable leverage for determining public policy, strikingly emphasized by the power vested in a handful of press barons and media controllers who enjoy (as Harold Laski once said) the harlot's privilege of power without responsibility.

There is another aspect to this problem, namely the incompatability between 'possessive individualism' and the sharing of common citizenship. If the former creed is completely dominant, then the quest for private acquisition and consumption must tend to undermine the values of citizenship. The ill effects of this situation have already been noted in relation to the diminishing returns of private affluence. The 'positional goods' described by Fred Hirsch (1976), such as second homes, second cars, private beaches, etc., both create congestion costs and deprive others of satisfactory access to scarce resources and amenities. One ends up with the Galbraith picture of a family driving their expensive car along congested roads to share an elaborately packaged picnic by a polluted stream. As the competition for positional goods grows stronger, costs escalate and inequalities grow, while common interests get neglected.

The destruction of the values of common citizenship has grim effects. It is hard not to believe that the growth of crime, violence, and social alienation owes something at least to the existence of private affluence amidst public (and private) squalor. The safe use and shared enjoyment of many resources which nature has bestowed or which society has collectively accumulated – such as water, air, coastlines, the streets, parks and meeting places of cities, knowledge and art – gets eroded by private violations and appropriations, which in some countries are now removing even police protection from the common realm.

To correct this unbalanced situation, it is necessary to consider what realm of common citizenship should be marked out and distinguished from the private domain in such a way as to create a viable democracy. This task will be tackled through a brief survey of the application of the idea of citizenship to the economic and social functions of government under modern conditions.

Economic functions

A basic need here is to redefine the sensible but confused notion of the 'mixed economy'. One reason for the disrepute of this term lies in the state's apparent failures to achieve economic growth and to manage public enterprises successfully; but these activities are no longer an adequate test of the public interest in the management of the economy.

There seems to be little virtue in public ownership for its own sake. It is pointless where a public corporation follows, perhaps less efficiently, much the same policies as a private company would do. Such cases are legitimate targets for privatization, unless there are quite different policies which the corporation ought to be following. The objective of government (and the interest of citizens) ought to reside not in ownership *per se*, but in the imposition of certain policy goals and restraints upon the conduct of all economic enterprises. Public ownership is needed when it is the only or much the best way of applying this dictum.

One basic issue is how far the public interest requires control over the direction and pace of economic change. Some control (as was said earlier) is essential to avoid very disruptive and harmful social impacts. In principle it is surely right to insist upon the gradual introduction of any innovation which will initially create much unemployment, destroy much existing capital or compel many people to change their jobs and homes. The purpose is not to block all change or prop up all existing interests, but to make sure that such change can be made socially beneficial rather than disruptive. At the same time, government officials have to be wary of thinking that they can anticipate future consumer wants successfully. In principle it seems desirable to let firms discover their own markets, provided any harmful side-effects are controlled.

The public interest in technological development has been most perversely treated in terms of human values. To subsidize highly expensive technologies for the sake of international competition has often proved both economically wasteful and environmentally suspect or dangerous. However, there should be a stronger public interest in the development of socially and environmentally beneficial innovations. This is the best *rationale* for the existence of a large publicly supported scientific establishment.

At present big business corporations represent large concentrations of politically unaccountable wealth and power. They control from remote centres the livelihood of hundreds of thousands and the viability of entire communities. Unfortunately it is difficult to influence big commercial decisions sensibly or effectively through a system of general laws. Hence the existing tendency to *ad hoc* government interventions, often supported by public subsidies for lessening the adverse impact of economic retrenchment and redundancies. In the future more systematic policy influence will need to be exercised and to be linked with trade and import policy, so as to get a fairer balance between the advantages of world trade and the havoc which it can cause within a national economy. For this purpose, there seems to be no alternative to the corporate devices of joint decision making between government and 'peak bodies' within industry. Only this process will need to be supervised by systematic parliamentary reviews of the policies being followed and of their costs and benefits. Equally, government will probably need a reserve power to give a directive to a private corporation in certain circumstances, as it now has (in an ill defined way) with public corporations; and it may need the right to appoint representatives to the board of any large corporation, subject to the essential qualification that these representatives have an adequate and defensible policy mandate.

The mismatch between political democracy and economic inequality has become especially marked over the operations of these large private corporations. The profits which they make are no longer just the result of entrepreneurial skill but rest upon great social accumulations of scientific knowledge and technological skills, and upon the exercise of organizational and financial power upon a world scale. The plan of the Swedish Social Democrats to transfer by stages the ownership of big corporations to their workers represents a logical development in the evolution of Scandinavian efforts to realize democratic values (Scase, 1983).

There are many difficulties with workers' ownership of big firms, such as the large number of workers and the complexity of the business; but without going into specifics, it seems desirable at the least to require corporations to develop systems of co-ownership (Nove, 1983).

Ideally a new form of constitution would be introduced for all big businesses. Authority would be vested in a board representing management, workers, consumers and government. Experience unfortunately suggests that a complex constitution blunts the edge of management or leads to a transfer of effective power from the nominal board to an appointed chief executive. Some blunting of private managerial power is of course necessary to widen the criteria on which decisions are taken and to prevent a narrow interpretation of organizational interest; but since competitive economic conditions will not simply disappear, some structural compromise between social and managerial goals becomes desirable in practice.

Government policies for sustaining employment are particularly important. In a world where (even in 'affluent' countries) there are large unmet social and environmental needs, and where essential investment in infrastructure is often inadequate, it is socially perverse to accept the necessity for substantial unemployment, early retirement, extensive job sharing, etc., as a market necessity. The satisfactions of a more leisured society will also be more acceptable if they are introduced by small stages. In any event the right to work is one of the most basic elements of common citizenship and long-term unemployment is a grave affront to human dignity. Thus full employment policy has to be reasserted as a fundamental obligation of modern governments.

A simplistic but quite fashionable concept of market philosophy leads to a false definition of 'productive' work. It is assumed that if a profit cannot be made, the activity in question has no economic justification because individuals do not want it enough to pay for it. However, many profitable activities have unwanted side-effects which need to be compensated for by the non-profit sector, and many unprofitable activities benefit latent or absent clienteles such as future generations. Moreover, many public services (such as health and education) will be provided largely upon a non-profit basis as a matter of deliberate political choice. It seems strange to argue that, for example, the provision of dialysis machines for kidney sufferers through a public health service is less productive of economic welfare than a profitable supply of toy dolls or new cocktails.

184

The future role of government

Any full employment policy has to reckon with its financial costs and inflationary effects. Such effects cannot be shrugged off on the grounds that the employment generated is in some sense productive, which it may not always be. The extra costs have to be met through either higher taxation or reduced private consumption; but their impact will be lessened to the extent that extra resources are beneficially utilized and the costs of rapid market adjustment are reduced. Thus an effective employment policy necessarily requires a most skilful and discriminating form of public planning. Once again it must be said that such planning will only be feasible if most citizens come to accept and share a set of common goals and values.

Social functions

The 'welfare state' may refer either to a basic level of services and facilities provided for all citizens, or to a safety net available for those who fall below some minimum level of subsistence. It can of course mean, and often does so in practice, some mixture of these two concepts. The debate on this subject has been going on for a long time and is entangled with other issues.

Government can provide support in cash and services in kind. These two functions raise different issues. Cash support is implemented through social security schemes which offer a minimum level of income in a variety of situations, such as unemployment, sickness and old age. The tendency in Western societies has been to enlarge and make more comprehensive the range of contingencies thus covered. On the other hand, the level of subsistence provided varies from the generous (e.g. Holland) to the mean but is generally far from adequate. The treatment of different contingencies also varies, for example old age pensions are usually better protected and less conditional than is support for unemployment or sickness. This particular distinction seems to rest less upon the influence of pressure groups than upon public opinion and ideology.

The tacit issue behind social security debates is the extent of economic inequality that is acceptable in a modern democracy. Obviously there can be no easy or dogmatic answer to this question, since so many relevant factors and competing concepts of justice are involved. However, it is a reasonable proposition that the distribution of net incomes ought not to be so broad as to jeopardize the concept of equal political rights and shared citizenship. This consideration might, although opinions will differ, suggest a maximum differential of perhaps three to one.

185

Political theories of modern government

In practice the distribution of incomes depends upon a mixture of social security, taxation and minimum wage legislation. The growth of public expenditure has joined with the resistance of middle and higher income taxpayers to reduce tax thresholds and to make taxation less progressive. Widespread recourse to indirect taxation adds to this effect, save where luxury goods are highly taxed. As a consequence in many (but not all) Western societies, the total impact of government intervention upon income distribution has become only very mildly and unevenly progressive. Since the inequalities of capital wealth are far greater, as well as often being taxed more lightly or not at all, one can conclude that modern democracies are a long way from placing reasonable limits upon the extent of economic inequalities.

Okun (1975) among others has argued persuasively that in the USA the inequality of income is much greater than the need for 'incentives' can possibly warrant. The example of Scandinavian countries, which have combined prosperous economies with re-distribution of wealth, suggests the same conclusion. Political factors which have been discussed earlier, such as the electoral weight of middle-income groups and the skill of higher-income groups over avoiding taxation, create obstacles to redistribution which are hard to remove. All that can be suggested here is that the principles of political and civic equality require stronger measures for reducing inequalities of income, and still more obviously for achieving a gradual redistribution of wealth through the taxation of capital and schemes of industrial partnership or co-ownership.

Social security policies have to be combined with taxation policies in order to achieve standards of minimum and maximum income. What the minimum should be must depend upon the resources of a given society and its profile of wealth distribution, but inequalities ought at least to be constrained within some democratically defensible set of limits.

Liberal individualists regard the provision of social services as a less efficient way of combating inequalities than would be a re-distribution of incomes, since the latter method enables the poor to buy what they want rather than what government chooses to provide. The imposition of 'technocratic' standards upon captive clienteles (Ch. 6), the frequent ability of middle-class groups to extract more benefit from public services, and the absorption of resources for the convenience of the official providers (Ch. 4) all lend support to this line of argument. Income redistribution once achieved is an apparently more rational means of promoting equality than the direct provision of services.

The future role of government

There are still stronger reasons for concluding otherwise. One such is the difficulty of breaking a cycle of poverty simply by cash injections. Some recipients at least will spend a cash benefit upon immediate consumption rather than upon meeting the needs of their children or other dependents, who will remain under-privileged. The creation of a more responsible society would change this picture but such a society takes time to create. Moreover many recipients live in degraded environments which can only be improved by much collective effort. No doubt it is preferable that this improvement should be carried out with or through the co-operation of local residents, but once again co-operative action encounters particular difficulties in degraded environments and needs strong support from remedial public services.

A still weightier argument is the case for regarding some public services as being fundamental to the concept of citizenship. This argument is strong in relation to education, health and to some extent housing. If public provision of such services were confined to the impoverished, the direct redistributive effect would be stronger; but the services themselves would in practice be less adequate and social segregation would be greater than under a system of universal provision. No doubt there is a case for permitting some degree of private provision, so that individual preferences can be allowed for and some alternative option exists when public provision proves unsatisfactory. All the same, the extent of such privatization has to be carefully limited and controlled if the quality of education or health for example, and the concept of common citizenship, are not to be undermined by the exit of the wealthy. Deteriorations within the British health service, once a proud example of a good universal service, show how easily this result can occur. Once again we are dealing with the erosion of social norms by the successive thrusts of egoism, and it is the protection of those norms and traditions which claim priority in a fair democracy.

The applications of a citizenship criterion certainly extend well beyond individualized services such as health and education. They extend in principle to all activities which, in T. H. Green's famous phrase, can remove obstacles to the good life for members of a society. As W. A. Robson (1976) points out, a 'welfare society' should be widely understood to embrace opportunities for collective enjoyment, such as the theatre and the arts, and measures to improve the collective environment, through town planning and other means. One important index to the welfare of any society is

187

the quality and safety of its 'public domain' − the streets, parks, community buildings, etc., which provide the meeting places for a vital common life. The quality of the public domain does not show up in figures of economic growth. Its deterioration in high growth countries is eloquent testimony to the erosion of the norms of citizenship by private acquisition. Without shared citizenship, economic development will eventually become pointless and self-destructive.

The arguments in this section have been perhaps more specific and controversial than might be expected in a study of political theories. To return to base, the analysis here presented rests upon the premise that some features at least of the corporatist state are here to stay. It will be impossible to put the clock back to old-fashioned pluralism, let alone to *laissez-faire*. Corporatism can easily become simply a shield for international capitalism, or alternatively (as happened before) the framework for a repressive military regime. If the future is to be different, the basic problems of political accountability and social justice posed by corporatism have to be faced. They have to be faced anyway if democratic values are to be made viable or meaningful. But of course the question remains as to how governments can be equipped for new tasks without falling prey to the many dysfunctions which theorists have suggested. This is the subject to which the final chapter turns.

8

APPROACHES TO POLITICAL REFORM

THE MORAL BASIS OF GOVERNMENT

The previous chapter discussed the future role of government and this chapter is largely concerned with the consequent case for a reform of political institutions. However, many people will be wary about any theories which assign extensive responsibilities to governments. Have not earlier chapters of this book revealed the frequently perverse, narrow and short-sighted behaviour of governments under the influence of free-riding individualism, group pressures, bureaucratic self-interest and the corporate influence of big business and strong unions? Can one expect governments swayed by such pressures to follow enlightened and humanist policies? Indeed, is not government often as much a cause as a cure for social problems?

To meet this criticism, one must show how reforms in political and economic institutions could improve the performance of government and strengthen its civic and democratic basis. Reforms require changes in social values and public opinion, and it is therefore incumbent upon any reformer to state the ethical basis of his proposals. The previous chapter may appear to require that government rest upon a collectivist and conformist type of social ethic. This was not the author's intention. He sees his proposals as resting upon individualist and liberal beliefs, adapted to the circumstances of modern societies. It is worth explaining why this is so, in terms of the theories in this book.

An appeal to the individualist tradition in Western political thought may seem paradoxical in the light of my earlier critique of public choice theory, but this is not really so. Those theorists concentrate heavily upon the collective results of individuals pursuing their private and self-regarding interests. They thereby discard or minimize the possibility of individuals making responsible judgements which take account of the welfare of others and of society generally. Morality is treated by many of these writers as a hard to explain or idiosyncratic preference for altruism, which may modify but need not negate conclusions reached on more 'realistic' assumptions. Some writers in this school recognize and defend the rights of individuals to their existing entitlements and possessions on utilitarian grounds; but this defence hinges upon the alleged impossibility of comparing the welfare of individuals, an assumption which produces a very restrictive view of public policy and which ignores the ethical link between individual rights and responsibilities.

The public choice theorists may claim that they are only pursuing a scientific inquiry and not making moral judgements, and in the hands of a craftsman like Olson (who keeps his assumptions fairly plausible), the results are some important insights into the problems and limitations of collective action; but the explanations do not cope well with the influence of social values and norms upon individual behaviour, or the way in which individual interest itself is understood and defined. Much individual behaviour is not self-regarding in a narrow or calculated sense, but is motivated by desires for social recognition or approbation.

However, the appeal to social norms is a quite inadequate *ethical* response to theories of egoism. Although individuals may act unselfishly and sometimes rise to acts of personal heroism under the influence of social norms, the collective power of the group may be used selfishly and aggressively or be appropriated by leaders for their personal gain or power. Hitler's soldiers fought with bravery and self-sacrifice for a xenophobic nationalism and a leader lusting for power. The use of individual judgement and moral responsibility to criticize social norms is an essential part of the Western liberal tradition and itself constitutes a social value of great, albeit precarious importance – since this value has continually to be asserted against the pressures for conformity.

Unlike primitive societies, modern Western ones reveal considerable evidence of change and conflict over social values. This change offers much scope for the critical exercise of individual judgement and responsibility, and hence for the review and reform of existing institutions. In appropriating the notion of 'rational action' to the instrumental advance of self-interest, the public choice theorists have done a disservice to this liberal rationalist tradition. This tradition stresses the significant role of reason over the harmonization of interests and the responsible exercise of individual freedom. Stripped of these conditions, the individual is a bundle of desires and tastes, not a person capable of meaningful choice.

Pluralist ideals also reflect the concept of a moral and rational individualism, through giving pride of place to associations of individuals which arise spontaneously and without coercion. This theory, as its critics have shown, is not a realistic description of how many powerful groups form and operate. Individual self-interest plays a strong part, and coercion if not direct is often present in the form of the high costs of non-co-operation. All the same, the pluralist ideal is not meaningless or non-existent as a motive to action. It shows up in the form of voluntary action which is motivated by the individual's own judgement of social needs and not by pressure of public opinion. Such behaviour may be a minority element in Western political life, but it is a crucial element in any reform movement.

Pluralism has suffered from an excessive distinction between the moral basis of 'intermediate institutions' and that of government or the state. The former are credited with a strong element of freedom whereas the latter is seen as an instrument of coercion. In fact however, motives of free assent and coercion are or can be present in both cases. The ultimate reliance of government upon coercion need not prevent assent being given to laws which are reached by methods regarded as tolerably fair. Rational dissent from many of the laws or policies of a state is quite consistent with moral support for its institutions. Such support is more probable if citizens themselves participate to some extent in the making and implementation of laws, are tolerably informed about their purposes, and are free to voice their dissent and to ask for justification of the actions of government. A society without too wide disparities of wealth and power is more likely to induce an effective and responsible exercise by individuals of their political rights. The same conclusion will hold if government is seen to be mindful of the welfare of the less fortunate and respects the value of personal development. These points are little more than the ABC of an active democracy, but they are consistent in principle with the ethics of individualism even though their application gives scope for dissent.

The ethical basis of corporatism lies in an appeal to the principles of social solidarity and national unity. Nationalism can be invoked as a quest for successful economic performance and military strength within the world arena. However, the pursuit of these goals can lead to considerable inequality and instability in the state's economic system and to conflicts between domestic and international economic interests, both of which results will damage the goal of social consensus or cohesion. In these circumstances, the moral appeal to nationalism can become an artifical or xenophobic cloak for dominant economic interests.

191

Corporatism represents a concerted use of economic power. Its justification requires that this concerted power be used to steer economic change in desirable directions, and to share the consequent benefits and costs equitably among all members of society. Otherwise there could be no moral rationale for corporatism as opposed to some explanation of it as a historical necessity. Thus the creation of new forms of accountability for the exercise of this power, and the application of stronger principles of social justice, become necessary elements within the ethics of corporatism.

The theories discussed in earlier chapters are primarily concerned with the exercise of power on behalf of variously defined interests – whether those of the individual, the organized group, corporate bodies or the nation state. Social values often enter into these theories as rationalizations or legitimations of power relationships, although they also appear as sources of social cohesion in versions of pluralism and corporatism. Thus social values can form part of political explanations. But ultimately, the only defensible basis for an ethical theory lies in the responsible exercise of individual freedom. In this ethical sense, pluralism and corporatism deal with the claims and conflicts of different sources of individual rights and obligations.

This analysis may at least suggest the need to base reform proposals upon a defensible ethic of individual rights and obligations which take account of the conditions of modern societies. Moreover it seems likely that modern democratic government will become unworkable unless it can command a stronger and more broadly shared ethical support. In this sense the moral basis of government is not an optional extra to other motives for political behaviour but the indispensable core of a working democracy.

PARLIAMENTARY AND GOVERNMENTAL REFORM

It is beyond the scope of this book to go fully into the many complex issues which arise with any attempted reform of the system of government. Moreover, the issues obviously vary for every country. My aim must be the more modest one of suggesting some approaches to reform which accord with the analysis and conclusions of the previous chapter. The basis for these ideas is the nature of the future role of government and the need to revive the institutions and practices of political democracy.

In the first place, governments will need to develop a much

improved capacity for policy making and planning. This proposition may seem a platitude, but governments are at present ill-
equipped for performing this difficult task.

Secondly, the operations of government need to be more
effectively decentralized. This conclusion follows from the first
one, since if the role of central government is to be broad it
becomes the more important that it should not also be deep. In
other words, wherever possible operational powers ought to be
devolved upon regional or local governments, in order to prevent
the expansion of central bureaucracy and the consequent clogging
and confusion of the 'planning function'. Still more fundamentally, decentralization is needed to express political and social
values, provided that it takes democratically coherent forms. This
issue is considered in the next section.

Thirdly, if some form of corporatism is here to stay (although it
may be modified and redirected), it is essential to ensure that its
institutions and processes are made accountable, and that the
exercise of public powers by representative bodies is more closely
related to the overall balance of government objectives.

Any reform of political institutions should start with the role of
legislative assemblies or parliaments. In the last few decades, there
have been numerous experiments with parliamentary reform which
have brought about some modest improvements in the oversight of
public expenditure and administrative operations (Crick, 1964;
Coombes, 1976). But these efforts fall well short of what is
required. In parliamentary systems, they run up against the
entrenched forces of party discipline and political career structures
which give complete priority to the recruitment and support of the
government in power. Consequently reviews by parliamentary
committees polarize too easily along party lines and aspiring
politicians have little incentive to uphold parliamentary rights
whenever this spoils their chance of office. Where there is a
constitutional separation of powers, as in the USA, members of the
legislature can act more independently. Unfortunately, their strong
powers of administrative oversight are largely exercised on behalf
of entrenched interests.

In parliamentary systems, a possible reform would be to
establish by law a dual career structure for politicians, such that the
chairmen and some of the members of review committees have a
guaranteed status and pay, and some protection from dismissal
as a result of party changes. Such measures would have to beware
of unduly constraining governments from pursuing their
policies when in office through the obstruction of parliamentary

committees. The present danger, however, is surely the reverse — that parliament as a collective institution is all too weak in relation to the government of the day.

One purpose of parliamentary review is to oversee the complex institutions of a corporatist type of society, so that the representativeness of these institutions is periodically tested and their exercise of public power is kept within defined limits. An associated function is to prevent governments from interfering erratically with institutions which they have themselves created. For example, it is a widely accepted principle that public corporations (and the same system should be applied in future to all big business organizations) should have a considerable freedom of managerial action within the limits of 'strategic guidelines' laid down by government. In practice, such bodies become exposed to frequent *ad hoc* interventions by ministers or departments. Some such interventions are doubtless defensible, but it should be a parliamentary function to monitor and check their incidence and to substitute periodic reviews of the corporation's competence and effectiveness over its assigned task.

Another goal of parliamentary review is to study a variety of opinions upon the economic, social and environmental issues of the day. Such a mandate necessitates an openness to the representations of all bodies which wish to be heard, and in particular to those bodies which are absent or weakly represented within the processes of administrative consultation. A mandatory requirement that due attention be given to the views of such groups, in particular voluntary and 'cause' groups, would go some little way to remedy the defects of 'unequal pluralism'.

To review the goals of public policy effectively, parliamentarians need collectively to possess a variety of qualities. They will need enough connection with the dominant interests and attitudes of society to avoid the danger of unrealism, while being alive to new social movements and minority opinions. They will need to be well informed about policy issues without becoming a chamber of specialists. They will have to combine some degree of judicial open-mindedness with the infusion of original and unorthodox opinions. Clearly such a blend of personal qualities is unlikely to be realized within a fallible political institution, but its design should take account of these considerations.

Undoubtedly the best institution for forwarding these purposes would be a well-designed upper house or chamber. The complexity of modern government and the case for some check upon the decisions of the popularly elected lower house, have led to widespread acceptance of the need for a bicameral legislature; but the composition and powers of the upper chamber remain subjects of considerable difficulty. If directly elected, it duplicates and conflicts with the lower house. A hereditary chamber lacks legitimacy and probably competence, while one nominated on the advice of party leaders, as in Canada, is open to patronage and favouritism.

The most successful upper houses are probably those, such as the German and Swiss, which contain nominees of the states within a federation. In all countries and not only in formal federations, the representation of smaller governments within a national assembly is a valuable way of implementing the objective of political decentralization. It helps to ensure that national laws and policies are made with due regard to the advice of those who will often be charged with their application and interpretation, and it corresponds to a 'bottom-up' rather than a hierarchical conception of government. However, the consequent control of centralized initiative by localized interests may also be too restrictive, if the latter are given a completely dominant place within the upper house.

Another familiar theory is to design the upper house as a 'parliament of industry' or functional assembly to represent the principal occupations of the society. This idea might seem to accord naturally with the logic of corporatism, but it has never been implemented in a democratic society. A strong objection to this proposal is that it might simply replicate and confirm the influence of strong economic interests upon government, thus completely contradicting one of the main objectives of parliamentary oversight of the administration. On the other hand, such a house might be designed to achieve more balanced representation of functional groups, and more open compromises between them, than can occur through administrative bargaining. In any event, there would be considerable value in introducing into parliament more individuals from the sciences, arts and professions and people drawn from a wider range of occupations than the few groups which dominate political recruitment.

Consequently, the upper house should be designed so as to get a desirable mix of membership. For example, half of the members might be representatives of state or local governments, while the other half might be elected at large from all occupational groups in the society, plus representatives of the unemployed and retired. Alternatively and preferably, these geographical and occupational proportions could be lower, and perhaps a third of the members might consist of individuals chosen in some way for their distinction and originality. Room might also be found for leaders of voluntary organizations and learned societies. The guiding aim would be to create a second chamber having specific political roots but also a diverse and talented membership, so that it could competently act as the 'grand inquisition of the nation' into the conduct of government. Such a body should still be given only limited powers to delay new legislation or to challenge financial policies. The lower house, as reflecting the current state of party politics, would continue to be dominant in these matters.

Reform of executive government itself turns upon the need to articulate more successfully the nature of the planning and policy-making function. The sections on planning in the chapters on pluralism and corporatism can be used to support a conception of 'strategic planning', whose purpose is to specify the goals, parameters and incentives which will guide the work of operational agencies and economic institutions. Such planning needs to steer a course between dogmatism and ineffectiveness: to avoid the pathologies of elaborate bureaucratic controls, while influencing organizational behaviour in the desired directions. Its methods and purposes have also to be justified before the critical scrutiny of parliament and public opinion.

Clearly these are most difficult prescriptions to achieve in practice, but some reforms should significantly assist their realization. One basic problem is the dichotomy between political and bureaucratic inputs into the policy-making process which was discussed in Chapter 6. The political inputs have a short time span because of electoral considerations, and an erratic character through changes of party government. These features are particularly marked in periods of strong political conflict and uncertainty over values, and some protection needs to be afforded against the high economic and human costs of frequent policy reversals. Conversely, the bureaucratic inputs into the policy process are more durable but easily become static or ritualistic; when successful they build up a strong independent momentum, but they may also wither through lack of political relevance. Temporary political advisors, as their testimonies reveal, have much difficulty over influencing the bureaucracy, but bureaucratic planning units often lead a cautious, submerged existence far from the political light of day.

There are great advantages therefore in the creation of mixed planning units, staffed partly by politically appointed experts sensitive to the goals of the current leadership and partly by bureaucratic experts who bring a somewhat more neutral and long-term viewpoint. Another valuable device is the use of an advisory council of independent experts with power of access to government information and with the right to have their reports published and presented to Parliament. A good example is the Netherlands' Scientific Council for Government Policy. (This and other innovations in planning are discussed in Baehr and Wittrock (1981).)

Planning and policy-making units need to possess a cellular rather than a hierarchical structure. Theirs is an activity where Victor Thompson's (1963) belief that the authority of knowledge should supersede the authority of hierarchy deserves the fullest possible application. In the previous chapter, it was also urged that government policies should integrate a diversity of factors and perspectives (economic, social and environmental). However, to create a large central planning staff in one office, working to a prime minister or president, is a monolithic and overloaded procedure. Experience suggests that this arrangement either fails or leads to the dominance of economic over other goals. Thus it seems preferable to establish a separate planning staff for each principle sphere of responsibility, but to promote flexible arrangements for joint working and frequent interchange between the various planning units. Flexible forms of co-operation between the political chiefs of these units are equally necessary.

A related reform concerns the clarification of political and bureaucratic responsibilities. This issue was also discussed in Chapter 6, where it was suggested that a structural separation of policy making and operational functions, such as occurs in Sweden, is a way both of making senior bureaucrats more accountable for their acts and also of gaining more attention for the planning function. A structural split of this type also has the obvious danger of isolating the policy makers from the implementers of policy. Thus, like all organizational recipes, it is no panacea and has to be applied with skill and caution. However, it could help to reduce the confusion of responsibilities which often occurs in government departments, and the perversion of planning into detailed controls which easily occurs.

Further important issues concern bureaucratic education and ethics. Specialization of skills and functions has raised the barriers to policy co-ordination and evaluation. The cure for this problem has to be sought partly in the development of broader and more liberal forms of general education. However, government is unique in respect of the range and complexity of the criteria which are relevant to its policies. Consequently it has a particular need to promote forms of vocational and professional education which require experts to examine the wider implications of their specialisms and to build bridges between related subjects, such as town planning and architecture or economics and sociology. Also important is the sharing of 'contextual' knowledge about the economic, social and political characteristics of the society, and the encouragement of a critical perspective upon the function and methods of government itself.

Bureaucratic ethics entails the development of appropriate rules and conventions which should govern the discharge of public business. The special features of government – its coercive properties, its political accountability and in a democracy its linkage with the concept of civic equality – require these rules to be given much closer attention than has so far been the case.

Bureaucratic ethics tend to be highly pragmatic. Bureaucrats often see themselves as simply responding to diverse political pressures over which they have no control. This is not an accurate perception. Bureaucrats at the least influence public policies through the ways in which they interpret and execute political demands, but the ethical significance of this role is rarely admitted or considered. 'Impartiality' has always been a central value of bureaucracy. Today, this value has to be reinterpreted under complex conditions of competing political pressures and the pursuit of diverse policy goals. There is therefore need for a new code of bureaucratic ethics which will protect the interests of weak or dependent individuals and groups, and which will assist bureaucracy to perform its balancing role within the political system in a fairer manner. The development of such a code depends a lot upon the self-awareness and concern of bureaucrats themselves.

The working norms and conventions of bureaucracy are strongly tilted towards maintaining elaborate team work and collective decision making, and tend therefore to dampen or negate individual initiative. But if government is to perform its positive tasks well, individual initiative has to be encouraged. Indeed the apparent or alleged deadening of initiative in the conduct of public corporations has formed an important argument for privatization, and the exaltation of private enterprise further undermines the rewards for enterprise inside government. History gives examples of outstanding public servants who have exercised independent initiative and judgement, but they have done so for a smaller reward than business would offer, and often at risk to their careers for 'stepping out of line'.

Approaches to political reform

The encouragement of initiative depends partly upon structural reforms, such as more effective delegation to the heads of enterprises and operating units. It also depends upon establishing a much better understanding of the purposes for which such initiative should properly be exercised. In brief it requires, as does bureaucratic ethics, the restatement of a public interest philosophy. Senior bureaucrats have an obvious occupational and moral interest in concerning themselves with this subject, and it is a sorry reflection either upon them or their political environment that they so rarely do so. The restatement of a public interest philosophy cannot be vigorous or effective without the participation of bureaucrats themselves.

THE DECENTRALIZED STATE

The issue of political decentralization is of growing importance in modern Western societies. It can be confronted in several ways. Here it may be helpful first to suggest some general criteria which may be applied to the subject before turning to the context of actual institutions.

Economic criteria

Decentralization enables local communities to choose (through their representatives) that bundle of government services which they prefer, thus increasing the scope for consumers' choice within government. This argument is qualified by the requirement that local units of government should minimize 'externalities' (i.e. effects upon the residents of other areas) and should be reasonably efficient units for the services they provide − although differential charges and 'contracting out' of services provide possible ways of meeting these two problems.

The main problem about this economic theory is its inegalitarian effects. Since poor residents have restricted mobility and since rich residents may manage to use planning or other powers to keep poor people out of their areas, local government units will tend to become polarized economically, thus reducing the ability of poor areas to provide proper services − and restricting mobility as well. These effects are a grave drawback to the considerable autonomy of local government in the USA (Self, 1982, Ch. 3).

These ill effects can be largely avoided through measures of financial equalization provided by higher levels of government, subject of course to the brake upon local autonomy caused by a higher degree of financial dependence. A regional government

199

which possesses a balance of rich and poor areas can also perform this equalization function without becoming dependent upon central government; but if its resources are below the national average, it will need help itself over the provision of public services.

Political criteria

As Chapter 4 suggested, decentralization is often justified on the grounds that it disperses and thereby reduces the power of government. Equally of course it will reduce the effectiveness of government in all cases where a strong or concerted exercise of public powers is desirable. Thus the weight of this argument turns upon the balance between two opposing dangers and upon an assessment of the desirable role of government.

Earlier chapters have also suggested that the fragmentation of public powers increases the influence of strong economic interests and promotes 'unequal pluralism'. It can also lead to the inefficient and undesirable side-effects which are associated with 'disjointed incrementalism' and with neglect of the planning function in government. However, these criticisms apply much more to particular forms of decentralization than to the principle itself. Decentralization need not imply a widespread scatter of political and administrative authority, but can be conducted through the agency of multi-purpose and integrated regional and local governments. Again it can be made consistent with a considerable measure of co-ordinated planning at all levels of government.

Political decentralization can build upon the traditional case for popular participation in the work of government and upon the proposition that democracy has little meaning or prospect of stability unless its practices are widely diffused. The classical case for local self-government is much strengthened by the need to increase practical experience of the rights and duties of common citizenship. In Western societies where widespread anomie and helplessness can be traced at least partly to the centralization of political and economic power, this argument perhaps needs little demonstration.

At the same time, the case is still limited and qualified by the same values of common citizenship. Localized institutions carry a lower risk of populist forms of tyranny or dictatorship but are more open to the manipulations of narrow and self-interested oligarchies. The alternation of regimes or parties which is a normal or anyhow expected feature of national politics never penetrates at all into many elective local institutions. Thus, within a modern democracy, it is right and necessary that certain basic rights should be stipulated and guaranteed for all members of the society irrespective of residence.

The teasing issue for theories of decentralization has always been how extensive these rights should be and how rigorously they should be stipulated. On issues such as racial or other forms of discrimination, there seems good reason to accept a fairly rigid specification of universal rights and duties. Such measures fall within the principle of equality under the law. In respect of public services, or at any rate the more necessary ones, the case for laying down minimum standards which must be provided everywhere is also strong. But if these standards are pitched high, there will be little scope for local choice, initiative or experiment; nor will local representatives be effectively accountable for their uses of public money. If the standards are closely stipulated and enforced by central administrative agencies, bureaucratic power becomes extended and centralized and with it the dangers of ritualism and technocracy. Thus the concept of 'minimum standards' needs to be construed liberally rather than dogmatically, and in such a way as to prevent the imposition of uniform technical standards upon local communities.

Bureaucratic criteria

Chapter 6 discussed in some detail the contribution which decentralization can make to bureaucratic reform. It was pointed out there that political and bureaucratic decentralization were complementary, and worked together best where local governments were large enough to be professionally competent, but not so large as to resist political direction or to be devoid of a sense of political community. The dysfunctions of large bureaucracies create a powerful case for decentralization, if these requirements are met.

These considerations about decentralization have to be viewed within a historical context of rapid technological and economic change and of dramatic shifts in the international power structure. It is a familiar idea that we all live within a 'global village' forged by the growth of mass communications and mass production. Abundant evidence exists in the form of the vast international markets for standardized products, the spread of mass cultures within and between nations, the growth of world tourism (itself increasingly standardized), and so on.

Yet in other respects this global village is not truly global at all. It is split down the middle by the strong obstacles to intercourse between the members of rival power *blocs*, and it is divided by the gulf between the living standards of rich and poor nations. These divisive forces appear to be growing within the world, while within individual states the gap between rich and poor or between the beneficiaries and the casualties of economic development also seems to be widening. Thus the benefits of technology are very unequally shared, and the growth of mass culture tends to overlay and obscure profound differences of lifestyles, beliefs and values. Nor is the fact of easy world communications of itself very efficacious for spreading a better understanding of the nature of these diverse cultures.

Therefore the issue of decentralization has to be viewed within a changing political and cultural context. The power of most national governments has been diminished by the emergence of large blocs or systems of military and economic power. Within many states, national power is also being modified or threatened by the growth of sub-national movements and their demands for regional autonomy or sometimes for independence. It is true that the governments of the two developed 'superpowers', the USA and the USSR, continue to wield enormous power derived from their own great resources and their leadership of a heterogeneous bloc of allies or dependants. Some independent action by other governments is possible because of the diplomatic need of the superpowers to maintain large coalitions of supporting or acquiescent nations, and because the balance of nuclear terror sometimes allows lesser assertions of national power to be made with impunity. These conditions and the weight of history may serve to disguise the basic weakness of national sovereignty in the modern world.

Nationalism remains a potent sentiment and ideology, but one that often is not exclusively or strongly identified with existing states. It is drawn upon by regional movements in many parts of Europe, such as Scotland, Wales, Brittany, the Basque country, etc., which can appeal to historical traditions of autonomy that have revived with the decline of European empires and nation states. Within the USA, most blacks and hispanics seem to feel a deeper ethnic than American identification. The dependent nationalities which constitute many of the republics of the USSR may not have forgotten their more traditional loyalties. In any case, nationalism within enormous and diverse federations is not of the same character and intensity as it once possessed in the more compact European states. In those states, both in Western and Eastern Europe, nationalism can still draw upon hostility to external domination, but its positive force is more doubtful.

Sub-national or regional movements also provide a focus for cultural resistance to the domination of mass culture and homogenized markets. Regional cultures sometimes seem fragile and limited in appeal, but they may draw strength from the cultural counter-movements discussed in the previous chapter. It seems probable that the many groups experimenting with alternative lifestyles or seeking more traditional or distinctive values will continue to grow. Regionalism both nurtures and is nurtured by these movements.

Political institutions gain considerable survival value from the mere facts of a long existence and an accumulated network of interests and loyalties. Thus it is hardly to be expected that nation states will easily wither away or be replaced by other political structures. None the less it may eventually prove the case that effective power moves both upwards and downwards from the national level in some parts of the world. A 'Europe of the regions' is at least one possible vision of the future, whereby a considerable strengthening of European political institutions would be accompanied by a devolution of powers to regional or sub-national governments. A political basis for regionalism already exists in a lopsided manner in the United Kingdom and France, and on a more systematic basis in Germany and Italy, while the smaller European and Scandinavian countries would each constitute a natural unit within a broader European system. Whether realistic or not − and currently it looks highly unrealistic − the creation of such a European political system might accord very well with goals of political decentralization and cultural diversity.

Within either a federation or a unitary state, the structure of decentralization is unlikely to be tidily arranged according to the principles discussed earlier. Probably the last clear example of a symmetrical structure was the Napoleonic creation of departments and communes, a system which has proved to have enormous survival value. Irrational boundaries and obsolete divisions of power among state and local governments cannot be shifted easily, short of revolution, although there are marked differences in the reformist tendencies or capacities of national governments. Moreover, it is a reasonable pluralist belief that some protection should be assured to existing regional and local institutions. All the same, there are situations and periods where decentralized institutions need to be changed if they are to work effectively, and the criteria discussed earlier offer guidelines for this purpose.

In any event, the uneven spread or intensity of sub-national loyalties must sometimes preclude the application of uniform principles. For example, Wales is a weak economic unit and, lacking a natural centre or integrated communications, its geography is very ill suited for purposes of self-government. However, the satisfaction of the Welsh sense of cultural identity and political aspirations may be a lot more important than are criteria of economic or administrative efficiency. This is the type of issue that no theorizing can adequately resolve. No one can easily predict how much 'autonomy' will satisfy a nationalist movement, or what use the people in question will make of such self-government or perhaps full independence as they achieve. It does seem to be the case that successful nationalism, when widely and deeply felt, has energizing effects which may overcome economic handicaps or at least produce a poorer but happier society – especially if sacrifices are shared equally.

This discussion is not meant to suggest that a federal or even confederal constitution is superior to a unitary one. That question depends upon the scale and diversity of the total system – upon whether, for example, one is envisaging a European federation or a continuation of largely independent national states. It also depends upon the ability of a national state to accommodate sub-national movements, such as those of Scotland and Wales within the United Kingdom, without introducing a partial form of federalism.

Moreover existing federal systems are not generally well designed for achieving a desirable balance between central planning and the devolution of powers. The duplication of the full panoply of legislative institutions at two levels of government creates considerable difficulties for effective planning at the centre, and can place too much stress upon the devolution of legislative rather than executive powers. A system like the West German one, where the *Land* governments are responsible for executing federal laws as well as their own and there is considerable co-operation between the two levels, can minimize these problems.

By contrast, unitary states have the advantage of flexibility over adapting the structure and powers of local institutions to the changing role of government; but this advantage needs to be controlled by some constitutional recognition of the rights of regional and local institutions and the means by which they may be changed. As was said earlier, it is important that these institutions be given appropriate representation within the national parliament, so that government policies are made with their advice and consent.

Approaches to political reform

The reform proposals in this chapter offer no more than guidelines for the evolution of political institutions. They cannot be made more precise because the world itself is changing. For example, the principles of political decentralization have to be applied under conditions both of growing international interdependence and stronger sub-national or regional movements for autonomy. The impacts of these developments upon the structure of nation states cannot be closely foreseen.

A further question is the capacity of political institutions to steer the course of economic and technological change into more beneficial channels. In principle the scope for such beneficial action is enormous. Modern technology is both efficient and malleable. There is no intrinsic logical or economic obstacle to switching the vast resources of sophisticated skills now harnessed for military purposes into the goals of feeding the hungry, renewing urban infrastructure, improving welfare services and protecting the future environment of the planet. In ordinary human terms, there is work enough to be done to render absurd the proposition that mass unemployment and enforced idleness are necessary evils; and the social and moral claims of the tasks waiting to be done need little demonstration.

Technology can also be adapted to the goal of decentralization, broadly defined. There is already a flourishing literature on the scope for decentralizing the generation of energy and the use of natural resources. Another large literature deals with methods of decentralizing the management and control of economic enterprises. These possibilities cannot be reviewed here, but essentially their appeal lies in strengthening the capacity of local or regional communities to order their own lives in a more stable and far-sighted manner, instead of retaining a high dependence upon erratic changes in the world economy and the remote decisions of large organizations. Any consequent losses of technological and economic efficiency would be offset by the gains of a fuller and more stable use of local resources. The greatest value of a decentralized system would be the enhancement of political participation and the values of common citizenship in action, subject to the need to balance fairly the rights of broader and narrower communities.

The concept of government itself is capable of a changed interpretation. Its association with coercive action and bureaucratic overload needs at least to be considerably modified, if new social energies are to be released and if a more willing endorsement is to be given to public policies and decisions. The conditions for achieving a more active and informed democracy have been discussed, but these prescriptions and the associated idea of a stronger measure of effective equality will suggest to some a Russian-like vision of conformity, backed by the force of public opinion rather than the voluntarist spirit of free co-operation. It would be unrealistic to deny the relevance of public opinion and social norms if civic rights and duties are to be taken more seriously. It therefore becomes the more necessary to encourage to the full smaller and more participatory forms of collective action, such as co-operatives of many types and voluntary organizations.

Wolin (1960) feared that political philosophy was dying because the interests and values of the general community (with which such philosophy deals) have become subordinated to those of sectional groups and organizations. In a different way and from a Marxist perspective, Therborn (1976) analyses the construction of an 'ideological community' by Durkheim, Parsons and other sociologists as a way of combating the conflict of interests and sense of alienation within Western capitalist societies. These and other studies correctly perceive this weakness and poverty of community spirit. Community spirit, however, can be reinvoked in very different ways, ranging from the maximum possible reliance upon voluntarist and local bodies, working with the encouragement of government, to the promotion of a centralized state, supported by an assertive and intolerant nationalism.

Optimistic visions of the future could certainly be considered unrealistic in terms of some of the theories discussed earlier. These theories might suggest that nation states are locked inescapably into a highly competitive arena. The prosperity and safety of a nation state depends upon effective performance within this arena, and social and environmental goals (however desirable) have therefore to be treated as completely subsidiary to this primary goal. Such an explanation can build either upon a presumed natural law of human egoism and assertiveness, or upon a concept of structural or historical determinism. Even if the corporate state is riven by conflicting interests which will defeat its goals, it could still be claimed that its behaviour cannot be changed until the system breaks down and new structures form.

Without accepting such a pessimistic forecast, the accumulated structure of power and perceived interests do present a formidable barrier to the creation of a more beneficent state. For example, while many people may work voluntarily for nuclear disarmament, they are confronted by the interests of all those whose jobs and profits are enmeshed within a military system. The fact that equivalent opportunities *could* be provided in other ways is a somewhat abstract notion in terms of an immediate balance of interests. Moreover, in this and other cases, a change of policy is also inhibited by widespread popular inertia or fear of tampering with an authoritative policy based upon secret information. The fact that even so the anti-nuclear movement has gained so many adherents, and has elicited so much sacrifice of private interests for its cause, is itself a refutation of the hard-headed assumptions often made by public choice and some pluralist thinkers. Moreover the strength of the peace movement may also be considered some evidence of the ability of moral ideas to capture ground from material interests, when one reflects how unequal in resources are the contending sides.

Many of the proposals made in these last two chapters encounter the same problem. Ideas of political reform or new conceptions of government which disturb existing interests have a hard row to hoe. The influence of ideas can still be important where these offer a possible alternative to further deterioration in the life of society. When an appropriate structural shock occurs, their time may come.

GUIDE TO FURTHER READING

The reader who wants to study further any of the four schools of political thought discussed in Chapters 3 to 6 inclusive will encounter a formidable volume of literature. It may therefore be helpful to set down a selective list of books dealing with each main school of thought about modern government, together with a brief comment about the work in question. In compiling this list, I have been more concerned to put down some interesting or original works dealing with both the theory and the practice of modern governments than to list textbooks or to attempt a comprehensive coverage. In passing, it should be noted that good textbooks on these subjects are anyhow hard to come by, and original works will do more to stimulate the reader's interest and understanding. Full references for the books listed here can be found in the bibliography.

Public choice theories usually build upon economic or logical models of rational behaviour which distinguish them from the more empirical theories or generalizations associated with studies of pluralism, corporatism and bureaucracy. These three subjects also overlap, since pluralism can be claimed to evolve into corporatism, and modern bureaucracy has both pluralist and corporatist features.

Most books on public choice theories and nearly all books on modern pluralism are American, whereas most of the books on corporatism and many on bureaucracy are European or use European examples. This circumstance may suggest to the reader that pluralist analysis has more validity for the USA and corporatist analysis for European nation states.

CHAPTER 3 THE INDIVIDUALIST STATE

Some knowledge of economics or mathematical logic is clearly useful for anyone tackling this literature, but the individual with little or very limited knowledge of this kind can still in most cases follow the argument if he skips the mathematical illustrations. Numbers 1, 3, 4 and 8 are all fairly easy to read, and number 9 is helpful for understanding the general approach of economists.

1. Thomas Schelling *Micromotives and Macrobehaviour* is a good introduction to the indirect effects of individual choice.
2. Dennis Mueller *Public Choice* is a competent textbook using fairly easy economics.
3. Mancur Olson *The Logic of Collective Action* is the classic statement of the 'free rider' problem, with some persuasive illustrations.

Guide to further reading

4 Anthony Downs *An Economic Theory of Democracy* designs and tests a model of the rational behaviour of voters and politicians.

5 James Buchanan and Gordon Tullock *The Calculus of Consent* analyzes the costs and benefits to the individual of government coercion.

6 Albert Hirschman *Exit, Voice and Loyalty* shows how individual behaviour differs in political and economic contexts.

7 P. M. Jackson *The Political Economy of Bureaucracy* is a useful summary of this subject, seen largely from a public choice standpoint.

8 Charles Schultze *The Public Use of Private Interest* effectively applies economic logic to the design of public policies.

9 Brian Barry *Sociologists, Economists and Democracy* compares the results of economic and sociological investigations into political behaviour.

10 Charles Rowley and Alan Peacock *Welfare Economics* is a strong critique of the Pareto principle and welfare maximisation (but difficult for non-economists). A more readable argument for restricting government action in the name of individual liberty is F. A. Hayek *The Constitution of Liberty*.

CHAPTER 4 THE PLURALIST STATE

Although pluralist ideas are widely pervasive, there are few works dealing specifically with pluralist theories. Much of the literature is empirically based in the functioning of American institutions. The more general works listed are those by Dahl (number 1), Self (6) Braybrooke and Lindblom (8), and MacPherson (10).

1 R. A. Dahl *A Preface to Democratic Theory* discusses the historical origins and character of democratic pluralism.

2 R. A. Dahl *Pluralist Democracy in the United States* represents the high tide of belief in a beneficent pluralism.

3 R. A. Dahl *Dilemmas of Pluralist Democracy* (published 15 years later) outlines the drastic reforms needed to salvage pluralism.

4 T. J. Lowi *The End of Liberalism* is a vigorous attack upon the subversion of general laws by arbitrary administration and special interests.

5 Grant McConnell *Private Power and American Democracy* is a well-documented study of the appropriation of public power by private interests.

6 Peter Self *Administrative Theories and Politics* examines the diverse nature of administrative and organizational behaviour in different political contexts (also relevant to Bureaucracy).

7 E. N. Suleiman *Politics, Power and Bureaucracy in France* shows the interplay of pluralism and elitism in French administration (also relevant to Bureaucracy).

8 D. Braybrooke and C. E. Lindblom *A Strategy of Decision* analyzes

and defends the incremental nature of policy-making in a pluralist society.

9 William Kornhauser *The Politics of Mass Society* is a vigorous statement of the need for intermediate groups as a defence against the tyranny of mass society.

10 C. B. MacPherson *The Political Theory of Possessive Individualism* is a powerful critique of the influence of the concept of private property upon liberal and pluralist thinking (equally relevant to reading for Chaper 3).

CHAPTER 5 THE CORPORATIST STATE

There seem to be no good general works on the nature of corporatism, and the best starting point is collections of essays.

1 P. C. Schmitter and Gerhard Lembruch (eds) *Trends Towards Corporatist Intermediation* (an ugly title) contains Schmitter's interesting description of the subject. See also the essays of Offe and Jessop.

2 Suzanne Berger (ed.) *Organizing Interests in Western Europe* has good contributions on different countries from Offe, Schmitter, Berger and Schwerin.

3 J. T. Winkler's article 'Corporatism' offers a nationalist explanation of corporatism.

4 James O'Connor *The Fiscal Crisis of the State* is a clear Marxist analysis of some causes of corporatism.

5 Manuel Castells *City, Class and Power* analyzes the impact of modern capitalism upon the planning of French cities and regions.

6 Colin Crouch *The Politics of Industrial Relations* and Leo Panitch *Social Democracy and Industrial Militancy* both give good accounts of the causes and failures of corporate bargaining in Britain.

7 Francis Castles *The Social Democratic Image of Society* by contrast explains the reasons for the success of corporate bargaining in Scandinavia.

8 Andrew Shonfield *Modern Capitalism* offers the best analysis and defence of the growth of corporatist planning in Europe in the 1960s. His later work, *The Use of Public Power*, tries to show where this planning went wrong and how it could be set right.

9 C. E. Lindblom *Politics and Markets* offers a persuasive theory of the relations between government and business which is more pluralist than corporatist (but relevant to both).

CHAPTER 6 THE BUREAUCRATIC STATE

This list concentrates like the chapter upon the political environment and character of bureaucracy. It moves from simpler to more complex works.

Guide to further reading

1 Martin Albrow *Bureaucracy* is a useful introduction to general concepts.
2 Eva Etzioni-Halevy *Bureaucracy and Democracy* is a clear discussion of a tangled relationship.
3 H. Jacoby *The Bureaucratization of the World* is a good historical exposition of the growth of bureaucracy in both government and business.
4 Charles Perrow *Complex Organizations* is a balanced account of organization theories which brings out some of the virtues and vices of modern bureaucracies (also relevant to Pluralism).
5 J. A. Armstrong *The European Administrative Elite* describes the attitudes and values of top administrators.
6 B. Guy Peters *The Politics of Bureaucracy* explains political-administrative relationships and strategies (also relevant to Pluralism).
7 Guy Benveniste *The Politics of Expertise* discusses the ability of experts to solve political problems.
8 Michel Crozier *The Bureaucratic Phenomenon* is an interesting study of bureaucratic stagnation in French public enterprises, explained by cultural values.
9 Vincent Ostrom *The Intellectual Crisis in American Public Administration* offers drastic 'public choice' remedies for the evils of over-centralized bureaucracy.
10 B. Schaffer and G. Lamb *Can Equity be Organised?* discusses, from a very different standpoint, the political and structural causes of administrative inequities.

REFERENCES

Albrow, Martin (1970), *Bureaucracy* (London: Macmillan).
Alt, James E. (1979), *The Politics of Economic Decline* (Cambridge: CUP).
Armstrong, J. A. (1973), *The European Administrative Elite* (Princeton, N.J.: Princeton University Press).
Arrow, K. J. (1963), *Social Choice and Individual Values*, 2nd ed. (N.Y.: Wiley).
Ashford, D. E. (1982), *British Dogmatism and French Pragmatism* (London: Allen & Unwin).
Australia, Parliament, Joint Committee of Public Accounts (1982), *Third Parliamentary Seminar: Parliamentary Accountability and Management of the Public Sector. Selection and Development of Senior Public Servants* (Canberra: AGPS).
Baehr, Peter R. and Wittrock, Björn (eds) (1981), *Policy Analysis and Policy Innovation* (London: Sage).
Banfield, E. C. (1961), *Political Influence* (Glencoe, Ill.: Free Press).
Banfield, E. C. (1968), *The Unheavenly City* (Boston, Mass.: Little, Brown).
Barker, Sir Ernest (1951), *Principles of Social and Political Theory* (Oxford: Clarendon Press).
Barry, Brian M. (1970), *Sociologists, Economists and Democracy* (London: Collier Macmillan).
Beer, Samuel H. (1965), *Modern British Politics* (London: Faber).
Beer, Samuel H. (1982), *Britain Against Itself: The Political Contradiction of Collectivism* (London: Faber).
Bell, Daniel (1978), *The Coming of Post-Industrial Society* (New York: Basic Books).
Bentley, A. F. (1949), *The Process of Government* (reprinted, Bloomington, Ind.: Indiana University Press).
Benveniste, Guy (1973), *The Politics of Expertise* (London: Croom Helm).
Berger, Suzanne (ed.) (1981), *Organizing Interests in Western Europe* (Cambridge: CUP).
Berry, Brian J. (1973), *The Human Consequences of Urbanization* (London: Macmillan).
Blaug, M. (1980), *The Methodology of Economics* (Cambridge: CUP).
Bottomore, T. B. (1964), *Elites and Society* (London: C. A. Watts).
Braybrooke, D. and Lindblom, C. E. (1963), *A Strategy of Decision: Policy Evaluation as a Social Process* (New York: Free Press of Glencoe).
Breton, A. (1974), *The Economic Theory of Representative Government* (Chicago, Ill.: Aldine).

212

References

Brittan, Samuel (1975), 'The economic contradictions of democracy', *British Journal of Political Science*, vol. 5, part 2, pp. 9–159.

Bruce-Gardyne, Jock and Lawson, Nigel (1976), *The Power Game* (London: Macmillan).

Buchanan, James M. (1965), *The Inconsistencies of the National Health Service* (London: Institute of Economic Affairs).

Buchanan, James M. and Tullock, Gordon (1962), *The Calculus of Consent* (Ann Arbor, Mich.: University of Michigan Press).

Burnham, James (1943), *The Managerial Revolution* (London: Putnam).

Castells, Manuel (1977), *The Urban Question: A Marxist Approach* (London: Edward Arnold).

Castells, Manuel (1978), *City, Class and Power* (London: Macmillan).

Castells, Manuel (1983), *The City and the Grassroots* (London: Edward Arnold).

Castles, Francis G. (1978), *The Social Democratic Image of Society* (London: Routledge & Kegan Paul).

Chapman, Brian (1959), *The Professions of Government: the Public Service in Europe* (London: Allen & Unwin).

Cohen, Stephen C. (1977), *Modern Capitalist Planning: the French Model*, 2nd ed. (Berkeley, Calif.: University of California Press).

Coombes, D. L. (1976), *The Power of the Purse* (London: Political and Economic Planning).

Cooter, Robert and Rapport, Peter (1984), 'Were the ordinalists wrong?', *Journal of Economic Literature*, June, pp. 507–30.

Crewe, Ivor M., Sarlwick, B. and Alt, J. (1977), 'Partisan dealignment in Britain 1964–1974', *British Journal of Political Science*, vol. 7, no. 2, pp. 129–90.

Crick, B. R. (1964), *The Reform of Parliament* (London: Weidenfeld & Nicolson).

Crosland, C. A. R. (1956), *The Future of Socialism* (London: Jonathan Cape).

Crossman, Richard (1975), *The Diaries of a Cabinet Minister* (London: Hamilton).

Crouch, Colin (1979), *The Politics of Industrial Relations* (Manchester: Manchester University Press).

Crouch, Colin (1983), 'New thinking on pluralism', *Political Quarterly*, vol. 54, no. 4, Oct–Dec, pp. 363–74.

Crozier, Michel (1964), *The Bureaucratic Phenomenon* (Chicago, Ill.: University of Chicago Press).

Dahl, R. A. (1956), *A Preface to Democratic Theory* (Chicago, Ill.: University of Chicago Press).

Dahl, R. A. (1967), *Pluralist Democracy in the United States* (Chicago, Ill.: Rand McNally).

Dahl, R. A. (1982), *Dilemmas of Pluralist Democracy* (New Haven, Conn.: Yale University Press).

Donoughue, B. and Jones, G. W. (1973), *Herbert Morrison: Portrait of a Politician* (London: Weidenfeld & Nicolson).

Downs, A. (1957), *An Economic Theory of Democracy* (New York: Harper & Row).

Downs, A. (1967), *Inside Bureaucracy* (Boston, Mass.: Little, Brown).

Dunleavy, Patrick (1981a), *The Politics of Mass Housing in Britain 1945–1975* (London: OUP).

Dunleavy, Patrick (1981b), 'Professions and policy change', *Public Administration Bulletin*, vol. 9, August, pp. 3–16.

Duverger, Maurice (1964), *The Idea of Politics* (London: Methuen).

Dye, Thomas R. (1972), *Understanding Public Policy* (Englewood Cliffs, N.J.: Prentice-Hall).

Eckstein, Harry (1973), *Division and Cohesion in Democracy: A Study of Norway* (Princeton, N.J.: Princeton University Press).

Elder, Neil (1970), *Government in Sweden* (Oxford: Pergamon Press).

Etzioni, Amitai (1961), *A Comparative Analysis of Complex Organisations* (London: Macmillan).

Etzioni-Halevy, Eva (1983), *Bureaucracy and Democracy* (London: Routledge & Kegan Paul).

Friedrich, C. J. (1940), 'Public policy and the nature of administrative responsibility', *Public Policy*, vol. 1, pp. 3–24.

Galbraith, J. K. (1957), *American Capitalism: The Concept of Countervailing Power* (London: Hamilton).

Gawthrop, L. C. (1969), *Bureaucratic Behaviour in the Executive Branch* (New York: Free Press).

Gerth, H. H. and Mills, C. W. (1948), *From Max Weber: Essays in Sociology* (London: Kegan Paul, Trench, Trubner).

Goldstein, Walter (ed.) (1978), *Planning, Politics and the Public Interest* (N.Y.: Columbia University Press).

Goldthorpe, J. H. (1968), *The Affluent Worker: Political Attitudes and Behaviour* (Cambridge: CUP).

Goodin, Robert E. (1982), *Political Theory and Public Policy* (Chicago: University of Chicago Press).

Goodsell, C. T. (1983), *The Case for Bureaucracy* (Chatham, N.J.: Chatham House).

Gough, E. N. (1979), *The Political Economy of the Welfare State* (London: Macmillan).

Grant, Wyn and McKay, David, (eds) (1983), 'Industrial policies in OECD countries', *Journal of Public Policy*, special issue, February.

Guttsman, W. L. (ed.) (1969), *The English Ruling Class* (London: Weidenfeld & Nicolson).

Halevy, E. (1928), *The Growth of Philosophical Radicalism* (London: Faber).

Hanf, Kenneth and Sharpf, Fritz W. (1978), *Interorganizational Policy Making* (London: Sage).

Hardin, Garrett (1968), 'The tragedy of the commons', *Science*, vol. 162, no. 3859, pp. 1243–8.

Harvey, David (1973), *Social Justice and the City* (London: Edward Arnold).

References

Hayek, F. A. (1944), *The Road to Serfdom* (London: Routledge & Kegan Paul).

Hayek, F. A. (1960), *The Constitution of Liberty* (London: Routledge & Kegan Paul).

Hayek, F. A. (1973), *Economic Freedom and Representative Government* (London: Institute of Economic Affairs).

Hayward, J. E. S. (1966), *Private Interests and Public Policy: the Experiences of the French Economic and Social Council* (London: Longman).

Heady, Ferrel (1966), *Public Administration: A Comparative Perspective* (Englewood Cliffs, N.J.: Prentice-Hall).

Heclo, Hugh (1974), *Modern Social Politics in Britain and Sweden* (New Haven, Conn.: Yale University Press).

Heclo, Hugh (1977), *A Government of Strangers: Executive Politics in Washington* (Washington, D.C.: The Brookings Institution).

Himmelweit, Hilde, Humphreys, T. P., Jaeger, M. and Kaliz, H. (1981), *How Voters Decide* (London: Academic Press).

Hirsch, Fred (1976), *Social Limits to Growth* (Cambridge, Mass.: Harvard University Press).

Hirschman, A. (1970), *Exit, Voice and Loyalty* (Cambridge, Mass.: Harvard University Press).

Hodgkinson, C. (1978), *Towards a Philosophy of Administration* (Oxford: Blackwell).

Hood, Christopher (1976), *The Limits of Administration* (London: Wiley).

Jackson, P. M. (1982), *The Political Economy of Bureaucracy* (Dedington, Oxon.: Philip Allan).

Jacoby, H. (1973), *The Bureaucratization of the World* (Berkeley, Calif.: University of California Press).

Jessop, Bob (1979), 'Corporatism, parliamentarianism and social democracy', in *Trends Towards Corporatist Intermediation*, P. C. Schmitter and G. Lembruch (eds) (London: Sage), pp. 185–212.

Kariel, Henry (1961), *The Decline of American Pluralism* (Stanford, Calif.: Stanford University Press).

Keating, Michael (1983), 'Decentralization in Mitterand's France', *Public Administration*, vol. 6, no. 3, Autumn, pp. 237–52.

Keeling, Desmond (1972), *Management in Government* (London: Allen & Unwin).

Keynes, J. M. (1936), *The General Theory of Employment, Interest and Money* (London: Macmillan).

King, Anthony (1975), 'Overload: problems of governing in the 1970s', *Political Studies*, vol. XXIII, nos 2 and 3, June, pp. 284–96.

Klein, Rudolph (1975), 'The National Health Service', in *Social Policy and Public Expenditure 1975: Inflation and Priorities*, Rudolph Klein, ed. (London: Centre for Studies in Social Policy), pp. 83–104.

Klein, Rudolph (1980), 'Costs and benefits of complexity: the British National Health Service', in *Challenge to Governance*, Richard Rose (ed.) (London: Sage), pp. 105–126.

Kornhauser, William (1959), *The Politics of Mass Society* (Glencoe, Ill.: Free Press).

Larkey, P. D., Stolfi, C. and Wise, M. (1981), 'Theorizing about the growth of government', *Journal of Public Policy*, vol. 1, no. 2, pp. 157–220.

Lasswell, Harold (1950), *Politics: Who Gets What, When, How* (reprinted New York: Pete Smith).

Laver, Michael (1981), *The Politics of Private Desires* (Middlesex: Penguin).

Leibenstein, Harvey (1966), 'Allocative Efficiency vs. X-Efficiency' *American Economic Review*, vol. 56, no. 3, June, pp. 392–415.

Lepawsky, Albert (1978), 'Style and substance in contemporary planning? The American New Deal's NRPB as a model', *Plan Canada* 18/34.

Leruez, Jacques (1980), 'Planning in an overloaded economy' in *Challenge to Governance*, Richard Rose, ed. (London: Sage), pp. 52–70.

Lindblom, C. E. (1965), *The Intelligence of Democracy* (New York: Free Press).

Lindblom, C. E. (1977), *Politics and Markets* (New York: Basic Books).

Lowi, T. J. (1979), *The End of Liberalism*, 2nd ed. (New York: W. W. Norton).

McConnell, Grant (1966), *Private Power and American Democracy* (New York: A. A. Knopf).

MacPherson, C. B. (1962), *The Political Theory of Possessive Individualism* (London: OUP).

Mannheim, Karl (1951), *Freedom, Power and Democratic Planning* (London: Routledge & Kegan Paul).

March, J. G. and Simon, H. A. (1958), *Organisations* (New York: Wiley).

Marx, Karl (1962), *Capital* Vol. I, English edition (Moscow: Progress Publishers).

Maslow, A. H. (1954), *Motivation and Personality* (New York: Harper).

Meynaud, Jean (1968), *Technocracy* (London: Faber).

Miliband, Ralph (1977), *The State in Capitalist Society* (London: Quartet Books).

Millett, J. D. (1966), *Organization for the Public Service* (Princeton, N.J.: Van Nostrand).

Mishan, E. J. (1967), *The Costs of Economic Growth* (London: Staples Press).

Mishan, E. J. (1971), *Cost–Benefit Analysis* (London: Allen & Unwin).

Mueller, Dennis C. (1979), *Public Choice* (Cambridge: CUP).

Musgrave, Richard A. and Peacock, Alan T. (eds) (1967), *Classics in the Theory of Public Finance* (London: Macmillan).

Nettl, J. P. (1965), 'Consensus or elite domination: the case of business', *Political Studies*, February, pp. 22–44.

Nie, N. H., Verba, S. and Petrocik, J. R. (1979), *The Changing American Voter*, 2nd ed. (Cambridge, Mass.: Harvard University Press).

Niskanen, W. A., Jr (1971), *Bureaucracy and Representative Government* (Chicago, Ill.: Aldine-Atherton).

References

Nove, Alec (1983), *The Economics of Feasible Socialism* (London: Allen & Unwin).

Nozick, Robert (1974), *Anarchy, State and Utopia* (Oxford: Basil Blackwell).

O'Connor, James (1973), *The Fiscal Crisis of the State* (New York: St Martin's Press).

Offe, Claus (1981), 'The attribution of public status to interest groups: observations on the West German case', in *Organizing Interests in Western Europe*, Suzanne Berger, ed. (Cambridge: CUP), pp. 123–58.

Offe, Claus (1983), 'Competitive party democracy and the Keynesian welfare state: factors of stability and disorganization', *Policy Sciences* (Amsterdam), vol. 15, pp. 225–46.

Okun, Arthur M. (1975), *Equality and Efficiency: the Big Tradeoff* (Washington, D.C.: The Brookings Institution).

Olson, Mancur (1965), *The Logic of Collective Action* (Cambridge, Mass.: Harvard University Press).

Olson, Mancur (1982), *The Rise and Decline of Nations* (New Haven, Conn.: Yale University Press).

Orwell, George (1955), *Animal Farm* (London: Secker & Warburg).

Ostrom, Vincent (1973), *The Intellectual Crisis in American Public Administration* (University, Ala.: University of Alabama Press).

Oulés, Firman (1966), *Economic Planning and Democracy* (London: Penguin).

Panitch, Leo (1976), *Social Democracy and Industrial Militancy* (Cambridge: CUP).

Parkin, A. (1982), *Governing the Cities: the Australian Experience in Perspective* (Melbourne: Macmillan).

Parsons, Talcott (1951), *The Social System* (Glencoe, Ill.: Free Press).

Peacock, A. T. and Wiseman, J. (1961), *The Growth of Government Expenditure in the United Kingdom* (Princeton, N.J.: Princeton University Press).

Perrow, Charles (1979), *Complex Organizations*, 2nd ed. (Glenview, Ill.: Scott Forsman).

Peters, B. Guy (1978), *The Politics of Bureaucracy* (N.Y.: Longman).

Peterson, Paul (1981), *City Limits* (Chicago, Ill.: University of Chicago Press).

Poulantzas, Nicos (1978), *Classes in Contemporary Capitalism* (London: Verso).

Pressman, J. L. and Wildavsky, A B. (1973), *Implementation* (Berkeley, Calif.: University of California Press).

Price, Don K. (1962), *Government and Science: Their Dynamic Relation in American Society*, 2nd ed. (New York: New York University Press).

Richter, Melvin (1964), *The Politics of Conscience: T. H. Green and His Age* (London: Weidenfeld & Nicolson).

Riker, William H. and Ordeshook, Peter C. (1973), *An Introduction to Positive Political Theory* (Englewood Cliffs, N.J.: Prentice-Hall).

217

Robinson, Joan (1948), *The Economics of Imperfect Competition* (London: Macmillan).

Robson, W. A. (1976), *Welfare State and Welfare Society* (London: Allen & Unwin).

Rose, Richard (1980), *Challenge to Governance* (London: Sage).

Rose, Richard (1984), *Understanding Big Government* (London: Sage).

Rowley, Charles K. and Peacock, Alan T. (1975), *Welfare Economics* (London: Martin Robertson).

Runciman, W. G. (1963), *Social Science and Political Theory* (Cambridge: CUP).

Sayre, W. S. and Kaufman, H. (1960), *Governing New York City* (New York: Russell Sage Foundation).

Scase, Richard (1983), 'Why Sweden has elected a radical government,' *Political Quarterly*, vol. 54, no. 1, Jan–March, pp. 43–53.

Schaffer, B. B., ed., (1975), 'The Problems of Access to Public Services,' special edition, *Development and Change*, vol. 6, no. 2.

Schaffer, B. B. and Lamb, G. (1981), *Can Equity be Organised?* (Paris: UNESCO).

Schelling, Thomas C. (1978), *Micromotives and Macrobehaviour* (New York: W. W. Norton).

Schmitter, P. C. (1979), 'Still the century of corporatism?' in *Trends Towards Corporatist Intermediation*, P. C. Schmitter and Gerhard Lembruch, eds (London: Sage), pp. 7–52.

Schnattschneider, E. E. (1960), *The Semi-Sovereign People* (New York: Holt, Rinehart & Winston).

Schultze, C. L. (1968), *The Politics and Economics of Public Spending* (Washington: The Brookings Institution).

Schultze, C. L. (1977), *The Public Use of Private Interest* (Washington, D.C.: The Brookings Institution).

Schumpeter, Joseph A. (1943), *Capitalism, Socialism and Democracy* (London: Allen & Unwin).

Schwerin, Don S. (1980), 'The limits of organization as a response to wage-price problems', in *Challenge to Governance*, Richard Rose, ed. (London: Sage), pp. 71–105.

Seidman, Harold (1980), *Politics, Position and Power* (New York: OUP).

Self, Peter (1974), 'Is comprehensive planning possible and rational?' *Policy and Politics*, vol. 2, no. 3, March, pp. 193–203.

Self, Peter (1975), *Econocrats and the Policy Process* (London: Macmillan).

Self, Peter (1977), *Administrative Theories and Politics*, 2nd ed. (London: Allen & Unwin).

Self, Peter (1982), *Planning the Urban Region* (London: Allen & Unwin).

Self, Peter and Storing, Herbert J. (1962), *The State and the Farmer* (Berkeley, Calif.: University of California Press).

Selznick, Philip (1957), *Leadership in Administration* (New York: Harper & Row).